Living on the Land

Living
ON THE
Land

INDIGENOUS WOMEN'S

UNDERSTANDING OF PLACE

Edited by **Nathalie Kermoal** &
Isabel Altamirano-Jiménez

AU PRESS

Copyright © 2016 Nathalie Kermoal and Isabel Altamirano-Jiménez

Published by AU Press, Athabasca University
1200, 10011 – 109 Street, Edmonton, AB T5J 3S8

ISBN 978-1-77199-041-7 (pbk.)   978-1-77199-042-4 (PDF)   978-1-77199-043-1 (epub)
doi: 10.15215/aupress/9781771990417.01

Cover image by Christi Belcourt, *Four Cedar Waxwings*. Courtesy of the artist.
Cover design by Natalie Olsen, Kisscut Design
Interior design by Sergiy Kozakov
Printed and bound in Canada by Friesens

Library and Archives Canada Cataloguing in Publication

Living on the land : indigenous women's understanding of place / edited by Nathalie
    Kermoal and Isabel Altamirano-Jiménez.
Includes bibliographical references and index.
Issued in print and electronic formats.

    1. Indigenous women. 2. Place (Philosophy). I. Kermoal, Nathalie J., 1964-,
author, editor II. Altamirano-Jiménez, Isabel, author, editor III. Horn-Miller,
Kahente, 1972- . Distortion and healing.

HQ1161.L59 2016   305.48'8   C2016-901373-1
                                           C2016-901374-X

We acknowledge the financial support of the Government of Canada through the
Canada Book Fund (CFB) for our publishing activities.

 Canadian Patrimoine
Heritage   canadien

Assistance provided by the Government of Alberta, Alberta Media Fund.

Government

Contents

Maps and Figures

Acknowledgments

We are grateful for the generous support of the Human Rights Education and Multiculturalism Fund and the Faculty of Native Studies at the University of Alberta, as well as for the participants' contributions.

We would like to extend a special thank-you to the three anonymous readers of the manuscript for their insightful comments and to Nicole Lugosi and Kristine Wray for their diligence and hard work in coordinating this project and preparing the final text. Thank you also to Naomi McIlwraith and J. D. Crookshank for the work they did in editing an earlier version of the manuscript as well as to the editors of Athabasca University Press for their diligent editorial work. And thank you to Christi Belcourt for giving us the authorization to use her amazing artwork on the cover of this book.

We are immensely grateful to you all.

Living
ON THE
Land

Introduction

Indigenous Women and Knowledge

Isabel Altamirano-Jiménez and Nathalie Kermoal

Inquiry into Indigenous knowledge, as a field of study, has grown at both national and international levels. However, some scholars have questioned whether Indigenous knowledge stands alone as a system, revealing the struggle to validate it vis-à-vis Western concepts and ways of knowing. Others have pointed out that Indigenous knowledge can be crucial to managing natural resources, mitigating climate change, and revitalizing communities. In looking closely at this body of literature, it is possible to argue that, as a system, Indigenous knowledge is interrelated with territory, kinship, identity, governance, economy, and education (Trask 2007; Moreton-Robinson and Walter 2009; Coulthard 2010). Although scholars have observed that this knowledge is connected to how people inhabit the world, less attention has been devoted to exploring Indigenous women's knowledge. In Indigenous societies, gender roles and responsibilities are delineated on the basis of protocols that shape the survival needs of the collective. The common preoccupation with the practical dimensions of Indigenous knowledge, however, has had the effect of decontextualizing it from the social, economic, political, environmental, and cultural processes in which it is embedded. Regardless of location and size, societies provide their members (men and women) with a sense of being in the world and with pathways to achieve status and recognition. Men and women often make use of different spaces and resources and, for this reason, they are knowers as well as keepers of specific knowledge. Differences between men and women's knowledge result not only from their specific activities and responsibilities but also from the historical and contemporary social context in which this knowledge is produced and mobilized.

Emphasizing Indigenous women's knowledge is important for several reasons. First, communities and individual experiences differ, and being an Indigenous woman is intertwined with lived experience and the worldview of her community. As noted by Aileen Moreton-Robinson and Maggie Walter, "Indigenous women's ways of being and belonging are derived from their relationship to country, humans, and ancestral beings" (2009, 5). To ignore the specific ways in which Indigenous women know is to undermine them as active producers of knowledge that participate in complex socio-environmental community processes. Second, from an Indigenous women's standpoint approach, it is important that we emphasize that places are connected to broader social and power relations. For example, gender cannot be separated from other systems of domination within which people operate and different degrees of privilege and penalty are accorded (Dhamoon 2015, 30). Power and penalty are accorded simultaneously within and among communities. Thus, a lack of attention to how such systems of domination work often means that Indigenous women's interests and concerns are concealed and erased within and outside their communities (Trask 2007, 296). Indigenous women's experiences are integral to decolonizing knowledge production.

The contributors to this book, the majority of whom are Indigenous, aim at grounding Indigenous women's knowledge in the land both historically and presently. They also explore the ways in which Indigenous women have resisted colonial attempts to assimilate and subordinate them. The chapters in this book represent Indigenous women's experiences beyond their domestic role and insists on connecting them to a variety of tasks within and beyond the household. To this end, the book aspires to prevent the continued neglect of Indigenous women's knowledge and contribution to their peoples and society at large. We do not mean to suggest by our emphasis on women's knowledge of land that women's participation in the production of knowledge is limited to the land and territory. Others have challenged prevalent representations of Indigenous women's domesticity by demonstrating how their work and labour have contributed to their urban households and communities' economy while subsidizing the market sector (Williams 2012). We do not theorize Indigenous knowledge as a practice either. Instead, the purpose of this book is to highlight the diversity of women's experiences by exploring and examining the lives of women as they are evidenced in oral history, interviews, economic processes, and life histories. The interpretative approaches pursued by the authors show the breadth of Indigenous women's knowledge while noting its ontological and epistemological commonalities (Moreton-Robinson and Walter 2009). As the editors of this volume, we think the complexity of Indigenous women's knowledge and experiences cannot be captured by a single methodological approach. In addressing the differences as well as the commonalities, this book seeks to reveal the systems of domination that shape women's interactions with the land, the environment, the community, and the knowledge production process. We argue that, far from being irrelevant, such systems have rendered Indigenous women's knowledge invisible and politically marginal. In paying attention to Indigenous women as knowledge holders, the contributors to this book anticipate opportunities for gendered social transformations and the decolonization of knowledge itself.

INDIGENOUS KNOWLEDGE

An extensive body of literature has been written on Indigenous knowledge since the 1980s. A literature review shows that Indigenous knowledge has been often defined in opposition to Western knowledge, whose origins can be traced back to the Enlightenment and the European scientific revolution of the sixteenth and seventeenth centuries. According to Linda Smith, the development of Western, rational, scientific knowledge was connected with colonialism and the "discovery" of the Indigenous Other by Europeans (1999, 59). Similarly, Mi'kmaw scholar Marie Battiste (2002) has pointed out that knowledge production from the West constitutes a form of imperialism that disregards and erases other types of knowledge.

Indigenous knowledge is often defined as "traditional knowledge" (TK), a label that emphasizes non-scientific, practical knowledge that is "handed down through generations by cultural transmission, about the relationship of living beings (including humans) with one another and with their environment" (RCAP 1996, 454; Berkes 2008, 9). This type of knowledge is not only specific to place but also cumulative, holistic, experiential, and dynamic (McGregor 2004; Kolawole 2005). Orally based Indigenous knowledge draws "on the knowledge of a population who have lived experience of the environments in question, and provide peoples with ownership of the development process" (Briggs and Sharp 2004, 661). Although these definitions emphasize the fact that Indigenous knowledge is socially and culturally transmitted, they continue to focus on the performativity of knowledge.

Though in the past Indigenous knowledge was regarded as an obstacle to development, in the 1990s it became an essential element of development policies (Agrawal 2004). Indigenous communities, academics, and to some extent governments insisted on the benefits of using Indigenous knowledge in the planning, management, and monitoring of land and resources. Policies passed by the Northwest Territories government, for example, challenged policy makers to "incorporate Traditional Knowledge into government decisions where appropriate" (Parlee 2012, 56). International conventions have noted the importance of protecting Indigenous knowledge. Similarly, in 2014 the United Nations Inter-Agency Support Group on Indigenous Peoples' Issues noted that Indigenous women could provide a unique and valuable perspective on the emergent water crisis (Inter-Agency Support Group 2014). The United Nations Declaration on the Rights of Indigenous Peoples (2007) stresses the right of Indigenous peoples to control and maintain their social and cultural differences by living according to their own historically developed ways of life. In 2012, a United Nations resolution further recognized "the value and the diversity of the cultures and the form of the social organization of Indigenous peoples and their holistic traditional scientific knowledge of their lands, natural resources and environment" (n.p.). Thus, Indigenous knowledge is closely considered in the search for appropriate and sustainable ways of managing resources. Many of these discourses imply that Indigenous peoples are the holders of some kind of magical secret that can save the world.

This increased attention to Indigenous knowledge also raises concerns over the hierarchical relationship between Western and Indigenous knowledge. Conflict often develops between Indigenous knowledge holders and scientists due to the insistence of Western knowledge on categorizing, organizing, and objectifying the knowledge (Kendrick 2003). For some pursuing the integration of Indigenous knowledge into Western knowledge, the process has become "a convenient abstraction, consisting of bite-sized chunks of information that can be slotted into Western paradigms, fragmented, decontextualized, a kind of quick fix, if not a panacea" (Ellen and Harris

2000, 15). In their attempts to universalize highly localized knowledge, actors have coopted what is essential to their interests while overlooking the power imbalances driving such cooptation (Wohling 2009, 2).

Others regard Indigenous knowledge as static and unchanging, while a few question the relevancy and even existence of such knowledge (Widdowson and Howard 2008; Flanagan 2008). The assumption that Indigenous knowledge is a relic of both an "idealized" and "backward" past is rooted in the colonial discourse of the nineteenth century (Nadasdy 2003; Howitt 2001), and was used to justify colonialism and land dispossession. Political, methodological, and epistemological differences are at the heart of the divide that exists between Indigenous knowledge and Western knowledge. Indigenous scholars have been extremely critical of the way scientists have treated Indigenous knowledge, noting that indigenous knowledge has been generalized or abstracted from specific context as a way to "scientize" it. As John Briggs notes, "such an approach misses the point of the special character of local needs" (2005, 110). Patrick Sikana and Timothy Mwambazi also argue, such an approach ignores the reality of the "socio-economic and historical situation of the local community in which the technology is applied" (1996, 108).

According to Arun Agrawal (2004), "it makes much more sense to talk about multiple domains and types of knowledge, with differing logics and epistemologies" than to focus on the differences between Indigenous knowledge and Western knowledge. He argues for "the recognition of a basic political truism" based on the usefulness of knowledge to different peoples instead of a focus on "the sterile dichotomy between Indigenous and Western, or traditional and scientific knowledge" (5). By concentrating on a productive dialogue that safeguards the interests of those who are disadvantaged, one is able to go beyond labels and "make intellectual space for Indigenous cultural knowledge systems that were denied in the past" (Rigney 2001, 9).

Scholars have established the need to deconstruct the hegemony of Western knowledge in order to emphasize Indigenous ways of being in the world and ways of knowing. Indigenous knowledge systems have developed over millennia and are grounded in living relational schemas. Relationships not only highlight the strong attachment Indigenous peoples have to their homelands but also underline the ontological framework that land occupies in those relationships (Coulthard 2010, 79). These relationships are reciprocal and develop among people as well as between people and non-human beings.

The moral code, norms, and laws governing those relationships are based on the principles of respect, reciprocity, and obligation (Trask 2007; Kuokkanen 2009). The norms, laws, and systems of governance that guide these relationships at the level of the family, community, and human and non-human interactions are specific to place (Cajete 2000, 1995; Kuokkanen 2009) and are more than a set of practices. As such this knowledge is not fragmented into silos or categories; rather, ontologies, epistemologies, and experiences are interwoven into this system.

Indigenous knowledge draws on different sources such as stories, dreams, visions, practices, and experiences (Young-Ing 2008). Similarly, Marie Battiste and Sa'ke'j Henderson (2000) note that the interconnection of aspects of Indigenous knowledge is communicated in oral tradition, songs, artifacts, stories, dances, and ceremonies (9). From these points of view, the legitimacy of Indigenous knowledge comes from social relationships and cannot exist without them. These relationships are not only embodied by human beings but also by animals, plants, spirits, water, and mountains.

Indigenous ontologies have not been destroyed by colonization although they are worn out by it (Coulthard 2010). Inuvialuk activist Rosemarie Kuptana (2008) argues that because Indigenous knowledge reflects unity rather than fragmentation, when something new is learned "the new knowledge is incorporated into a holistic worldview and becomes part of the explanation of the entire ecosystem as a whole, and explains the working of the ecosystem and not just an isolated particle" (n.p.). From these points of view, Indigenous knowledge evolves and changes over time and these new forms are a valid expression of indigeneity (Wohling 2009, 3) that continue to guide alternative visions of social relationships and coexistence (Coulthard 2010). Indigenous knowledge can be useful to operationalize a past in the face of contemporary colonialism. As such, Indigenous knowledge is a source of resistance and decolonization. In *Dancing on Our Turtle's Back: Stories of Nishnaabeg Re-creation, Resurgence, and a New Emergence*, Leanne Simpson (2011) stresses the importance of "researching back" Indigenous intellectual traditions. She calls for Indigenous peoples to "delve into their own culture's stories, philosophies, theories and concepts to align themselves with the processes and forces of regeneration, revitalization, remembering, and visioning" (148). Thus, rather than returning to a frozen Indigenous past, it is about reclaiming Indigenous knowledge to make sense of the present and imagine future possibilities. As Kahente

Horn-Miller demonstrates in her chapter, "Distortion and Healing: Finding Balance and a 'Good Mind' Through the Rearticulation of Sky Woman's Journey," stories have the potential to strengthen families and communities and provide a better understanding of the role women play in the governance of the community.

INDIGENOUS WOMEN'S STANDPOINT

Although scholars have done an important job in conceptualizing Indigenous knowledge, they have paid less attention to how knowledge is specific to place and differs according to gender, age, sexuality, livelihoods, and experiences of colonization. These factors have an impact on individuals' access to knowledge and ability to use it. Gender differences raise particularly important issues. Indigenous women's ways of knowing are shaped by their livelihoods and shared experiences of racism, colonialism, and by their experiences as leaders, mothers, sisters, and grandmothers. The "Indigenous women's standpoint" approach developed by Maori scholar Aileen Moreton-Robinson (2000), focuses on Indigenous women's knowledge and is informed by a feminist paradigm (1). According to Moreton-Robinson, at the centre of this methodological paradigm is a shared positioning among Indigenous women and an acknowledgment that they also have diverse individual experiences. She argues that "the intersecting oppressions of race and gender and the subsequent power relations that flow from these into the social, political, historical and material conditions of our lives [are] shared, consciously or unconsciously. These conditions and relations discursively constitute us in the everyday and shape the problems Indigenous women confront" (5). As Moreton-Robinson puts it, a "different way of being human" and the colonized status of Indigenous women provide us with a unique vantage point from which to analyze colonizing power (7).

Privileging Indigenous perspectives involves understanding that being *Indigenous* and being *woman* are derived from the relationships established with place, spiritual beings, humans, and the environment. Men and women inhabit, experience, and belong to the world and as such they are holders of knowledge. This knowledge and belonging to the world are based on the interconnections among the social, political, spiritual, economic, and natural spheres.

In Indigenous societies, gender roles and responsibilities stem from and are part of broader relationships. That is to say, Indigenous peoples and societies differentiate between the roles that women and men assume based on social interactions and survival needs of their collective society (Cohen 1999). Feminist scholars have explored how men and women have differential knowledge of natural resources. Gender differentiation and specialization means that the Indigenous knowledge and skills held by women often differed from those held by men; this affects patterns of access, use, and control of land and resources and results in different perceptions of landscapes and priorities (Agarwal 1992). Others have shown that although men often have privileged access to resources, women have specific knowledge of resources that allows for the survival of the household (Rocheleau 1996; Wangari, Thomas-Slayter, and Rocheleau 1996). However, Indigenous women's knowledge expands beyond the activities done by women and involves a system of inquiry that reveals Indigenous processes of observing and understanding and the protocols for being and participating in the world.

Because Indigenous knowledge is inherently tied to land, there are particular landscapes, landforms, and biomes where ceremonies are held, certain stories recited, medicines properly gathered, and transfers of knowledge properly authenticated (Morphy 1995; Basso 1996). The knowledge held by Indigenous women is lived and embodied, is a process of sharing social life, histories, economic, and political practices. Because relationships to land and identity have been mediated by colonial regulations and policies, Indigenous women's knowledge and experiences have been underpinned by a variety of personal and communal experiences and gender processes.

As the contributors to this book show, such processes shape how knowledge, knowledge sharing, and revitalization take place. Each chapter in this book converses with these different manifestations and weaves the threads of legibility and illegibility through stories, histories, struggles, and resistance. Although the chapters mainly focus on Canada, the endeavour to stimulate a transnational conversation is also present. Altamirano-Jiménez enters these dialogues as a Zapotec scholar teaching in Canada and Kermoal enters as a Breton historian working with Métis people in Canada. We are both committed to building ethical and collaborative relationships with Indigenous scholars and communities and to centering the experiences and voices of Indigenous women. The book is organized relative to the various dimensions of Indigenous women's knowledge. It begins with examinations of Indigenous oral history and experiences, and follows with explorations of Indigenous women's knowledge of the land and the political, social, legal, and economic implications of misrepresenting such knowledge. The colonial inequalities of the past that continue on into the present become apparent in legal cases, cartographic approaches, and grievances about the loss of land. The authors show that challenging and displacing hegemonic Western knowledge is required to enable other forms of literacy and knowledge to coexist. This book is a tribute to Indigenous women's profound and expansive literacy and knowledge.

In chapter 1, Kahente Horn-Miller shows how ancient stories provide teachings for contemporary Kanien'kehá:ka women regarding their roles and responsibilities. Horn-Miller, who comes from a matrilineal culture, refers to herself as Sky Woman's great-granddaughter, and as such she—as well as the other women in her community—passes down Sky Woman's knowledge. Combining first-hand knowledge with cultural and communal creation stories, Horn-Miller demonstrates how traditional learning helps to strengthen families and communities, generating new possibilities to resistance. According to the author, "it is in the interactions between Sky Woman's life as a theory of being and our life in actual practice that her experience provides special insights" for understanding the role of Indigenous women in governing and sustaining communities.

The fact that stories have the political potential to resist the everyday exercise of power is also addressed in chapter 2. Shalene Jobin, of Cree and Métis descent, writes that her grandmother's learning and passing on of Cree stories and teachings was a way of resisting assimilation and cultural genocide after attending a residential school. Jobin notes that the Cree stories that her grandmother recorded convey teachings "about ways of being in the world, ways of interacting with other humans and animals, and ways of being in relationship with the land." In their respective chapters, Horn-Miller and Jobin emphasize how Indigenous knowledge continues to guide women's resistance as well as provide alternative visions of social relationships.

In chapter 3, Carole Lévesque, Denise Geoffroy, and Geneviève Polèse are concerned with knowledge and the roles Naskapi women play in the development of the Naskapi cultural and ecological heritage. Through interviews with elders from the Kawawachikamach community in Northern Québec, the authors identify four main organizing principles of the knowledge and expertise of men and women and show how social laws govern the rules around knowledge and who is a holder of knowledge. Neither Indigenous knowledge nor laws are confined to knowledge of the environment. Both are rooted in different ways of knowing and that knowledge is simultaneously gendered and spiritual.

Although Indigenous women's knowledge has continued to exist and guide their lives, it has also remained largely "invisible." As the contributors to this book show, this invisibility is not an accident but is rather an expression of the power relations that flow into the social, political, and historical structures that shape Indigenous women's lives and the challenges they confront in the present. For instance, large-scale resource development rarely takes into consideration the socioeconomic and cultural implications that such projects have for communities as a whole, to say nothing of the impact on women in particular. Little attention has been paid to Indigenous women's knowledge in resource management or land use studies despite the fact that Indigenous communities in Canada and beyond have retained many aspects of their traditional resource use and allocation systems: including how and what to harvest in specific seasons and how to produce, prepare, and preserve food. Most of the research in the area of resource management has focused on male-dominated activities, and as a result we have relatively scant understanding of the role that women play in the gathering and processing of resources. As Brenda Parlee and Kristine Wray note in chapter 7, contemporary studies still reflect the idea of "man the hunter." An idea that has been reproduced in the legal recognition of Indigenous rights in Canada.

In chapter 4, Isabel Altamirano-Jiménez and Leanna Parker analyze how the model of the male breadwinner was also replicated in the case brought against Nicaragua by the Awas Tingni community. Based on research conducted in the Atlantic coast region of Nicaragua in 2008, the authors explore the use of mapping in securing land rights and how it not only tends to impose a western understanding of land and resources on Indigenous communities but it also rests on a frozen understanding of Indigenous traditional economic activities. These authors show that the cartographic legal approach unevenly benefits certain groups of people and redefines Indigenous peoples' relationship to the land. This approach is even more problematic for Indigenous women, who have already seen their land rights eroded through colonialism. Neither the law nor geography are neutral, they are embedded in Western knowledge and values. Altamirano-Jiménez and Parker argue that if Indigenous mapping is to benefit Indigenous peoples, maps must be presented in ways that articulate the legal systems of Indigenous peoples.

Similarly, in chapter 5, Nathalie Kermoal notes that, in the wake of the 2003 Supreme Court decision in *R. v. Powley*, Métis rights are often framed around male activities such as hunting and fishing, rarely taking into consideration Métis women's roles and responsibilities. By focusing on the medical expertise of Métis women in western Canada, Kermoal presents a compelling case for the connections women have with the environment. Instead of always positioning women at the periphery of inquiries, she proposes to centre Métis women's knowledge for greater empowerment of communities. Kermoal urges scholars to undertake gender-sensitive research to understand how Métis women conceptualize their relationships with the land, and how these conceptualizations have changed over time, in order to better understand identity and territory. She argues that effective environmental consultation requires a holistic approach, which should centre on Métis women, as their knowledge may provide a deeper and richer perspective on the land.

In chapter 6, Kathy Hodgson-Smith and Nathalie Kermoal move away from "man the hunter" and discuss the traditional occupancy and land use study experience of the Métis of northwestern Saskatchewan. This land use study included the work and knowledge of women and provided valuable insights about women's activities and their longstanding relationship to the territory and to the land. The study demonstrated that Métis women's activities adapt to changing conditions and when faced with challenges due to appropriation or regulations, alternatives are created and developed.

On the basis of research carried out between 2007 and 2011 with seven communities in the western Arctic, Brenda Parlee and Kristine Wray argue in chapter 7 that the representation of women in the spheres of natural resource management, including the management of barren ground caribou, has in large part been obscured by stereotypes of the past. As they point out, the oversimplified image of "man the hunter" in management and policies narrows "our understanding of the place of caribou in the lives and livelihoods of peoples in the Canadian North" and has a tendency to "discount, rather than embrace, the complexity and diversity of the relationships that exist in northerly communities between human beings and the environment."

Parlee and Wray's findings also apply to fishing, as Zoe Todd demonstrates in the final chapter. Drawing on research conducted in Paulatuuq, Northwest Territories, Todd examines the intersections of women's knowledge of harvesting, fishing, and food security. She found that "these activities are crucial to a sense of continuity, providing opportunities for Paulatuuqmiut to connect with memories of the past, to create and sustain relationships with other people and with the environment, and to pass knowledge along to children and grandchildren." In a time of climate change and potential resource exploration, this knowledge is vital to guide decision making at the local, territorial, and federal level.

The chapters in this book explore different dimensions of Indigenous women's knowledge in different locations and through different disciplines. In the questions raised and the possibilities offered, these chapters call for transforming knowledge, colonial power imbalances, and male-dominated political processes. We hope to contribute to expanding the intellectual space for the visibility of Indigenous women's knowledge.

REFERENCES

Agarwal, Bina. 1992. "The Gender and Environment Debate: Lessons From India." *Feminist Studies* 18: 119–58.

Agrawal, Arun. 2004. "Indigenous and Scientific Knowledge: Some Critical Comments." *Indigenous Knowledge and Development Monitor* 3 (3). http://www.iss.nl/ikdm/ikdm/3-3/articles/agrawal.html.

Basso, Keith. 1996. *Wisdom Sits in Places: Landscape and Language Among the Western Navajo*. Albuquerque: University of New Mexico Press.

Battiste, Marie. 2002. "Indigenous Knowledge and Pedagogy in First Nations Education: A Literature Review with Recommendation." Paper prepared for the National Working Group on Education and the Ministry of Indian and Northern Affairs. http://www.afn.ca/uploads/files/education/24._2002_oct_marie_battiste_indigenousknowledgeandpedagogy_lit_review_for_min_working_group.pdf.

Battiste, Marie, and James (Sa'ke'j) Youngblood Henderson. 2000. *Protecting Indigenous Knowledge and Heritage: A Global Challenge*. Saskatoon: Purich Publishing.

Berkes, Fikret. 2008. *Sacred Ecology: Traditional Ecological Knowledge and Resource Management*. Philadelphia: Taylor and Francis.

Briggs, John. 2005. "The Use of Indigenous Knowledge in Development: Problems and Challenges." *Progress in Development Studies* 5 (2): 99–104.

Briggs, John, and Joanne Sharp. 2004. "Indigenous Knowledge and Development: A Postcolonial Caution." *Third World Quarterly* 22 (4): 661–76.

Cajete, Gregory. 2000. *Native Science: Natural Laws of Interdependence.* Santa Fe, N.M.: Clear Light Publishers.

Cohen, Alex. 1999. *The Mental Health of Indigenous Peoples: An International Overview.* Geneva: Department of Mental Health, World Health Organization.

Coulthard, Glen. 2010. "Place Against Empire: Understanding Indigenous Anti-Colonialism." *Affinities: A Journal of Radical Theory, Culture, and Action* 4: 79–83.

Dhamoon, Rita. 2015. "A Feminist Approach to Decolonizing Antiracism: Rethinking Transnationalism, Intersectionality, and Settler Colonialism." *Feral Feminisms* 4: 20–38.

Ellen, R., and H. Harris. 2000. "Introduction." In *Indigenous Environmental Knowledge and Its Transformations,* edited by R. A. Ellen, P. Parkes, and A. Bicker, pp. 1–33. Amsterdam: Harwood Academic Publishers.

Flanagan, Tom. 2008. *First Nations? Second Thoughts.* Montréal and Kingston: McGill-Queen's University Press.

Howitt, Richard. 2001. *Rethinking Resource Management: Sustainability, Justice and Indigenous Peoples.* London: Routledge.

Inter-Agency Support Group on Indigenous Peoples' Issues. 2014. "The Knowledge of Indigenous Peoples and Policies for Sustainable Development: Updates and Trends in the Second Decade of the World's Indigenous People."

Kendrick, Anne. 2003. "Caribou Co-Management in Northern Canada: Fostering Multiple Ways of Knowing." In *Navigating Social-Ecological Systems,* edited by Fikret Berkes, Johan Colding, and Carl Folke, pp. 241–68. Cambridge: Cambridge University Press.

Kolawole, Oluwatoying Dare. 2005. "Mainstreaming Local People's Knowledge: Implications for Higher Education in the South." *South African Journal of Higher Education* 19: 1427–43.

Kuokkanen, Rauna. 2009. "Indigenous Women in Traditional Economies: The Case of Sámi Reindeer Herding." *Signs: Journal of Women in Culture and Society* 34 (3): 499–503.

Kuptana, Rosemarie. 2008. "Relationship Between Traditional Knowledge and Intellectual Cultural Properties: An Inuit Perspective." In *Department of Canadian Heritage Discussion Papers. Traditions: National Gatherings on Indigenous Knowledge–Final Report.* www.traditions.gc.ca.

McGregor, Deborah. 2004. "Traditional Ecological Knowledge and Sustainable Development: Toward Co-Existence." In *In The Way of Development: Indigenous Peoples, Civil Society and the Environment,* edited by Mario Blaser and H. A. Feit, pp. 72–91. New York: Zed Books.

Moreton-Robinson, Aileen. 2000. *Talkin' Up to the White Woman: Indigenous Women and Feminism*. St. Lucia: University of Queensland Press.

Moreton-Robinson, Aileen, and Maggie Walter. 2009. "Indigenous Methodologies in Social Research." In *Social Research Methods*, edited by Maggie Walter, pp. 1–18. Oxford: Oxford University Press.

Morphy, Howard. 1995. "Landscape and the Reproduction of the Ancestral Past." In *The Anthropology of Landscape: Perspectives of Place and Space*, edited by Eric Hirsch and Michael O'Hanlon, pp. 184–209. Oxford: Clarendon.

Nadasdy, Paul. 2003. *Hunters and Bureaucrats: Power, Knowledge and Aboriginal State Relations in the Southwest Yukon*. Vancouver: University of British Columbia Press.

Parlee, Brenda. 2012. "Finding Voice in a Changing Ecological and Political Landscape: Traditional Knowledge and Resource Management in Settled and Unsettled Claim Areas of the Northwest Territories, Canada." *Aboriginal Policy Studies* 2 (1): 56–87.

Rigney, Lester-Irabinna. 2001. "A First Perspective of Indigenous Australian Participation in Science: Framing Indigenous Research Towards Indigenous Australian Intellectual Sovereignty." *Kaurna Higher Education Journal* 7: 1–13.

Rocheleau, Dianne E., and David Edmunds. 1996. "Women, Men and Trees: Gender, Power and Property in Forest and Agrarian Landscapes." *World Development* 25: 1315–71.

Royal Commission on Aboriginal Peoples. 1996. *Report of the Royal Commission on Aboriginal Peoples*. Vol. 4, *Perspectives and Realities*. Ottawa: Minister of Supply and Services.

Sikana, Patrick M., and Timothy N. Mwambazi. 1996. "Environmental Change and Livelihood Responses: Shifting Agricultural Practices in the Lakes Depression Zone of Northern Zambia." In *Sustaining the Soil: Indigenous Soil and Water Conservation in Africa*, edited by Chris Reij, Ian Scoones, and Camilla Toulmin, pp. 107–16. London: Earthscan Publications.

Simpson, Leanne. 2011. *Dancing on Our Turtle's Back: Stories of Nishnaabeg Re-creation, Resurgence and a New Emergence*. Winnipeg: Arbeiter Ring Publishing.

Smith, Linda Tuhiwai. 1999. *Decolonizing Methodologies: Research and Indigenous Peoples*. London: Zed Books.

Trask, Milani. 2007. "Indigenous Women and Traditional Knowledge: Reciprocity Is the Way of Balance." In *Women and the Gift Economy: A Radically Different Worldview is Possible*, edited by Genevieve Vaughan, pp. 293–301. Toronto: Inanna Publications and Education.

United Nations. 2007. "United Nations Declaration on the Rights of Indigenous Peoples." New York: United Nations.

———. 2009. "United Nations' Panel on Traditional Knowledge on Water." New York: United Nations.

———. 2012. "Resolution Adopted by the General Assembly: 66/142 Rights of Indigenous Peoples." New York: United Nations.

Wangari, Esther, Barbara Thomas-Slayter, and Dianne Rocheleau. 1996. "Gendered Visions for Survival: Semi-arid Regions in Kenya." In *Feminist Political Ecology: Global Issues and Local Experiences*, edited by D. Rocheleau, B. Thomas-Slayter, and E. Wangari, pp. 127–54. New York: Routledge.

Widdowson, Frances, and Albert Howard. 2008. *Disrobing the Aboriginal Industry: The Deception Behind Indigenous Cultural Preservation.* Montréal and Kingston: McGill-Queen's University Press.

William, Carol. 2012. "Introduction." In *Indigenous Women and Work: From Labor to Activism*, edited by Carol Williams, 1–26. Illinois: University of Illinois Press.

Wohling, Marc. 2009. "The Problem of Scale in Indigenous Knowledge: A Perspective from Northern Australia." *Ecology and Society* 14 (1): 1.

Young-Ing, Greg. 2008. "Indigenous Knowledge and Intellectual Property Rights in Context." In Canada, Department of Canadian Heritage, *Discussion Papers for Traditions: National Gatherings on Indigenous Knowledge.*

CHAPTER ONE

Distortion and Healing

Finding Balance and a "Good Mind" Through the Rearticulation of Sky Woman's Journey

Kahente Horn-Miller

Like all women, I am Sky Woman's great-granddaughter. I come from a matrilineal culture, the Kanien'kehá:ka, or "people of the flint," to whom Europeans gave the name Mohawk. In our oral history, we tell the story of Sky Woman; it is through the telling of her story that we learn about our roles and responsibilities as women. As we embody her life, and learn from our mothers, we are also passing on her knowledge.

The story opens in the Sky World at the beginning of time and tells of the relationship between the young Sky Woman, whom we know by the name Awe(n)ha'i' ("mature blossoms"), and her family and the people of that world. It describes how she was treated because she was special and gifted, how she learned the ways of her people, and about her relationship and marriage to the keeper of the Tree of Light.[1] The story is the first place where the clans appear, ceremonies and songs, the medicine game of lacrosse, and where Sky Woman's corruption takes place, leading to her descent to the earth world below. The challenges Sky Woman faces affect her both physically

---

1 The Tree of Light refers to the life forces of nature. The keeper of that tree is essentially the power of creation, the source of all life.

and emotionally, throwing off her sense of balance. As she deals with each of these challenges through critical engagement with herself and those she loves, Sky Woman learns how to think for herself, how to be respectful of others, how to endure suffering. It prepares her for what is to come.

This first part of the story teaches us about creating a Sky World on earth, one where respect for all living things is enacted in daily life. The story teaches us that Sky Woman has a history, a family, and a place where she belongs. We are reminded that we come from somewhere and that the Sky World is very similar to the world as we know it. It is understood in our culture that to be healthy in body, mind, and spirit you have to have a sense of your own history and identity. My own version begins with Sky Woman's descent. She is pregnant, alone, scared, and bewildered. Yet she is acutely aware of her surroundings. This is her story.

Sky Woman's Story

There are those who say I fell, was pushed, or jumped through a hole under the great tree and began my fall to the earth world below. Only I know the truth. This is the story as I lived it, and I am telling you what I remember.

It seemed like I fell a long time before anything happened. I opened my eyes, and I could see the water birds from the world below coming up to meet me. The Heron and the Loon were the leaders, with their wide wings expanded in full flight. All of their wings combined to create a large, soft cushion for me to land on. I could feel the softness of their feathers and the strength of their wings under my feet. I felt safe, but I was also shocked at my circumstances and how my life had suddenly changed. I wondered, what was to become of me? I was let loose, like a baby lynx in a briar patch, in a world I didn't know. I felt no fear, only concern for the safety of my baby, mixed with sadness. I rubbed my belly and spoke to her.

"Little one," I said, "I love you very much and I will protect you. We are now in a different world. You will never meet your grandmother or grandfather. You will never meet your father, but I am here and I will always love you and look after you."

I kissed my fingertips and touched my belly softly as tears gently rolled down my cheeks and fell on her.

I went to the edge of the platform created by the birds' wings and peered over the edge. Far below, my eyes were met with brilliant blue. The blue was from a great expanse of water reflecting the sunlight, and it was both beautiful and almost too much to bear. There appeared to be no land. I wondered to myself, where I would stand in this world?

In the depths beneath us, I could see water animals grouped together, looking up and talking to one another. I knew that they were talking about me and wondering what to do. Suddenly Otter gasped for air and dove under the surface of the water. Much time passed, and eventually his body slowly rose. He was dead.

I gasped and cried out, "Oh, Otter has died trying to save me!"

I wanted to hold his soft head in my arms and tell him I was grateful he had given his life to try to save me. I felt helpless watching from above. Then I saw Beaver being take a gasp of air and go below the surface. A long time later, his body slowly surfaced. I cried out again, with fresh tears on my cheeks as I wept for Beaver. I wanted to hold him and thank him for giving up his life to try to save me.

Next, I saw Muskrat gasp for air and dive below. A long time later his body slowly rose to the surface. I closed my eyes and let the tears fall down my face into the folds of my dress. I felt so sad that these water beings had died trying to save me. I wondered again what was to become of me.

Suddenly from far below I heard a cheer erupt from the assembled animals. Muskrat had succeeded! In his lifeless paws were specks of dirt from the ocean floor. One of the animals pried the dirt from Muskrat's clenched paws and gently placed the dirt on Turtle being's back. Immediately, Turtle's shell began to grow bigger. Soon the shell became big enough for me to stand on. I was gently lowered and my feet touched the first earth.

"Thank you, water beings, for saving me and my baby," I said. "I am grateful to you all for what you have done and brought to this world."

"I am going to sing you a song and dance for you, to show you how thankful I am for all that you have done."

I readied myself, hummed a few bits of the first song in preparation. The animals gathered around me, their eyes wide and their ears open. The air was alive.

The Formation of Turtle Island

I began to dance the women's shuffle dance and sing the planting songs I had learned from the women of the Sky World. I was heavy with child, but I still shuffled counter-clockwise, making the earth spread out on the Turtle being's back. I placed the tobacco and strawberry plants in the soil.

"Hey ya, hey ya," I sang in a loud clear voice. I wanted all the animals to know how grateful I was for what they had done for me, and for the earth to be patted down, firm and smooth.

My baby kicked, keeping the beat of the song inside me. I held my belly as I continued to dance. With each part of the song my voice grew louder and clearer. I turned my face up to Elder Brother Sun and let his loving smile warm my face. I looked up to the Sky World and sang for my mother and father. I sang for my husband, who had misunderstood me and challenged me as I tried to help interpret his dream. I sang for the fate I had been dealt. But we had arrived safely. As I sang and danced I felt stronger and stronger. I began to heal from my hurt and sorrow at being misunderstood by my husband. I understood him and was grateful for what he had given to me, my unborn baby.

The Turtle being's shell continued to grow, and the earth spread out in all directions with my songs and dances. As I danced, the roots and seeds from the Sky World that were caught in my hair fell to the newly formed earth, while my dancing feet covered them over with good, black earth. Immediately tiny green shoots began to appear. New life was beginning on earth! It was as though my relatives in the Sky World were with me planting in my garden, ensuring that my baby and I wouldn't starve.

I looked down and around me in wonder at the new life growing. Corn stalks began to appear, growing taller and forming silken hair that peered from their crowns. As the minutes went by, beans and squash also appeared. I could see all kinds of herbs, fruits, medicines in the ground around me. The air started to smell of the fragrant aromas of rich black soil and lush plant growth. I could see bright red strawberries and large flat tobacco leaves as well. I knew that as long as I had the sacred medicines, along with the corn, beans, and squash to eat, my baby and I would be fine.2

The animals appeared and sniffed delicately at the new growth. I stood still and spread my arms out, welcoming the animals to taste what had come from the Sky World.

"Come and eat!" I said. "I have planted all the things we will need on this earth to survive. My relatives from the Sky World made sure we would not starve. I have planted them as we did together in the Sky World and I want to share them with you."

Fox came forward and sniffed at the green leaves of a plant. He tasted them and then began to eat.

"Mmmm. These are good," he said.

Rabbit, Bear, Wolf, and Deer all came forward and began to eat. For a time there was silence punctuated by sounds of smacking lips and grunts of happy feasting. I was exhausted. I lay down to take a nap and prepared for the birth of my daughter.

My Baby-Faced Lynx

I woke up to strong labour pains coursing through my back and belly. I was scared for the first time. The labour pains felt like a rope was tied tightly around my waist. I cried out for my mother.

"Mother," I said, "I miss you! I wish you were here with me to help me, and to see your new grandchild come into this new world!"

After the shock of the first labour pains, my sensibilities kicked in. I had seen women give birth in the Sky World, so I knew what I had to do. I squatted over a pile of soft grasses. I made it through each contraction as it came to me, breathing with the pain, counting my breaths. I called out to my mother every once in a while so that she would hear me:

"Mother! Mother! She is coming!"

Then came the final pushes and I could feel the head of my baby come through. There was a loud gushing noise and then she fell into the softness beneath me. I bit the umbilical cord loose, birthed the placenta, and prepared to bury it, as was the custom of my ancestors. I looked around me for a tree near to where she had been born. As I dug the hole, I said some words and sang the song of creation. As a reminder to my daughter of where she came from, our mother the earth, I gently placed into the ground the sac which had nourished her.

"Hey ya, hey ya," I sang in a loud clear voice. I wanted my relatives above to hear me and know of the birth of their granddaughter.

My little Baby-Faced Lynx, as I called her, was beautiful. She took to my breast right away, and nursed for a long time as she lay on my belly. I touched her hair; her soft head was so tiny in my palm. She had a nice little round soft bum and tiny toes which she flexed in pleasure as she drank my warm milk. I spoke to her:

"I love you, my little one. I will always look after you and give you food to eat. I will always try to make you happy. I will always do everything I can to heal you."

I closed my eyes and we drifted off to sleep, I could feel her little quick heartbeat and her shallow breaths. We slept. When I awoke my daughter had grown. She grew fast and as time passed she became a young woman.

Life with My Daughter

My Baby-Faced Lynx loved to walk and explore the earth. As a child she had many playmates and her life was full of happiness. The animals would take on human form and play games with her. As she grew and became too old for child's play, she began to explore the earth more widely. Sometimes I would not see her for a whole day. But she always came home.

When my daughter reached puberty, she was given the name Iakotsition-teh (One Flower Has Arisen). One night as I was sleeping, I had a dream in which Uncle appeared to me. He told me that I was to watch over Iakotsi-tionteh carefully. Three beings in human form would appear to her and want to marry her. I was to tell her that she was not to be tempted, but to wait for a fourth young man who would appear. This man was to be her husband.

I asked Uncle, "How will she know that this fourth man is the right one?"

"She will know because she waited and took her time."

When I woke up the next morning, I talked with my daughter.

"My daughter, I love you. You are going to be a woman soon. I have to tell you that when you are out in the world wandering the earth, men will appear to you. They will want to be with you. You must come to me and ask my permission first."

Iakotsitionteh said, "Yes, mother. I will do that."

She's a good girl.

One day my daughter came back from her wanderings and told me of a man she had met. He had asked her if she wanted him for a companion. She had told him that she had to ask me first. Upon hearing of this, I said no. This same thing happened two more times. I said no again and again.

One day the West Wind came to visit. He appeared in human male form. I watched as his eyes admired the beauty of my daughter. That night he appeared in my daughter's dream and continued to do the same for two more nights. Each morning when she awoke she told me about her dream and the handsome young man who appeared to her. She told me she was in love with him and that they had agreed that they wanted to be life partners. I thought about this and about what Uncle had told me. I agreed to the marriage.

That night the West Wind came to Iakotsitionteh and lay beside her. In the morning I found two crossed arrows on her belly. I knew that my daughter was pregnant with twins. Iakotsitionteh awoke and gasped. Her belly began to swell as the babies grew rapidly inside her. I was so happy I was going to be a grandmother. I rubbed my daughter's belly.

"My grandchildren, I love you. You are going to be arriving soon in this world. There is a lot to see. I will make sure you are happy and well fed. You will never need for anything at all. I will make sure you stay healthy and strong."

My daughter rubbed her belly and smiled at me. The babies caused my daughter a lot of discomfort. It seemed like they were always in conflict. We could hear the two babies arguing and fighting inside her womb. I did all I could to help my Iakotsitionteh through her pregnancy and get ready for the birth.

One day I heard my daughter cry out in pain. I felt something in my gut that I had never felt before—apprehension. I ran to my daughter and helped her to lie down. Her belly had dropped and I could see her struggling through contractions. Suddenly she pushed and one baby came out the normal way, from between her legs and fell to the soft pile of leaves below. She groaned loudly as this happened. Then she opened her eyes wide, grabbed my hand, and fell over as the other baby came out of her armpit.

I helplessly watched my daughter, as she bled to death before me. The light faded from her eyes. I cried as I could do nothing to save her. I called out to my relatives in the Sky World for their help:

"Why have you done this? Why is my daughter dead? I have lost what I loved the most! Help us."

I cried as I picked up the twin boys, washed them and wrapped them. They looked at me with their soft brown eyes, and I remembered my beautiful Baby-Faced Lynx and how she suckled in those first few minutes of her new life. Tears rolled down my face and fell into the folds of their coverings. I lay the babies down and then went to prepare my daughter for burial as I had seen my relatives do in the Sky World.

I lovingly washed my Iakotsitionteh and dressed her. I sang songs as I did this and spoke words of love.

"My daughter," I said as tears fell down my face, "I loved you greatly. Many loved you greatly. You are going to be missed by me, and all others who had a chance to know you in your short time on this new earth. We watched you as you were born and grew into a beautiful young woman. We watched you as you played on this earth and worked in the gardens tending to the plants with loving care."

I stopped for a minute to think about my pretty little Baby-Faced Lynx daughter. The way she looked up to me as I taught her about the plants and medicines that grew around us. The memory of her innocent face brought tears to my eyes.

"Your presence on the earth will be missed. But you are going to a place where you will be loved. You will have warmth and life again in ten days' time. Your ancestors in the Sky World will watch over you and care for you as I did. Your life there will be rich with happiness. Your body will nourish the earth and give life to the new plants and animals."

With my words and songs I sent her on her way back to the Sky World. I buried her in a grave and prepared to look after my grandsons.

My Twin Grandsons Do Their Work

My boys, as I called them, looked alike, but were very different in their temperament. Many know them today as the right-handed and left-handed twins. One was kind and thoughtful, the right hand; the other was selfish and scheming, the left hand. Teharonhia:wakon, "He who grasps the sky with both hands," was the kind one, and Sawiskera, "Flint crystal ice," was the scheming one.

As I came to see later, the differing minds of the two boys came to characterize the two types of beings on the earth. There are those whose minds are solely turned toward the earth and bring disruptive influences to it and try to take control over it, like Sawiskera. There are those who always know where they come from and try to protect things on earth and always think of others first, like Teharonhia:wakon.

I misunderstood this aspect of my grandson, Teharonhia:wakon. His belief in letting people think for themselves and come to a conclusion on their own I mistook for a kind of apathy and uncaring. It made me angry and I began to favour my other grandson, Sawiskera. I did not think of the boys equally, which I realized much later was a misguided understanding. I had this fault, much like my husband in the Sky World.

Throughout their lives the two boys were in constant disagreement about many things. I told the boys, "Look, you two are frustrating me. Why don't you work it out? Play a game to resolve things or find another solution." I shook my head and sighed, "Sometimes you boys remind me of your grandfather, who was so misguided."

In those times I would think of my Iakotsitionteh and peace would come back to me. I was reminded of my purpose, to be diligent and look after my grandsons. I began to look forward to the days we spent together. Life with my twins was also filled with happiness and laughter. We would go for long walks.

"What's this, Tohta?" they would ask.[2]

I spent long periods explaining about the plants and animals on the earth and how they came to be there. I was filled with joy to see their young minds at work. The boys played with the little animals and made games for themselves. I encouraged them along as I could see their hunting and gathering skills developing. The boys also learned how to cultivate corn, beans, and squash as they helped in the garden. These earliest times with the boys were good ones.

Some time had passed and the boys were approaching adulthood. I was weeding my garden on a beautiful warm day when Sawiskera came to see me.

"Tohta, can you show me how to make a bow and arrow?" he asked with a mischievous grin.

So I made him a set just like the ones I had witnessed my relatives making in the Sky World.

"Now look, grandson, you are supposed to use this only for hunting food," I told him.

But, a short time later, Teharonhia:wakon came to me and told me of what his brother had done with the bow and arrow. Teharonhia:wakon said, "My brother Sawiskera has been impatient with our mother. He has taken the sharp arrow you made him and cut off our mother's head. He laid her head to the side of her body and she is not whole and not prepared for her travel back to the Sky World."

He shook his head and looked at me with troubled eyes as he spoke, "Sawiskera was not thinking of her but of his own frustration at her death. I buried her in the ground again and new life has sprung up from her grave." I sighed and closed my eyes for a minute. I had an image of my daughter

---

2 *Tohta* is a term of endearment used to refer to one's grandmother or grandfather. The word comes from the longer word *Aksotha*, meaning "all that I am," with reference to one's lineage.

before me. "Your brother is still troubled by your mother's death," I said, opening my eyes. "What he has done has caused you to do the right thing in return and because of this, your mother will always be remembered as She Who Always Leads."

As I spoke Teharonhia:wakon leaned in to listen.

I went on, "Your mother, even though she didn't live long, was the first being to be born on this earth. She visited this world only for a short time and now is on her return journey to where she came from. Before leaving, her body will bring forth new life, much like she did when she gave birth to you. In this way she shows us by example how the cycle of life is renewed. This is good."

The troubled look on Teharonhia:wakon's face disappeared and he looked at peace again. Teharonhia:wakon then asked me to make him a bow and arrow just like his brother's. I did so. I tried to treat the two boys equally. At the same time, I knew how different they were, and I tried to keep them apart so that they could both develop their own gifts. It went on this way for some time. I grew older, and the twins grew into men.

One day after wandering the earth, my grandson Teharonhia:wakon came home with seeds. He spoke to me.

"It is time for me to do the work I have been destined to do. I will make sure that we always have food to eat."

"I see that you have much work to do. I think you should be alone and away from me and your brother. This way we will not be in your way."

I think Teharonhia:wakon took that to be my blessing, and he left and built a lodge on the other side of the Turtle Island. I watched him go with pride and sadness because he was a connection to my Iakotsitionteh. I still had one grandson nearby. Sawiskera, I could see, was troubled or different and needed my constant guidance.

Earth Is Created

Teharonhia:wakon spent time creating many beautiful things on the earth. From a distance I could see many changes in the world. New plants began to appear where there had been none before. Birds that sang beautiful songs could be heard in the trees. New animals named Moose and Buffalo began to wander through the forest. Other animals like the Porcupine and Raccoon began to appear. I looked out from my shelter and wondered what my grandson was doing. I decided to go and visit Teharonhia:wakon to see for myself.

When I arrived with my other grandson, Sawiskera, Teharonhia:wakon offered us something to eat. When we were done, he took us outside his lodge and showed us what he had created.

"All that you see here is for us to share in," he said. "We have enough to survive, but we have to look after it." I was impressed with the good work my grandson had done.

"You have created many great things," I said, "wonderful sweet berries, healing herbs, and wonderful animals to eat. Your work is good."

I could see that my other grandson was jealous. By his actions, Sawiskera challenged his brother to work toward perfection. Sawiskera hid the animals that his brother had created. He put all the four-legged animals in a cavern where they went in for hibernation. Now he had his own steady supply of food. One day Teharonhia:wakon came to me.

"Grandmother, have you seen all the animals that I created? I am hungry and would like to eat."

"Your brother has been bringing me delicious meats to eat. Perhaps you should follow him to find out where he gets them from."

Teharonhia:wakon did so and found out what his brother had done with the animals. He set them free, but before doing so, he made them wild so they wouldn't be as easy to catch.

I continued to keep my distance to see if the twins could continue to sort out their differences. As they matured, I saw that the twins begin to share in each other's gifts. Teharonhia:wakon gave Sawiskera food in exchange for half of his disruptive power; this diminished his power by half, and he could no longer change the work of his brother.

After a time Teharonhia:wakon created the men-kind and of course the women-kind out of the red clay and gave them a portion of his life, of his mind, and of his blood. Teharonhia:wakon showed these First People, or Onkwehonwe, all that he created. He instructed them to continue the work of creation, make it beautiful, and to cultivate mother earth—a mission given to my granddaughters. Teharonhia:wakon also instructed Onkwehonwe not to take it for granted but to be thankful.

Sawiskera continued to make his own animals and plants, which were opposites of those created by his brother. Many were found to be harmful and poisonous to humans and the Onkwehonwe had to take care in their use. I took the time to teach the women-kind which plants were useful to women's work. I also taught them the planting cycles so their families would never go hungry.

In time Sawiskera created his own race of beings out of the red clay and the white foam of the sea, which gave his beings lighter skin. He did not have the same skills as his brother Teharonhia:wakon, and Sawiskera was unable to give them life. It was Teharonhia:wakon who gave these beings a bit of his life, his blood, and his mind. These beings Teharonhia:wakon said were not Onkwehonwe but would be called human beings and would be of two minds, two opposites, like the twins themselves.

One day Teharonhia:wakon had had enough of the deceitful actions of his brother, Sawiskera.

"Sawiskera, I am tired of your constantly undermining my work. Let's have a game of dice to decide this once and for all."

By this time I was too old and didn't have enough energy to get involved. I thought that this was a good way to resolve their differences. As I understood it, the dice game would decide who would take care of the night and who would take care of the day and keep the boys out of each other's way. The two brothers met on a mountaintop. Teharonhia:wakon was victorious.

Teharonhia:wakon took pity on his brother and built him a hut on the Sky Road. As the loser of the game of dice, Sawiskera was no longer allowed to come to earth during the daytime and disrupt the work of Teharonhia:wakon. With this, time was now split into day and night. It was now Sawiskera who controlled the night.

He had to watch all those who were spirits on their way to the Sky World pass before his door. When Sawiskera came out at night, he couldn't see very well. And so he was not able to cause as much trouble. With this new arrangement Teharonhia:wakon happily continued his work of creation.

My Journey to the Sky Road

Day by day I could feel myself aging and weakening. I knew I would soon go back to my relatives in the Sky World. I looked forward to seeing my mother and father again, and my daughter, Baby-Faced Lynx. One day I tried to get up, but I was too weak. I lay for a long time listening to sounds of the animals and the winds rustling through the grasses outside my lodge. I felt at peace. I knew I had done all I could on this beautiful earth—I had brought the beginnings of life and planted them in the soil. I had birthed my daughter and looked after her babies after she was gone. I had tried to be a good grandmother to Teharonhia:wakon and Sawiskera. I closed my eyes for the last time, took a deep breath, and fell asleep forever with a smile on my face.

My spirit remained on earth for ten days. In that time my grandson Teharonhia:wakon found my body and honoured me by putting my body in the night sky across the road from his brother Sawiskera. That way I could continue the good work that I had done during my lifetime and watch over Sawiskera to keep him from making too much trouble. This way I became grandmother moon. I gave Sawiskera a little light to work by at night. In this new lofty position, I also let women-kind know when to plant, when to do ceremonies, and when to birth. And most important, I keep women focused on their monthly cycles.

I don't have to worry about Sawiskera anymore. In the daytime the Onk-wehonwe have their councils and ceremonies, which only go from daybreak to sunset. They are pretty strict about doing that work during daylight hours. So Teharonhia:wakon takes care of that business very well. It is those things that one does at night that need to be balanced. In these hours things can go bad. As well, it is at night that our children are conceived. I know this because I watch over the women. And I keep an eye on the mischievous one, Sawiskera.

From my place on the Sky Road, I look over the earth where my daughter is buried, and her granddaughters and their daughters, and their daughters. My connection to my great-granddaughters continues. I made a promise to these women that they would see me every twenty-eight days. And so it is through their cycles that we have stayed in touch, all the way through time. This is what reminds them of their gifts and place on this earth.

DISCUSSION

The writing of Sky Woman's story took a few months to complete. The piece made me reflect upon my own life experiences and roles as mother, daughter, aunty, and sister. Putting myself in her place and envisioning what she must have felt and saw as she went through her life gave me special insight into my own experiences and that of the nine women living at Kahnawà:ke whom I was interviewing at the time. It helped me to understand the teachings better, and now I share them with you. This is my gift to my great-granddaughters.

I learned a certain way of being from my mother, of what it means to be a strong and independent woman, a community member, a mother: what it is to be Kanien'kehá:ka. The story of Sky Woman is told throughout the

Haudenosaunee confederacy, of which the Kanien'kehá:ka are a part.³ It is told to children and adults, written into books, painted, drawn, and woven into daily life. Although details of the story have shifted over time, certain basic elements remain the same and serve as the core of the Sky Woman narrative.⁴

It is in the interactions between Sky Woman's life as a theory of being and our life in actual practice that her experience provides special insights. As Sky Woman strives to create a heaven on earth, the corruption and the healing that she experiences move her and her world forward. She is to us mother, grandmother, peacemaker, mediator, elder, and finally Grandmother Moon, who watches over all women for time eternal. These roles represent Sky Woman's outer identity. In the words of her story, however, we glimpse her inner identity: we see her as she sees herself because we are her and she is us.

Her story also shows us that Sky World is a place where animals, humans, and spirits coexisted in mutual respect and where everything was provided for our survival, just as it is on earth. The principles of respect and equality are foundational and crucial to our survival. These principles are also illustrated in Haudenosaunee cultural, social, and spiritual life—in the clan system, matrilineal descent, consensual decision making, the cycle of ceremonies, and traditional songs and dances, to name a few. They are also embodied in the language. For example, there are no words in the languages spoken among the Haudenosaunee to describe a concept such as hate. Instead of saying "I hate you," we use the expression "ke ia ta kwa'swens" ("This person's being repulses me and I withhold my respect"), which comes from the root word for "being" or "body." In our language the root word for body and being is "iat." When we speak about someone, our language most often refers in some way to the person's body, mind, or spirit. The expression "ke ia ta

---

3 The name Haudenosaunee means "people of the long house." The confederacy consists of six nations—the Oneida, Onondaga, Seneca, Cayuga, and Tuscarora, in addition to the Kanien'kehá:ka (or Mohawk, as they were formerly known)—that joined together in the spirit of peace and mutual coexistence.

4 In his book, *The Rotinonshonni: A Traditional Iroquoian History Through the Eyes of Teharonhia:wako and Sawiskera* (Syracuse University Press, 2013), Brian Rice, a Kanien'kehá:ka, incorporates most known core elements of the Sky Woman story as part of his retelling of the larger epic of the establishment of the Haudenosaunee confederacy.

kwa'swens" focuses on the person's state of mind while maintaining respect for the person as a whole. One can also find the themes of respect and equality in the social, spiritual, and material culture, where respect for all living things is depicted in family relationships, ceremonies, wampum belts, the design elements on clothing, and much more. Our concept of equality comes from the natural world. No one human, animal, or object is better than any other. Rather, we are all part of a whole. Through time, however, these core elements of respect and equality have changed and become distorted. Often, one has to look closely, and with someone's guidance, to see them clearly.

Distortion is a major theme of Sky Woman's story. And, as in Sky Woman's story, the distortion of Haudenosaunee mother culture has taken place over centuries. This mother culture—the original culture, from which modern-day Haudenosaunee derive—speaks to the power of our women in our society. Kanien'kehá:ka women recognize that we have a closer tie to nature than men do, as we are the ones who bring forth new life and our spiritual, social, and societal responsibilities reflect this close connection. Our responsibilities work in counterbalance to those of men. Through the effects of colonization, however, our natural abilities and responsibilities have been eroded and our identities and self-perception have been negated, disregarded, re-visioned, and reconstituted according to the ideals of another people.[5]

Distortion in this context refers to the tendency of people to fall out of balance with themselves and the world. Being in balance in all things is referred to as having a "good mind." As seen earlier, Kanien'kehá:ka language references the body, mind, and spirit of the individual. The social, spiritual, and political aspects of society work in harmony to maintain balance

---

5 In many cases, we have come to believe what someone else says of us and taken it on as our own "truth." An example of this is seen in the idea of using blood quantum as a measure of how "Indian" one is. Many of our own people believe that this is an accurate measure of Indigenous identity when, in fact, as seen in old adoption practices of my ancestors, the notions of race and blood "purity" have no place in our traditional concept of identity and belonging. The adoption and integration of non-Kanien'kehá:ka people served to replenish and balance communities. The use of blood quantum as a measure of identity by our people reflects a changed thinking. Instead of relationships between all things being equal, they are now hierarchical. Therefore, as we became unbalanced, our families and communities became unbalanced.

within. As we saw, Sky Woman's own mind undergoes a certain distortion and rebalancing as she goes through life. This is what is referred to at the beginning as corruption. It is from these events that we learn how to live our lives in balance.

The social and political distortion of the role of Indigenous women is seen in the earliest narratives written about our people. Euro–North American historical thought consciously programmed the story of Haudenosaunee women out of the colonial narrative. Our history is viewed in terms of two loci of European patriarchy: religion and politics. Thus women became invisible in external and internal political maneuvering. This comes from the European's discomfort in dealing with women leaders and the authority and discretion of women's councils, a discomfort that sought, successfully, to repress the true extent of our political influence. As a result, when colonists were confronted with examples of Haudenosaunee women's influence and the threat it presented to the colonial project, they silenced and legislated away the legitimacy of our role, erasing it from historical documents and national histories. We are forced to mine these inaccurate documents for what they don't say about women and fill the gaps by talking to our elders, guessing and looking at ourselves in relationship with the natural world.

My version of Sky Woman's story in the first person actualizes Kanien'ke-há:ka women's lived experiences. Even though it was supposed to have taken place a long time ago, her story speaks to lived experiences that take place today. Each time I work on the story, I think of my own roles as mother, daughter, aunt, and community member. This work has enabled me to appreciate my own roles and understand them clearly. The writing of her story animates what I learn from women of my family and community. This is why her story is retold to our children. Her story brings to life the teachings from their families and other community members. Conversely, the rewriting of her story is augmented by the lives of the nine Kanien'kehá:ka women at the centre of my doctoral dissertation, which examines how Kahnawà:ke women express their Kanien'kehá:ka identity. The nine women I interviewed, who ranged in age from twenty-nine to eighty-six years, reflect a broad spectrum of women of this community. They are artists, educators, businesswomen, elders, and according to them, what is most important is that they are grandmothers, mothers, daughters, aunties, and sisters.

I used these stories to inform aspects of Sky Woman's experiences that I have not experienced and could thus not personally relate. Sky Woman's feelings and reactions are imbued with their experiences. She is in these nine women, and they are in her. As a result, Sky Woman's story resists or goes beyond feminism as a comment on colonial patriarchy and articulates a larger ideological framework of resilience. Her story, and its rearticulation, speaks to the idea of Indigenous womanism, in which traditional roles of women are empowered and valued. When asked whether they identified with feminism, most of the women of this study said no. Upon reflection of my own rejection of feminism, I have come to understand that what it is that Indigenous women are struggling with is not a social, spiritual, and political inequality with the opposite sex in our societies. Many of us see this as the purview of white Western feminism. We are dealing with the much larger struggle of the impacts of colonization in which sexism and patriarchy are a part. As we have awakened our own voices to this matter, white Western feminist theories no longer apply. At one time, we relied on feminism to enable us to articulate our struggle. We are now, however, working toward articulating our own theories and methods in combating colonialism through the broad spectrum of thinking called Indigenous womanism.

A reawakened Haudenosaunee womanhood leads to a second major theme of Sky Woman's story—healing. Distortion appears in many forms throughout the story. In the end, we see how this serves to teach us a lesson about ourselves as the characters achieve balance. Over the course of her life, Sky Woman finds healing and happiness time and time again, and it is usually through the enactment of her role as mother and grandmother. At every point we see her give thanks to the natural world for what it provides and its role in sustaining life. Ultimately, it is through the characters' journeys that foundational principles of the narrative are communicated. We learn that healing comes with balance and a good mind.

There is a definite view of the other in the Sky Woman story. In this case, it is the spirits who view Sky Woman as the outsider yet treat her as an equal. Even though she is different, she is given respect. In turn, she provides respect through her own actions. The idea of reciprocal respect can be seen in the historical record, where newcomers to the Americas were given food and shelter and taught how to survive in this land.[6] As Sky Woman describes

---

6 The principle of mutual co-existence was articulated in the Two Row Wampum Treaty of 1613, an agreement made between the Haudenosaunee and the Dutch government that became the foundation for the Haudenosaunee approach to all newcomers to North America. The agreement is based on peaceful co-existence,

her life, we gain understanding of the fundamental roles and responsibilities of Kanien'kehá:ka women. Women are recognized as different from men, with a different and equally significant purpose in life. Just as the Sky Woman story is a metaphor for Kanien'kehá:ka women, Kanien'kehá:ka women are a metaphor for Mother Earth, which provides everything necessary for survival. Through our ability to procreate, we represent the power of creation. This symbiotic relationship is articulated in traditional symbols, songs, and ceremonies of my people. Sky Woman's story itself also presents stark evidence for a contrast in world views and values. It is used as a reminder of the distortion of Indigenous ways by colonization.

My version is written in the first person and as such is a performative interpretation of what Sky Woman saw and felt about her fall, the development of Turtle Island, and so on. I choose this method of telling her story specifically because it is our story, lived in distortion in our everyday lives and the lives of our children. Her life is our life, as we live it to this day. We are her great-granddaughters, but our story is no different. We became distorted and are now in the process of healing. This version has all these elements, but, more important, it contains teachings from the everyday lives of women who live in my community. Every woman's story offers a clear connection, a path to the Sky Road where our Grandmother, Sky Woman, lives and watches over us. It is through this story that we reconnect with our ancestors in the Sky World.

Conclusion

Haudenosaunee women's traditions derive from the narrative that begins in the Sky World. There are many different stories about how the earth was created. Creation stories reflect divergent world views and the varied elements interwoven in a people's physical, ideological, and personal relationship with their environment. Built upon the basic need for survival, where everyone gets to be fed, to be happy, and to be healed, these stories tell how people created their own heaven on earth and provide a path to the future. The foundational principles of respect for the self and each other, equality, and personal responsibility for the future generations not yet born

---

sharing, and reciprocity, in which neither party seeks to impose its ways on the other. The relationship is symbolized in wampum belts by two purple rows with a white row between them.

form the Haudenosaunee women's tradition contained in this story. It is through this story that we come to understand and explore these principles at a theoretical level. And when we look around us at our communities, we see them in practice. If one looks closely, one can see that they continue to provide for the governance of the Haudenosaunee under the direction of the Mothers. This is what I saw as I explored the lives of the nine women in my original study.

Sky Woman's story also shows us what is at the root of what it means to be a good Haudenosaunee woman. In today's world, being a good woman is passed down intergenerationally in different ways, including the telling of this version of the narrative. Her story reminds us of our connection to our ancient mother who governs over us. As Sky Woman watches out for the cycles of birth, life, death, and rebirth, she ensures that we remain true to our feminine essence and integrate distortion and corruption into growth and healing.

The Sky Woman narrative provides many good examples of the good life and how corruption and distortion can be healed. We saw corruption when Sky Woman left the Sky World and healing when she was rescued by the water birds. We saw corruption when Muskrat died trying to get mud from the bottom of the ocean and healing when Sky Woman performed the first dance on Turtle's back. We saw corruption when Baby-Faced Lynx died in childbirth and healing when Sky Woman took over the raising of her grandsons. By these examples and many others we learn from Sky Woman how to look after the plants and animals, the children, and our future generations. From her story, we learn how to turn adversity into healing and opportunity, how to be decent to one another, and how to be rational and deliberative human beings.

It is apparent that many of our women no longer remember fully what it means to walk the good path of womanhood. There are many influences on how we perceive our identity as Indigenous women that affect our ability to be good mothers and ultimately decent human beings. Our identity as Kanien'kehá:ka women became clouded by theories of individuality that worked to distort our self-perception and corrupted us to the point that we lost our way. The path that Sky Woman maintains has been obscured. Understanding what lies behind these influences will help us strip away prescribed and projected colonial identities. Over time, people have omitted women from the historical record and said unkind things about us. Little of it has to do with us, as women, yet their work has served to structure the lives of not only Haudenosaunee women but all Indigenous women in such a way as to continue the destruction of mother culture. Yet, if one talks to our women today, they tell a version of their lived stories that is similar to the one Sky Woman handed down to us long ago. This tells us that somewhere she is alive in each and every one of us. This is where Sky Woman comes from in the first place and as long as Indigenous women exist, she'll be here trying to assert her essence.

CHAPTER TWO

Double Consciousness and Nehiyawak (Cree) Perspectives

Reclaiming Indigenous Women's Knowledge

Shalene Jobin

Those very same hands stroke the face of a child
Warrior within, not meek or mild
Every step that she takes is clearing the way
Inspiring a change, for generations today.

These lyrics—from "Okisikôwak," a song written and performed by the Indigenous women's music trio Asani—speak to the strength and power of Indigenous women.[1] They suggest that, every bit as much as men, women are warriors, fighting for positive change for Indigenous people. The destruction of Indigenous knowledge and Indigenous identity has been a fundamental objective of colonial policies in Canada. Significantly, Indigenous women have resisted the Canadian state's colonial objectives, holding on to their Indigenous teachings and seeing the importance of passing this knowledge on to future generations. In this chapter, I attempt to shed new light on

---

1 "Okisikôwak"—the Cree word for "angels"—is the fifth track on Asani's CD *Listen* (Outside Music, 2009). A micro-documentary about the making of *Listen* is available at http://youtu.be/MEz74GCVopc.

questions concerning the subjectivity and mode of resistance of Indigenous peoples. In particular, W. E. B. Du Bois's notion of double consciousness can help us understand some of the impacts of forced attendance in the Indian residential school system. Drawing on the recollections of my Nehiyaw (Cree) grandmother, I explore how the passing down of Indigenous women's knowledge through stories is an act of resistance to double consciousness. Residential schools aimed to produce subjects who had internalized the goals of colonial institutions—people who saw themselves through the eyes of the colonizer, seeking recognition and therefore mimicking non-Indigenous ways of being. This systematic program of forced assimilation, I will argue, created a double consciousness within the minds of many Indigenous people that threatened Indigenous knowledge systems. As the stories and teachings of my grandmother illustrate, women resisted the imposition of this double consciousness by passing on Indigenous women's knowledge, central in which is the relationships of women to the land broadly conceived—including relationships to the air, water, earth, and other nonhuman beings.

DOUBLE CONSCIOUSNESS

What does it feel like to be a problem? This is the fundamental question that Du Bois raises. The notion of double consciousness is developed in his seminal text, *The Souls of Black Folk* (1903). Du Bois wrote within the context of the early Jim Crow era in the United States, which had its origins in the 1870s, during the period of Reconstruction following the Civil War. The Jim Crow laws—which remained in force until the mid-1960s—created a system of racial apartheid that forced the segregation of African Americans in schools and other public places, on transportation, and in residential neighbourhoods, as well as restricting African American suffrage (Gooding-Williams 2009, 3). In the face of these new laws, the prominent turn-of-the-century educator Booker T. Washington argued that blacks should avoid political confrontation and set aside the pursuit of higher learning and instead develop a program focused on what Du Bois (1903, 42) aptly described as "industrial education, conciliation of the South, and submission and silence as to civil and political rights." Washington believed that if blacks learned a trade, this would enable them to succeed within a capitalist system, and their entrepreneurial success would bring suffrage. Du Bois was critical of this approach for numerous reasons, including the negative effect that submission to legislated inferiority would have on the psyche of blacks (see Gooding-Williams 2009, 90–94).

In the opening chapter of *The Souls of Black Folk*, Du Bois poses the fundamental question, "How does it feel to be a problem?" In his view, this feeling arises because African Americans have learned to see themselves as the "white world" sees them:

> [African Americans are]... born with a veil, and gifted with second-sight in this American world,—a world which yields him no true self-consciousness, but only lets him see himself through the revelation of the other world. It is a peculiar sensation, this double-consciousness, this sense of always looking at one's self through the eyes of others, of measuring one's soul by the tape of a world that looks on in amused contempt and pity. One ever feels his two-ness,—an American, a Negro; two souls, two thoughts, two unreconciled strivings; two warring ideals in one dark body, whose dogged strength alone keeps it from being torn asunder. (Du Bois 1903, 3)

The sense of "two-ness," of an internal struggle between two warring selves, is one of the devastating effects of racial prejudice and systemic injustices. As Robert Gooding-Williams (2009, 80) suggests, Du Bois's initial question can be stated another way: "How does it feel to be denied the normative status of membership in American society through the betrayal of the sublime ideal of reciprocity?" Gooding-Williams describes Du Bois's double consciousness as "the feeling of seeing oneself from the perspective of the other, or white, world, where that perspective has been conditioned and qualified by the racially prejudiced disclosure of Negro life"—a "revelation of the other world," implicit in which is "the application of standards-based, evaluative judgments (of 'measurings' of one's soul) to a picture of the Negro biased by amused contempt and pity" (80). Within this racially prejudiced world, black persons see themselves not as they are but instead judge themselves mistakenly, in the way that the white world sees them (81–82). This viewpoint produced a false consciousness, in which African Americans during this era evaluated themselves against standards not of their own making. For Du Bois, then, the answer was not to accommodate but to insist that white Americans overcome their prejudice and grant political and civil rights to African Americans.

The Souls of Black Folk, as a canonical text, and double consciousness, as an important theoretical concept, have been analyzed by many different authors. Léopold Senghor takes up the notion of double consciousness by seeing the need, first, to rid the African American and white American minds of the "degenerate black child" and then to replace this idea with an authentic view of African civilization (Adell 1994, 29). As Senghor explains, "In short, it is a question of both an internal and external transformation of the African American. Internally, through education and training; externally, by an increasingly strong pressure exerted on public opinion and on the American government" (Senghor 1977, translated and quoted in Adell 1994, 30). In Senghor's perspective, double consciousness was created, in part, by the false consciousness of an inauthentic view of African Americans and African civilization.

As Sandra Adell observes, Du Bois recontextualizes the Hegelian view, in which "consciousness, if it exists at all, is always a double consciousness. It is always seeking to reconcile itself with its Other. It is always striving for 'true self-consciousness.'" As she goes on to point out, "in this philosophical paradigm, the Otherness with which the Negro seeks to reconcile himself is one of the elements that constitutes his essence as a social and psychological being" (Adell 1994, 19). Rodney Roberts (2007, 100) sees in Du Bois's concept of double consciousness the suggestion that, in contrast to blacks, whites do have a true self-consciousness: "White consciousness is a one-ness. In single-consciousness there is no dependency for self in the relation to some other world, there is no other world—there is only *my* world." This reading of the notion of double consciousness shares something with feminist sociologist Dorothy Smith's concept of the "bifurcation of consciousness," according to which subordinate groups (such as women) become accustomed to seeing the world from the perspective of a dominant group (such as men). This bifurcation occurs because the dominant perspective "is *embedded* in the institutions and practices of that world. Conversely, the dominant group enjoys the privilege of remaining oblivious to the worldview of the Other, or subordinate group, since the Other is fully expected to accommodate to them" (Appelrouth and Edles 2010, 321). Judged as inferior both by race and by gender, Indigenous women are doubly vulnerable to the assimilationist policies of a patriarchal state.

INDIGENOUS DOUBLE CONSCIOUSNESS AND RESIDENTIAL SCHOOLS

Du Bois wrote during a time when segregation and racial prejudice were a normative reality for both blacks and Indigenous peoples in Canada and the United States. The Royal Proclamation of 1763, in which King George III claimed British sovereignty over North America, acknowledged the rights of "Nations or Tribes of Indians" to govern themselves and to retain title to their lands. By the time of Confederation, however, these principles had been largely forgotten. As Sir John A. Macdonald reportedly argued before the House of Commons on 8 December 1867, the government should "undertake the onerous duty of the protection of the Indian inhabitants from white aggression, and their guardianship as of persons under age, incapable of the management of their own affairs" (Canada 1967, 200, cited in Milloy 2008, 7). The national Indian policy promoted segregation until these "Indian inhabitants" were civilized enough to be enfranchised and assimilated into the larger Canadian polity. In 1920, a bill was introduced into Parliament that would amend the Indian Act so as to provide for the involuntary enfranchisement of Indians deemed suitable by an official of the Department of Indian Affairs. Commenting on the need to expedite enfranchisement, Duncan Campbell Scott, the deputy superintendent of the department from 1913 to 1932, stated to a special committee of the House of Commons in 1920: "I want to get rid of the Indian problem. . . . Our objective is to continue until there is not a single Indian in Canada that has not been absorbed into the body politic, and there is no Indian question, and no Indian Department and that is the whole object of this Bill" (quoted in Titley 1986, 50).[2]

This type of sentiment has influenced Canadian policy regarding Indigenous peoples, which operated through a combination of segregation and assimilation. Segregation was achieved through the reserve and pass system: the state moved Indigenous peoples onto separate pieces of land separating peoples from their full territory, and a person wishing to leave the reserve was required to obtain a pass from the local Indian Agent. The primary method used to achieve the state's goal of assimilation was forced attendance at Indian residential schools, the earliest of which date to the mid-nineteenth

---

2 Titley cites LAC, RG-10, vol. 6810, file 470-2-3, vol. 7, Evidence of D. C. Scott to the Special Committee of the House of Commons examining the Indian Act amendments of 1920, p. 63 [N-3]. Enfranchisement meant that a person lost his or her status as a registered Indian. Although policies varied somewhat over the years, enfranchisement could likewise be involuntary if a Status Indian moved off the reserve for an extended period of time, or acquired a post-secondary education, or served in the Canadian military. In addition, an Indian woman who married a non-Indian man lost her status.

century. The residential school system, funded by the federal government and run by churches, is arguably the most horrific program ever created in Canada.[3]

As the final report of the Royal Commission on Aboriginal Peoples notes, although the residential school system was originally designed for Indian children, it "would eventually draw children from almost every Aboriginal community—First Nation, Métis, and Inuit—across the country" (RCAP 1996, 1:172 [chap. 6, sec. 8]). The system included boarding schools for younger children, aged eight to fourteen, as well as industrial schools for older children, which were established in order to train Indigenous people in various trades. In the opinion of the commission, "the schools—80 of them at the high point—were the centrepiece of the assimilation strategy" (1:172). An essential element in this strategy was the erasure of language. Although early missionaries often favoured the use of Indigenous languages as a vehicle for conversion, students at residential schools were strictly forbidden to speak their native tongue and could be harshly punished for doing so. Instead, they were forced to speak only in English or, at some schools, in French.

In 1894, the Indian Act of 1886 was amended to enable the committal of Indigenous children, by the government, to attend residential school:

> The Governor in Council may make regulations which shall have the force of law, for the committal by justices or Indian agents of children of Indian blood under the age of sixteen years, to such industrial school or boarding school, there to be kept, cared for and educated for a period not extending beyond the time at which such children shall reach the age of eighteen years. ("An Act to Further Amend the Indian Act," RSC 1894, c. 32, s. 11: 138[2])

In addition, the Governor in Council was empowered to make regulations that would punish parents and children for non-compliance:

> Such regulations, in addition to any other provisions deemed expedient, may provide for the arrest and conveyance to school, and detention there, of truant children and of children who are prevented by their

---

3 Survivors of this system took the churches and government to court resulting in the Indian Residential Schools Settlement Agreement, "the largest class-action settlement in Canadian history" ("Residential Schools," Truth and Reconciliation Commission of Canada, n.d., http://www.trc.ca/websites/trcinstitution/index.php?p=4.

parents or guardians from attending: and such regulations may provide for the punishment, upon summary conviction, by fine or imprisonment, or both, of parents and guardians, or persons having the charge of children, who fail, refuse or neglect to cause such children to attend school. ("An Act to Further Amend the Indian Act," RSC 1894, c. 32, s. 11: 137[2])

These powers were reinforced in 1920, when another amendment to the Indian Act made attendance at residential school mandatory for all Indian children aged seven to fifteen ("An Act to Amend the Indian Act," RSC 1919–1920, c. 50). The violation of human rights inherent in such forced removal of children from their families has since been acknowledged by the United Nations.[4]

Residential school policy was envisioned by the state as a three-part process of separation, resocialization, and assimilation. First, the state-sanctioned view of Indigenous peoples as "savage" and backward justified the removal of children from their homes and communities. Second, a strict curriculum and regimented program were created with the intent of resocializing children—teaching them to feel ashamed of their culture and to strive instead to be whites. Third, policies were developed to assimilate certain graduates into the non-Indigenous world through enfranchisement, whereby the person would cease to be an Indian in the eyes of the government or society (RCAP 1996, 1:313 [chap. 10, sec. 1.1]).

In short, residential schools aimed to reshape not only the behaviour of Indigenous people but their very perception of the world and patterns of thought. The goal was to produce subjects so thoroughly alienated from their original language and society that the society would eventually cease to exist. Indigenous ways of being and knowing would be forgotten, and colonization would be complete. This system created a people who ceased to be "actional" agents of their own societies, causing them to behave as the non-Indigenous "other" and mimick non-Indigenous ways of being in order to seek colonial recognition. This goal has rightly been described as cultural

---

4 The United Nations Declaration on the Rights of Indigenous Peoples states that "Indigenous peoples have the collective right to live in freedom, peace and security as distinct peoples and shall not be subjected to any act of genocide or any other act of violence, including forcibly removing children of the group to another group" (United Nations General Assembly 2007, Article 7.2).

genocide.[5] Although, in the end, the state did not succeed in its efforts to eradicate Indigenous societies, its assimilation policies and practices and the double consciousness that these produced posed a severe threat to Indigenous knowledge systems.

LILLIAN WUTTUNEE

My grandmother, Lillian Wuttunee, was born in 1914 on the reserve of the Red Pheasant Cree First Nation, in the Eagle Hills area of Saskatchewan, not far from Battleford. All four of my grandparents attended residential school, but Lillian, who passed away in 2002, was the only one with whom I had the chance to discuss the experience. As a child she was sent to a residential school run by the Anglican Church. Even though Battleford Industrial School was virtually adjacent to the reserve, she was sent to Elkhorn Industrial School, in Manitoba, over 650 kilometers away. The location was problematic for many reasons. It was far from the territory where she lived, the land where she had learned to hunt, and the land where she knew how to harvest various medicines. The school was also too far away to allow her parents to visit, and most of the children spoke Ojibwe (Anishinaabemowin) as opposed to Cree. This distance and alienation from the other children made the experience a lonely one for Lillian. She regretted being so far away from her family. As she recalled:

> I was ten years old when I was sent to go attend the Indian Residential School at Elkhorn, Manitoba. I learned to speak Saulteaux while I was there for it is similar to Ojibwe and Cree. The children would say as I approached, "Here comes that Cree girl, watch what you say, 'cause she understands." So they couldn't talk about me.
>
> We only went to school for half a day because we also had to work. We did the laundry, washing in a big machine the many long tablecloths.

---

5 The Truth and Reconciliation Commission (TRC) of Canada explains cultural genocide as "the destruction of those structures and practices that allow the group to continue as a group" (TRC 2015, 1). They elaborate how for over a century "the central goals of Canada's Aboriginal policy were to eliminate Aboriginal governments; ignore Aboriginal rights; terminate the Treaties; and, through a process of assimilation, cause Aboriginal peoples to cease to exist as distinct legal, social, cultural, religious, and racial entities in Canada. The establishment and operation of residential schools were a central element of this policy, which can best be described as 'cultural genocide' (TRC 2015, 1)." (TRC 2015).

[. . .] Other days were set aside for darning and mending. [. . .] When I got older, I was placed to work in the bakery, where we learned to mix the dough in huge vats. I also worked in the dairy, churning butter, sometimes using my hands or using my feet turning the pedals. [. . .] I was an excellent seamstress from the time I was twelve. It was part of the curriculum that we work as well as learning reading, writing, and arithmetic.

We followed a strict ritual, going to bed at a certain time each night after kneeling to say our prayers. In the morning we would quickly hop out of bed and dress. Each of us had a locker along the wall, about sixteen inches wide. Every Monday morning we would be given salts from big jugs, meant to clean out our insides. I used to hate that, so I'd hold it in my mouth. As soon as the instructor had left the room I would race three floors down to the toilet and spit out the salts.

Boys and girls lived in separate dormitories and during meals ate at separate tables. My sister Maria was the supervisor's pet, while I used to get spankings from this same woman. Our hair was cut at an angle, and we all had bangs. This hairdo was called shingles.

Somedays I would just sit staring out at the high-board fences that surrounded the school. I was about fifteen or sixteen when I finally left to go back to the reserve. [. . .] During my stay at Elkhorn I made good friends, Edgarton Thunderchild, from the Thunderchild Reserve, and Helen and Agnes Eaglechief. But it was so nice to go home.[6]

Even if physical and sexual abuse were absent (or not revealed) in a residential school experience, cultural genocide persisted. For Lillian, the experience of residential school entailed emotional trauma the effects of which persisted into adult life, becoming visible in patterns of behaviour that suggest underlying conflicts about identity and self-worth. In her reminiscences, I observe illustrations of what Du Bois terms double consciousness in some of her actions. For example, while she and her husband, Gilbert, would speak Cree to each other, they made a point of speaking English to their children, even though their older children were fluent in Cree having spent their formative years in the Red Pheasant Cree community. In 1942 when it was time for the older children to start school, they moved from the reserve into Battleford, and Lillian began to spend a lot of time going through

---

6 My grandmother dictated these words, and all those that follow, to my mother, Loretta Jobin (née Wuttunee), on 27 February 1993, in Edmonton. My mother later transcribed them, and they are used here with her permission.

magazines looking at the latest fashions among white Canadians. Similarly, she would read books on proper table settings and etiquette. Lillian explains:

> Now, coming right off the reserve, I had to learn many new things myself. I immediately bought books to learn table etiquette and to teach myself how to dress in proper fashion. My minister came to me to invite us to a picnic (I didn't know what a picnic was). I dressed my children for this, putting a little suit with a white shirt on my son, while the little girls wore pink silk dresses. I was pregnant at this time. When we arrived at the picnic, everyone was dressed in shorts or blue jeans. I was angry with my minister for not telling me how to properly dress my children. I would not mix with the other women; instead I sat by myself, for I was in a bad humour. I never made the mistake of wearing wrong clothing again. Little did I know I had been enjoying picnics every day, as well as having a siesta under the trees near our home, when we had lived on Red Pheasant reserve.

Such anecdotes, sometimes retold at family functions, could simply be understood as endearing stories that explain an aspect of Lillian's character. Viewed in the light of Du Bois's concept of double consciousness, however, these stories, and others like it, point to the conflicts that result from the internalization of the standards of another culture through the forced attendance in the Indian Residential School System.

Through the experience of residential schools, Lillian was, as Du Bois put it, "gifted with second-sight" in the Canadian world. With this "gift," she saw herself, and received a sense of her worth as a woman, mother, wife, and human being, through the eyes of the white world. Sewing current fashions and mimicking white social norms allowed her to measure her soul "by the tape of a world that looks on in amused contempt and pity." When children arrived at residential school, not only was their hair immediately cut, but their clothes were replaced with uniforms. As sociologist Renée White points out, "Destabilization of national identity can occur by simply transforming the meaning of dress" (1966, 104). As she goes on to explain, in the process of acculturation, a person adopts the cultural markers, such as dress and manners, of the colonizing other, whether by necessity or by choice; in this way, markers that reveal the person's original cultural identity become "less visible and thus less reprehensible to the eye of the oppressor" (105). Perhaps Lillian's desire to dress and behave "in proper fashion" was a coping strategy, her attempt to be viewed and accepted by white Canadians as a fellow human being.

Figure 2.1 Lillian Wuttunee cooking a fish (n.d.).

At residential schools, children were imbued with a false consciousness: they were taught to regard white people as superior and to see themselves through the eyes of white disapproval. Viewing the world through the veil of this false consciousness, Indigenous peoples experienced a sense of inferiority. Frantz Fanon (1963, 228) writes that, given the belief in the superiority of the white man, the only destiny for a black man was to be white. Similarly, the only hope for Indigenous peoples was to succeed as far as possible in becoming white. The goal of residential schooling has indeed been described as "killing the Indian in the child." As the Aboriginal Healing Foundation explains, "In the context of residential schooling, 'killing the Indian' meant dis-connecting children physically, emotionally, mentally and spiritually from their language, culture and their communities and also, but most painfully, from their own sense of identity as being Indian" (Aboriginal Healing Foundation 2005, 44).

Physical dislocation occurred with the removal of children from their families and communities. Significantly, it also often meant removal from home territory and a break in relationships normally renewed through practices on the land. Following this physical separation, "emotional disconnection was achieved by teaching children that the parents, grandparents and Elders they so loved were savages, and their own bodies and racial characteristics were sinful and dirty" (Aboriginal Healing Foundation 2005, 45). Spiritual disconnection resulted from the forced assimilation of Indigenous children into a new religion, coupled with amendments to the Indian Act that outlawed traditional ceremonies. Forbidding children to speak their language and participate in their culture created mental disconnection. One effect of this mental disconnection, and an important aim of assimilation, was to stop the transfer of Indigenous knowledge to further generations. This process of disconnection left some survivors with deep-seated feelings of confusion because they felt that "being Indigenous was wrong" (Aboriginal Healing Foundation 2005, 47). In turn, this sense of ontological wrongness produced a false consciousness, in that survivors' understanding of their Indigenous identity was based on the warped views of residential school authorities, agents of the Canadian government, and the Canadian public. The stories of these survivors do not end here, however: resistance to assimilation and efforts to heal the double consciousness have occurred and continue to occur. As an important part of this process, residential school survivors and their descendants are reclaiming and sharing Indigenous knowledge.

For many Indigenous people, the response to assimilation and cultural geno-cide is not to struggle to merge the assimilated and the Indigenous self into one; rather it is to reclaim the Indigenous self and then to move forward in what Taiaiake Alfred (2009, 16) calls "a self-conscious traditionalism."[7] While Du Bois's concept of double consciousness is helpful for diagnosing the "problem," my grandmother's story cannot be fully understood in this way. In the life story she recounted, Lillian found it important to share Nehi-yawak (Cree) teachings, teachings she wanted me, her other grandchildren, and members of the community to know. This knowledge includes teachings about territory and how we are connected to the land.

Along with sacred stories and legends, personal stories, such as those told by Lillian, are one of the often-recognized styles of storytelling in Indigenous oral traditions (Wilson 2008, 97–98, citing Cree Elder Jerry Saddleback). By recounting the teachings she received from her grandmother, Lillian con-tributes to this collective narrative memory: she passes these teachings along to me and her other grandchildren while also linking us to our great-great-grandmother, who once recounted them to her. Songhees scholar Robina Thomas (2005, 240) talks about how important this sense of connection is to her: "My Grandmothers' stories are the essential core of my being. The stories are cultural, traditional, educational, spiritual, and political." As she explains, storytelling "also taught us about resistance to colonialism—our people have resisted even when legislation attempted to assimilate our children. All stories have something to teach us. What is most important is to learn to listen, not simply hear, the words that storytellers have to share. Many stories from First Nations tell a counter-story to that of the documented history of First Nations in Canada" (241). The literature on oral histories points to their living nature. As Julie Cruikshank (2005, 27) argues, these histories cannot be relegated to a "freeze-dried" past: they are continually reanimated by the specific nuances and wisdom imparted by the storyteller. Oral history should be seen as a social activity (Cruikshank 1998, 41), which gives us tools to live well.

---

7 Alfred (2009, 16) writes: "I am advocating a self-conscious traditionalism, an intel-lectual, social, and political movement that will reinvigorate these values, principles, and other cultural elements that are best suited to the larger contemporary political and economic reality."

My grandmother's stories illustrate a type of teaching and learning very different from the one offered within the somber walls of residential schools. These teachings stem from her knowledge of the ways of her people, her connection to the land, and her identity as a Cree woman. Despite the forced assimilation she experienced at residential school, my grandmother hung on to the knowledge she learned from her own grandmother and passed that knowledge on to her granddaughters, thereby weaving five generations of Wuttunee women together. Lillian understood the need to protect and reclaim the knowledge collectively held by her Cree ancestors. Her recounting of that knowledge is an act of resistance to assimilation, one that insists on the importance of collective narrative memory. As she explained:

> My father's mother, Marie, first taught me to set snares. She was the younger of the two sisters that my grandfather had for wives before he died in 1904. When the missionaries came to the reserve, he was told he could only keep one wife and so Marie moved into a separate house. It was behind my parents' home, but when it caught fire and burned down, she moved in with us.
>
> I used to follow behind her as she gathered medicines and listen as she told me what they were used for. I was very young and can only recall her saying, ayîkotâsima [This is Frog Pants] and this is good medicine. She would wrap the different medicines in a little calico cloth, and just by smell alone she could tell the names of the different roots and herbs. She also used to dig for Seneca roots, which she would tell me she was going to sell to Chinese people. Having being taught to taste the leaves and barks on the bushes of the berries we picked, I could tell you blindfolded a chokecherry from a raspberry or Saskatoon bush.

My grandmother chose to record this account for her descendants. She understood the importance of natural medicines and the knowledge that her grandmother carried as a Cree woman. Her story of how her grandmother taught her to set snares also demonstrates that Indigenous women played a vital part in hunting and hunting-related activities: these functions were not the sole prerogative of men. This is important, as the significant roles that Indigenous women play in hunting are too often ignored (Kuokkanen 2011, 227). Her narrative speaks to a different lived experience, one that is not outside the norm within my grandmother's world view. Lillian shared a few other hunting stories:

I was alone for five years before my sister Maria came along. I used to entertain myself by snaring rabbits. When I got a little older, I would also set traps on the lakes for muskrats and then wade in the water to retrieve my catch. One time, I was setting a trap and I forgot to set it off before slinging it over my back. It caught me right on my bum. I screamed and cried and jumped around until my grandmother heard the commotion. "What's the matter, *nosim*?" she asked. "I'm caught, I'm trapped. It's got my bum," I howled. This caused quite a few laughs to the people on the reserve for years to come.

I was quite the little hunter. I also trapped a weasel. It was yellow-brown for it was during the summer. I couldn't have been too old for it looked ferocious to me, and I didn't dare go too close to it in case it scratched me, so instead I decided to get my father. "There's something in my trap," I said to him. "I don't know what it is but it's a wicked animal." My father tried to keep a stern face and agreed to go and see it with me. When he got to the trap, he held the weasel with a stick while stepping on the trap with his foot to release it. The weasel's fur was useless to us in summer for to be paid anything the fur had to be white. I would hunt for everything, even gophers, and I helped to clear my uncles' fields of them.

As a young girl, my grandmother not only learned how to hunt, but she took pride in her skills. Her words also speak to the importance of humour and learning about humility.

Sharing personal stories is one way that Indigenous knowledge can be passed on; another method is through the sharing of Indigenous legends. Stories about Wîsahkecâhk, the trickster, are often considered sacred stories. These legends share teachings about ways of being in the world, ways of interacting with other humans and animals, and ways of being in relationship with the land. My grandmother's *nohkôm* (grandmother) shared Wîsahkecâhk stories with her.[8] These are my grandmother's words:

---

8 According to tradition, these stories were to be told during the winter. Lillian wanted these stories shared. When thinking through the ethics of publishing her Wîsahkecâhk account (and after talking and receiving approval from advisors, including a Cree Elder), I felt reassured when I found that a version of this legend was already in print, one told by the Rock Cree of northwestern Manitoba (Brightman 1989, 31–32) and it reminded me of the reach of Wîsahkecâhk legends throughout the expanse of Cree territory.

My grandmother always wore black. A black skirt and blouse, moccasins, and a black handkerchief tied around her head. She spoke only Cree. She still had good eyesight for I remember she could spot an insect from across the room.

"*Nohkôm*," I'd tell her, "you are so beautiful."

"*Kayâsês nôsisim*," she'd answer. "Long ago, granddaughter, I used to be a beautiful young woman."

"You're still beautiful, *nohkôm*," I'd reply and ask her to tell me a story, which she would do only in the winter, for she said it was bad luck to tell them in the summer.

"Okay," she'd answer, "but first sit there until I finish smoking."

I would watch as she filled her little clay pipe with tobacco and stare as she took each puff, waiting patiently for her to finish so that she could tell me a story. Finally she'd begin:

Wîsahkecâhk was walking in the woods when he heard some laughter. Being inquisitive by nature, he followed the sounds until he came across a flock of little birds.

"Why are you laughing, brothers?" he asked them.

"We have headaches," they answered, "and so we are throwing our eyeballs up into the trees."

"What happens then?" Wîsahkecâhk asked his feathered friends.

"We have only to shake the trees and our little eyeballs fall back into our heads, and so we cure our headaches," they answered him, for everything had to answer Wîsahkecâhk when he talked to them.

"I have a headache too," Wîsahkecâhk said.

"Oh, you must not say that just for the fun of it," the birds chirped. "Or something bad will happen to you," they added.

"I understand," Wîsahkecâhk said, before adding, "but I do have a headache."

The little birds did not believe him and so said, "We're warning you. You must not do this for nothing."

Wîsahkecâhk did not listen to the birds' advice. Instead, he threw his eyeballs up into the trees. Just then a fox was walking by and when Wîsahkecâhk shook the tree to get his eyeballs back, the fox caught them in his mouth and ran away. Wîsahkecâhk didn't really have a headache and now found himself without eyes. Being blind now, he stumbled to the different trees and touched their bark.

"Brother," he asked, "what kind of tree are you?" Each of the trees he touched identified themselves and told Wîsahkecâhk what kind of medicinal powers their bark, leaves, and roots were good for. Finally,

Wîsahkecâhk reached a spruce tree and, after feeling its bark, asked, "What kind of tree are you, my brother?"

"Minahik," the tree answered.

"You are just the tree I need," Wîsahkecâhk cried out in happiness. He climbed into its branches until he found its resin. He put it into his mouth and began to chew it until it finally became soft. From that he rolled out first one and then another eyeball and placed them into his empty sockets. He thanked the tree for giving him their medicine so that he could see once more.

Commenting on this legend, my grandmother said, "Now, it wasn't until I reached my seventies that I finally understood what that story was all about." She went on to say:

My grandmother never explained the curing part to me, for I was just a child. Instead, she told it to me like a story. The next night I would say to her again, "âcimow nôhkom" [Tell me a story, grandmother]. "Cêskwa" [Wait a minute], she'd answer, and she would go through the same ritual of smoking her pipe before beginning.

The story is indeed full of layered meanings. It speaks to proper (and improper) relations with other living things. It also speaks to Indigenous knowledge of the natural world and the availability of an abundance of medicines. In her account, Lillian explains the significance of one aspect of the knowledge found within this story, "Now, it wasn't until I reached my seventies that I finally understood what that story was all about" (1993). She explains the specific medicinal knowledge found within the story. She went on to say:

My grandmother never explained the curing part to me for I was just a child. Instead she told it to me like a story. The next night I would say to her again, "âcimow nohkôm" [Tell me a story, grandmother]. "Cêskwa" [Wait a minute], she'd answer and she would go through the same ritual of smoking her pipe before beginning.

As a child she understood certain teachings within Wîsahkecâhk stories, and as she grew older and her knowledge increased, her levels of understanding became apparent. This is part of the magnificence of Indigenous stories and the abundance of knowledge included within.

Conclusion

Settlers in settler-colonial countries have a home or mother country; for Indigenous peoples in Canada, we have no other home than this land. The primary objectives of Du Bois have been achieved; there are no longer unequal political and civil rights in America like those under the Jim Crow law. For Nehiyawak (Cree) people, although forms of self-determination have been achieved through acts of resistance, we have not achieved a post-colonial reality. The land left is only a postage stamp of our prior homeland. The gendered racism within settler colonial countries like Canada has resulted in a type of Indigenous double consciousness that has been amplified for Indigenous women. However, assimilation techniques like the Indian residential school system in Canada did not erase Indigenous knowledge or the importance of passing this knowledge on to future generations. Storytelling is one method that Indigenous peoples use to pass on this knowledge. Connection to the land and medicines found in nature are a few of the many important lessons contained within the stories my grandmother shared. Oral histories and storytelling are two ways to resist colonial attempts to erase Indigenous history and connection to territory. We need to tell more Indigenous women's stories: telling Indigenous stories affirms Indigenous identities, Indigenous ontologies, ways of being in the world, the complex roles of women in stewardship of the land, and our important roles in governance. Storytelling is one way to stand against double consciousness, by asserting the value of Indigenous women's knowledge systems. The history of opposition and struggle against colonial oppression has accomplished important gains; perhaps most significant are the psychological benefits achieved through resistance.

I would like to acknowledge the helpful feedback on earlier drafts of this paper from Nathalie Kermoal, Naomi McIlwraith, and Loretta Jobin. Parts of this chapter appeared in an earlier publication, "Cautionary Tales for Today: Wetigo Stories, Residential Schools, and Double Consciousness," *Journal of the North American Institute for Indigenous Theological Studies* 10 (2012): 77–88. Permission to use this material is gratefully acknowledged.

References

Aboriginal Healing Foundation. 2005. "Reclaiming Connections: Understanding Residential School Trauma Among Aboriginal People." Ottawa: Aboriginal Healing Foundation. http://www.ahf.ca/downloads/healing-trauma-web-eng.pdf.

Adell, Sandra. 1994. *Double-Consciousness/Double Bind: Theoretical Issues in Twentieth-Century Black Literature*. Urbana: University of Illinois Press.

Appelrouth, Scott, and Laura Desfor Edles. 2010. *Sociological Theory in the Contemporary Era: Text and Readings*. 2nd ed. Thousand Oaks, Calif.: Sage Publications.

Alfred, Taiaiake. 2009. *Peace, Power, Righteousness: An Indigenous Manifesto*. 2nd ed. Don Mills, Ontario: Oxford University Press.

Brightman, Robert. 1989. *Ācaðōhkīwina and Ācimōwina: Traditional Narratives of the Rock Cree Indians*. Hull, QC: Canadian Museum of Civilization.

Canada. 1967. *House of Commons Debates, First Session, First Parliament, 31 Victoria, Comprising the Period from the Sixth Day of November, 1867, to the Twenty-Second Day of May, 1868*. Ottawa: Queen's Printer, 1967.

Cruikshank, Julie. 1998. *The Social Life of Stories*. Vancouver: University of British Columbia Press.

———. 2005. *Do Glaciers Listen? Local Knowledge, Colonial Encounters and Social Imagination*. Vancouver: University of British Columbia Press.

Du Bois, W. E. B. 1903. *The Souls of Black Folk: Essays and Sketches*. Chicago: A. C. McClurg and Company.

Fanon, Frantz. 1963. *The Wretched of the Earth*. New York: Grove Press.

Gooding-Williams, Robert. 2009. *In the Shadow of Du Bois: Afro-Modern Political Thought in America*. Cambridge, Mass.: Harvard University Press.

Kuokkanen, Rauna. 2011. "Indigenous Economies, Theories of Subsistence, and Women: Exploring the Social Economy Model for Indigenous Goverance." *American Indian Quarterly* 35 (2): 215–40.

McLeod, Neal. 2000. "Cree Narrative Memory." *Oral History Forum / Forum d'histoire orale* 19–20: 37–61.

———. 2007. *Cree Narrative Memory: From Treaties to Contemporary Times*. Saskatoon: Purich Publishing.

Milloy, John. 2008. Indian Act Colonialism: A Century of Dishonour, 1869–1969. Ottawa: National Centre for First Nations Governance. http://fngovernance.org/ncfng_research/milloy.pdf.

United Nations. 2008. "Press Briefing: Permanent Forum Speakers Say Violation of Language Rights 'Cultural Genocide,' Call for Concrete Public Policy to Protect Indigenous Languages." United Nations: Meetings Coverage and Press

Releases. 24 April. http://www.un.org/News/briefings/docs/2008/hr4948.doc.
htm.

RCAP (Royal Commission on Aboriginal Peoples). 1996. *Report of the Royal
Commission on Aboriginal Peoples*. Ottawa: Minister of Supply and Services.
http://www.collectionscanada.gc.ca/webarchives/20071115053257/http://www.
ainc-inac.gc.ca/ch/rcap/sg/sgmm_e.html.

Roberts, Rodney. 2007. "Rectificatory Justice and the Philosophy of W. E. B. Du
Bois." In *Re-Cognizing W. E. B. Du Bois in the Twenty-First Century*, edited
by Mary Keller and Chester J. Fontenot, Jr., 88–111. Macon, GA: Mercer
University Press.

Thomas, Robina Anne. 2005. "Honouring the Oral Traditions of My Ancestors
Through Storytelling." In *Research as Resistance: Critical, Indigenous, and
Anti-oppressive Approaches*, edited by Leslie Brown and Susan Strega,
237–54. Toronto: Canadian Scholars' Press.

Titley, Brian. 1986. *A Narrow Vision: Duncan Campbell Scott and the
Administration of Indian Affairs in Canada*. Vancouver: University of British
Columbia Press.

Truth and Reconciliation Commission of Canada. 2015. *Honouring the
Truth, Reconciling the Future: Summary of the Final Report of the Truth
and Reconciliation Commission of Canada*. http://www.trc.ca/websites/
trcinstitution/File/2015/Honouring_the_Truth_Reconciling_for_the_Future_
July_23_2015.pdf.

UN General Assembly. 2007. "United Nations Declaration on the Rights of
Indigenous Peoples." http://www.un.org/esa/socdev/unpfii/documents/
DRIPS_en.pdf.

White, Renée T. 1996. "Revolutionary Theory: Sociological Dimensions of
Fanon's *Sociologie d'une revolution*." In *Fanon: A Critical Reader*, edited by
Lewis Gordon, T. Denean Sharpley-Whiting, and Renée T. White, 100–109.
Oxford: Blackwell.

Wilson, Shawn. 2008. *Research Is Ceremony: Indigenous Research Methods*.
Black Point, NS: Fernwood Publishing.

CHAPTER THREE

Naskapi Women

Words, Narratives, and Knowledge

Carole Lévesque, Denise Geoffroy, and Geneviève Polèse

By sharing their stories and knowledge, Naskapi women have played a key role in the reconstruction of the cultural and ecological heritage of their people. The Naskapi, who live in the subarctic region of the province of Québec, today represent about nine hundred people, most of whom reside in the village of Kawawachikamach, located about fifteen kilometres from the former mining town of Schefferville, along the 55th parallel (see map 3.1). The first written reports of the Naskapi date from the late eighteenth century. It appears that, at the time of the Europeans' arrival, the peoples to whom these reports refer did not form a single, integrated group rather they were several groups of hunters who ranged across the northern portion of the Québec Labrador peninsula (Lévesque, Rains, and de Juriew 2001). The evidence suggests that these were families or groups of hunters of Innu origin who, sometime around the mid-eighteenth century, had apparently migrated to the hinterland of the subarctic region from the North Shore of the St. Lawrence (where several Innu bands had settled). Initially few in number, the Naskapi are said to have comprised about three hundred people around 1830 (Lévesque et al. 2001).

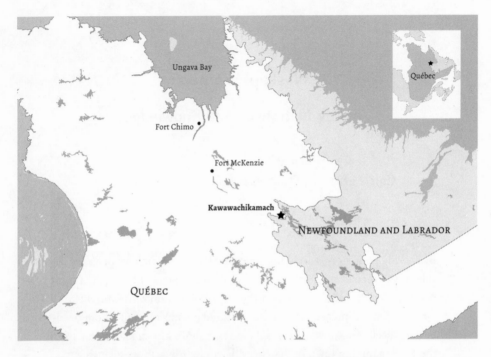

Map 3.1 Location of the Naskapi village of Kawawachikamach, northern Québec. Source: Laboratoire d'analyse spatiale et d'économie urbaine et régionale, Institut national de la recherche scientifique, Montréal.

In the mid-nineteenth century, Cree families from the James Bay region arrived in the area and joined the Naskapi families. By the end of the century, these peoples were travelling regularly to the trading post at Fort Chimo (now Kuujjuaq), on Ungava Bay, where they traded their furs for manufactured goods and food products (Turner, 1979). During his stay at Fort Chimo between 1882 and 1884, the American naturalist Lucien Turner ([1894] 1979) noted the presence of Naskapi Indians, who called themselves "Nenenot," or "true red men." Other sources state that these were indeed the ancestors of the Naskapi families living in Kawawachikamach today (see, for example, Cooke 1976; Graburn 1975; Mailhot 1983). At the time Turner wrote, the Naskapi differed from other Indigenous groups in the subarctic region because they preferred to hunt for caribou rather than trapping fur-bearing animals. In addition, because they did not attach themselves to a particular trading post but instead travelled to many trading posts over a wide expanse of territory (from Labrador east to James Bay and Abitibi, as well as south to the North Shore and the St. Lawrence valley), they preserved a certain degree of independence in their relations with both traders and missionaries, at least up to the early twentieth century. They are recognized in the oral tradition and in the literature as great travellers, and especially as highly skilled and prolific caribou hunters. Unlike many hunter peoples in the subarctic region, the Naskapi's adoption of a sedentary lifestyle is fairly recent, dating only from the 1950s (Lévesque et al. 2001).

This chapter is based on data from an ethnographic survey begun in 2000 and carried out in phases until 2012. The research involved several groups of Naskapi elders, both men and women, as well as a university research team.[1]

---

1 This ethnographic study was part of a broader initiative carried out by the Naskapi Development Corporation (NDC) aimed at revitalizing local cultural and ecological knowledge. At the request of the Institut national de la recherche scientifique, which is associated with the Université du Québec, we undertook this study in close collaboration with the community (see details p. 14 in the present chapter). The team of Naskapi elders brought together by the Naskapi Development Corporation included Jane Einish, Philip Einish Jr., Thomas Einish, Joseph Guanish, Luke Guanish, Sandra Guanish, Ann Joseph, Matthew Mameamskum, Ruby Nattawappio, Sandy Nattawappio, Donald Peastitute, John Shecanapish, David Swappie, Shinapest Tooma, Kathleen Tooma, Minnie Uniam, and Sandy Uniam. The team of researchers, under the leadership of Carole Lévesque and Denise Geoffroy, consisted of Nadine Trudeau, Marcelle Chabot, Muriel Paradelle, and Geneviève Polèse. Assisting the participants were translators Noat Einish, Philip Einish, and Silas Nabinacaboo.

The study was guided by two goals: to listen to and record Naskapi men's and women's words and knowledge and to create conditions favouring the equitable expression of views as well as knowledge sharing between men and women. Interest lies with the nature and scope of the information provided by Naskapi elders but also with the collaborative and reflective methodological approach underlying the discussion and research activities themselves. This approach reflects a firm commitment, on the part of everyone involved in the study—researchers and elders alike—to the co-production of knowledge on the culture and way of life of the Naskapi people.

The heritage that the Naskapi have undertaken to reconstruct for the benefit of future generations is closely associated with the final period of their lives as nomads, which they call the "Fort McKenzie time" and which lasted from 1915 to 1950. Several of the people who lived during this period are still alive today, and it is with these men and women that an ecological reconstruction exercise was launched in the early 2000s. We have organized our text into three parts to enable us to reconstruct some of the components of the universe of Naskapi knowledge. In the first part, we briefly summarize the categories of knowledge shared by Naskapi men and women. The second part examines the interface between men and women in the carrying out of their lives and in ensuring their subsistence. The third part takes a closer look at the area of medicinal plants, an area that is mainly the domain of women.

RESEARCH FRAMEWORK

Our research work is very much a part of the movement toward recognition of Indigenous peoples' knowledge that has developed and intensified over the past few decades. Indeed, since the early 1980s, interest in Indigenous knowledge has continued to grow (see, for example, Chabot and Lévesque 2001; Ellen, Parkes, and Bicker 2000; Lévesque et al. 2001; Lutz and Neis 2008; Menzies 2006). As Indigenous peoples have emerged as a political force both nationally and internationally, their knowledge has come to represent a key mark of identity for them and a new sphere of cultural and political affirmation. The legitimacy of this knowledge as a source of information that can be used to protect ecosystems and promote the responsible management of land and natural resources has been recognized on numerous occasions by the governments of many countries and by Canada, in particular. This recognition has also been manifested in the special provisions regarding the protection and potential use of this knowledge found in many international conventions, national environmental laws, and regional and local co-management strategies. We need only point, for example, to the provisions of the Convention on Biological Diversity (United Nations 1992), which urges member countries to take measures to recognize and protect traditional knowledge and to ensure that the application of this knowledge is considered in the areas of conservation and sustainable development.[2]

More recently, with the provisions of the United Nations Declaration on the Rights of Indigenous Peoples (United Nations 2007), earlier commitments with regard to Indigenous knowledge developed into universal human rights and were extended to all areas of Indigenous peoples' social, economic, political, artistic, and cultural lives.[3] Such developments confirm that Indigenous knowledge offers more than empirical information on the natural environment. It refers to the wide array of attitudes, abilities, and skills that its holders (both men and women) develop over the course of their lives in their social interactions and their social organization. It also testifies to particular ways of understanding the material and immaterial worlds and to the relationships of various kinds that exist among human beings, animals, and the land (see, for example, Berkes 1999; Descola 2005; Stevenson 1996; Turner et al. 2008).

Nevertheless, within this vast field, despite hundreds of studies from various parts of the world and the significant involvement of a number of Indigenous organizations, women's words have more often than not been ignored (Native Women's Association of Canada 2007, 3–4). In 2000, when

---

2 Article 8(j) stipulates: "Subject to its national legislation, [each Contracting Party shall] respect, preserve and maintain knowledge, innovations and practices of indigenous and local communities embodying traditional lifestyles relevant for the conservation and sustainable use of biological diversity and promote their wider application with the approval and involvement of the holders of such knowledge, innovations and practices and encourage the equitable sharing of the benefits arising from the utilization of such knowledge, innovations and practices" (United Nations 1992, 6). For a discussion of Indigenous environmental knowledge in the context of northern Québec, see Lévesque et al. (2004).

3 Article 31 (1) reads: "Indigenous peoples have the right to maintain, control, protect and develop their cultural heritage, traditional knowledge and traditional cultural expressions, as well as the manifestations of their sciences, technologies and cultures, including human and genetic resources, seeds, medicines, knowledge of the properties of fauna and flora, oral traditions, literatures, designs, sports and traditional games and visual and performing arts" (United Nations 2007, 11).

the members of the Naskapi Development Corporation undertook to set up a research project specifically concerning the properties of medicinal plants and herbs, an area of knowledge that was the responsibility of the women of the community, their initiative was bold and innovative (see Lévesque, Geoffroy, and Polèse 2006).

Moreover, our ethnographical studies also form part of a shift toward a knowledge society, which is placing more and more value on many different types of knowledge and on the skills and expertise of knowledge holders, regardless of who these knowledge holders may be (UNESCO 2005). The expression "knowledge society" or "information society" appeared toward the end of the 1990s with reference to the new conditions of learning and knowledge transmission made necessary by the emergence of information technologies. From this perspective, it became increasingly important for modern societies to invest in human knowledge and training and to focus on creativity and social innovation as much as on technological innovation. According to the definitions proposed by UNESCO, the knowledge society calls for development that is no longer centred only on economic growth but also on social development and human capital. Initiatives that aim at reconstructing knowledge that has disappeared or is in the process of disappearing, like the project undertaken by the Naskapi of Kawawachikamach, contribute directly to this new society by helping to document little-known systems of knowledge that may shed considerable light on the ways in which human beings of various origins and at different times have constructed their relationship to the world and the environment (Lévesque 2009).

ELEMENTS OF THE NASKAPI SYSTEM OF KNOWLEDGE

From the beginning to the middle of the twentieth century, Naskapi families' travel routes covered an area of 150 to 200 square kilometres, spanning the boundary between boreal forest and tundra in the eastern portion of the Québec-Labrador peninsula. In the winter of 1915–16, the Hudson's Bay Company established Fort McKenzie, a trading post in the heart of this region. Located inland some 150 kilometres south of Ungava Bay, the fort soon became a gathering point for many Naskapi families. For more than three decades, until the late 1940s, Fort McKenzie played a structuring role in the lives of these families of hunters, who came there to trade fur for tea, tobacco, flour, sugar, fabrics, ammunition, weapons, and other manufactured goods. At first, their visits took place mainly during the summer.

Hunting groups, generally consisting of three or four families (or about twenty people), spent the winter harvesting fur-bearing game in remote camps and then, in summer, met up with other groups at the fort. It became a regular gathering place over the years, especially for trading post employees, older people, and widows and their children. Ultimately, it became a place to which the Naskapi were rooted not only geographically but also in terms of identity (see Lévesque et al. 2001).

The Fort McKenzie trading post closed in 1948. The Naskapi population (some 190 to 200 people) then went back to live at Fort Chimo, on Ungava Bay. Life at Fort Chimo was very hard for the Naskapi, who found themselves in a less familiar environment, far from their usual hunting and trapping areas and from the places that they preferred for their camps. Many of them suffered from tuberculosis. Poverty now became rampant, and the reports of the teams of doctors and administrators that visited Fort Chimo at that time testified to the Naskapis' plight. The federal government began to take steps to resettle the group in the Schefferville area, where a new iron mine had begun operation in the early 1950s. The initial move to the Schefferville area took place in 1956 when the whole Naskapi population at Fort Chimo was moved by plane.

Although between then and the late 1970s, the Naskapi population was moved again several times in the region, because the government had not formally allocated territory to them, it was only after the signing of the Northeastern Quebec Agreement in 1978 that the Naskapi were granted rights to specific lands in the Schefferville region. They moved for the last time in 1984 to the brand new village of Kawawachikamach, where they built homes and have since been living (Lévesque et al. 2001).

When Naskapi men and women tell stories about the Fort McKenzie period, it is in hopes of transmitting the teachings and the memory of that time to the young people of their community:

> Young people have to know about nature so that they can find means of survival. It would be very useful for the community to pass the knowledge to the young. There needs to be a way to show our traditions to the youth; they need to see it. It is important to preserve the Naskapi culture. Our knowledge is the product of our observation of the environment during thousands of years and of these observations, influenced by our beliefs, values and customs. (woman, 2003)[4]

---

4 All comments from Naskapi elders were recorded in Kawawachikamach.

In telling these stories, embedded in which is their collective cultural heritage, the Naskapi identified four knowledge complexes that are in continual interaction with one another. We have classified these complexes as ecological, material, social, and spiritual knowledge.[5]

From an ecological viewpoint, the elders' narratives reflect an intimate knowledge of the natural environment in which they lived. They were closely familiar with the behaviour, habitats, diseases, predators, reproductive cycles, and migration patterns of the animals and fish:

> The wolves run in packs. They ambush the caribou. They go at the back
> of the herd, and then there is another pack that comes to the front.
> Once a pack spots a herd, they sneak up on it. When they howl, it is a
> message to other wolves to join in for the kill, just like a normal hunter
> gives direction to another hunter. They encircle the herd along with
> the reinforcements. Then they go in for the kill. Usually a wolf strikes
> behind the hind leg. This way it slows the caribou down. And then they
> go for the neck and the windpipe for the final kill. It lets the caribou
> get out of breath. Or when the wolf bites the hind leg of the caribou, it
> tires out the caribou. Then it goes in for the final assault. The wolf lives
> in harmony with us and with nature; it is also a keen hunter. The wolf is
> afraid of humans, but it has also been part of our roots and traditions for
> thousands of years. We live side by side with similar guidelines. When
> we hunt, we do not waste one bit of caribou; as well, the wolf respects its
> prey, and it doesn't leave anything behind either. The wolf does not waste
> anything, although it doesn't eat the bones or might leave some scraps
> for the birds. (Naskapi elder man, 2005)

Similarly, both men and women could easily distinguish the varieties of plants and trees—their properties, growth phases, and location, as well as the effects of climate on them. They also understood the solidity or flakiness and heat-storing capacities of the various rocks and minerals. They classified animals and plants according to their social, economic, or symbolic importance to the community. Caribou occupied a privileged position, both in

---

5 In identifying these four knowledge complexes, our intention is merely to systematize and synthesize the information that we gathered, rather than to propose a new system of categories for general use. Many of the researchers who have studied the topic of traditional ecological knowledge have suggested useful methods of classification, particularly Berkes (1999), Mailhot (1993), Menzies and Butler (2006), and Stevenson (1996). Here, however, we are referring more immediately to categories derived from anthropology and ethnology (see Leroi-Gourhan 1971 and 1973).

the material world, as the primary source of food and raw materials, and in the Naskapi cosmogony and spiritual world. The Naskapi attributed both human qualities and supernatural powers to the caribou:

> We greatly respect the caribou because it gave us life and it is always present among us. To attract the caribou and survive, we would sing and play the drums and dream. If an elder dreamt of his brother or his grandson, the description of the caribou hunting scene would take that person's name. (man, 2006)

> At the traditional feasts, nothing is wasted. Because nothing is wasted, that is how you honour the caribou because it provides food, shelter, lodging, warmth, toys, etc. An area might also be named after a success-ful hunt has taken place there. The caribou is very important so there is a name it is associated with for each season and for different moments during the year. (woman, 2005)

People's movements over the land, on foot or by canoe, also required a deep understanding of space, topography and geology, watercourses, and meteorological factors:

> We used the stars as guide when we went on a hunting expedition. The stars were our clocks and compass. We followed the stars: when they are in a certain area, we know that it is time to go. With the sun, we would put a stick in the ground, look at the shadow, and know at what point we have to be back according to where the shadow is—it was our sundial. (man, 2006)

From the material perspective, the elders referred to techniques of pro-duction, supplying food and materials, and consumption, as well as the tools, weapons, and medicines needed to carry out the activities required for survival and daily life. These might include harvesting methods, which varied with the type of game and the season, or everyday tasks such as food preparation, the treatment of hides and furs, the making of everyday and ceremonial objects and of clothing, the setting up of camps, and the trans-portation of people and supplies.[6] Again, the caribou stood at the centre of both material and spiritual life, which in turn rested on the principles of respect and reciprocity:

---

6 For a discussion of women's roles in Naskapi daily life, see Desmarais, Lévesque, and Raby (1994).

The elders taught young men how to prepare the pemmican. Once they
had the knowledge, as men, they would prepare the pemmican for the
elders. But everyone ate the pemmican; it is shared by everyone, even
the small kids. It is honoured because it comes from the caribou. It is so
sacred that you can't leave scraps behind, you have to devour everything.
The tradition is that, after the pemmican is done, there is the beating
drum ceremony to call upon the animals and to thank them. Once the
drum has been set up, the drummer has the first taste. Young people
were not allowed to be next to the drummer. People come and thank the
caribou for feeding them so well. Everyone is feasting away, and they are
thanking the animals and asking for more. (man, 2006)

From a social standpoint, the elders described methods of learning and
of transmitting knowledge from adults to children, the care that should be
given to children, women in labour, the sick, the injured, and old people,
the roles and responsibilities of each person in various circumstances, and
the mechanisms by which social cohesion was maintained. Children were
socialized to the need for mutual aid and solidarity very early on. Men and
women also emphasized the appropriate attitudes and behaviour of children toward their parents and of young people toward elders. The learning
covered not only ways of doing things but also ways of being, that is, the
ways of interacting with others in everyday life, during times of travel, and
in specific situations such as a birth or death:

Before a young person gets to start having knowledge, he has to fast
four days. Fasting opens the mind. During those days, the person fasting
drinks three different kinds of medicinal teas. After that, an elder can
start teaching some traditional knowledge. This normally takes place
in the bush. You have to be in good thoughts; the person who gets the
medicine has to be positive. (man, 1999)[7]

The fourth knowledge complex concerns the spiritual world and the Naskapi belief system, including communication with animal spirits, mental
attitudes, divination practices, rituals, songs and incantations, dream interpretation, and prayer. Such knowledge enables one to decipher the signs of
nature and to understand the place of human beings in the universe. As the
Naskapi elders indicated, the right to hold this knowledge was extended

---

7 Citations dated 1999 and 1985 originate from earlier work with the Naskapi that
has not been previously published.

only to those who were spiritually prepared to receive it, therefore the elders did not discuss it further. The ability to interpret and apply this knowledge is based primarily on a state of mind and on a profound understanding of the relationships between humans and animals and between humans and non-human entities that make up the Naskapi spiritual world. One of the elders described the purpose of drumming:

> Children used to ask the elders why they were using the drums and what the sounds meant. The elders said that they were singing of their dreams of what they dreamt, songs about caribou and other animals. The elders used to be able to tell what each sound meant. That is how they knew where the caribou was, because they would ask with their drums. They depended on the caribou. They would beat the drum before a hunting expedition. When an elder beats the drum, they listen and they know according to the sound, where the caribou is. It has been known that these songs really benefitted them. Sometimes these visions really happened. (man, 2004)

The Naskapi clearly did not view these knowledge complexes as mutually exclusive areas of expertise. On the contrary, they were closely interwoven with one another. Nor were they exclusive to the Naskapi: all hunting groups in the subarctic region developed similar knowledge systems (Descola 2005). Similarly, for the Naskapi, such knowledge complexes were not strictly gendered but rather formed the cultural universe of the group as a whole. At the same time, both men and women acknowledged the existence of gender differences. These differences must therefore be taken into consideration in efforts to reconstruct the Naskapi's ecological and cultural heritage.

The Interface Between the Female and Male Universes

The literature in the field of Indigenous knowledge, as well as the anthropological literature on hunter-gatherer societies, frequently reports a division of tasks between men and women and often identifies spheres of activities specifically associated with one or the other gender. The Naskapi are no exception to the rule. But when we listened to what women and men said during joint gatherings, we were able to identify four main organizing principles that were applied to the knowledge and skills of men and women: differentiation, complementarity, transfer, and integration.

It is not surprising to find that the narratives often reveal a fairly clear division of tasks between men and women. Men hunted, and women processed and prepared the game, maintained the camps, and looked after the children. Very early on, little boys and girls learned the roles and responsibilities that they would have throughout their lives, as well as the knowledge and skills that would be needed. Their parents and grandparents made them toys that foreshadowed their future tasks: bows and arrows, guns, and ammunition pouches for boys; dolls, clothes, and wood and bark containers for girls. When they were about ten or twelve years old, boys and girls learned to make and use a variety of real tools and other objects. This process of learning and teaching, which was usually conducted on an individual basis over a number of years, was also gendered: men taught boys, and women taught girls. The elders explained that this division of tasks gave children the foundation on which other, more complex and sophisticated learning would later rely. It also ensured the continued survival of the group as a whole:

> Young people were a big part of the family; they were given tasks that were obeyed. As soon as young children can walk, they are taught traditional practices and values. The whole group teaches the children since everyone has different skills. They must see how everything is done. When both girls and boys have learned these skills, the young boys have become hunters and the girls are able to take care of the camp. Then they are ready to find a mate. (woman, 2006)

The narratives also reveal a degree of complementarity between the female and male universes. We defined complementarity as an arrangement whereby one gender helped in the implementation of knowledge or skills that were clearly associated with the other gender. Complementarity thus pertained to the execution of certain tasks. For example, women played a secondary role in hunting caribou: the tasks they performed were important for the success of the hunt, but it was the men who planned and led the activities. Conversely, during childbirth, an event over which midwives took control, men performed supportive tasks, such as lighting fires, gathering wood, bringing food, and heating stones and water:

> One difficult time was childbirth while people were on the move. Everyone had to stop, the midwives were the elderly, and you had to keep the tent warm for two days after the baby was born, twenty-four hours a day. Women took care of the delivery. Men went to fetch wood. After delivery, two days later they were on the move. You needed to have moss for diapers; the baby was in a toboggan. During winter, it was important to keep the baby warm. Babies were breastfed. (woman, 2006)

Both men and women, jointly and separately, emphasized the element of complementarity, stressing the need for mutual aid that prevailed in various circumstances:

> The hard work that was done between genders was well organized; everyone chipped in. The children, the young people, the adults, the elders—everyone helped in the work. All the harder tasks, more physical tasks, are done by the men. All the straps of hide are made by the women, but the setting up is done by the man. The easier tasks, like cleaning the house, are done by the women. But some tasks are shared by men and women—the porcupine, for example, since it is an easy but long task. (woman, 2006)

Here, for example, women might play a complementary role in the construction of a fairly large object, such as a drum, by producing straps of hide, while the men assemble the drum (what the elder refers to as "setting up"). Similarly, although food preparation was a female activity, men would sometimes help with cleaning and butchering an animal, as in the case of the porcupine.

The third principle is that of transfer. In an environment often marked by severe conditions, both genders had to be able to manage under any circumstances. Knowledge primarily held by one gender was therefore taught to the other, as a backup measure. For example, women were taught to hunt so that they would be able to cope in the event of the extended absence (or death) of the males:

> Men taught women how to hunt for the periods when they were away. Women could kill caribou if the men were away. (man, 2006)

> When men weren't there, then women would hunt and install their nets on the ice and hunt ptarmigan. (woman, 1985)

For the same reason, knowledge about medicinal plants was taught to men, even though this domain was clearly identified with the female universe.

The fourth organizing principle is that of integration, which we define as a necessary combination of knowledge and skills to which men and women contributed in more or less equal measure. This sort of integration was involved especially in the creation of objects that required several types of materials and techniques, some of which were associated with women and some with men. A good example is the production of snowshoes, which called for both animal hides (processed by women) and wood (procured by men) and for the use of techniques such as tanning and smoking hides (done by women) and carving and modelling wood (done by men). Moreover, the end product—the snowshoes—were available for use by everyone. The toboggans used to transport children and supplies, as well as items such as meat, shotgun ammunition pouches, and carrying bags, are other examples of objects that required the collaboration of men and women.

The conceptual categorization that we have set out illustrates the fundamental structuring role that interpersonal relations played in the learning and application of Naskapi knowledge and skills. Simply noting the simultaneous existence of the male and female spheres does not adequately capture the complexity of the underlying social dynamics. An examination of this knowledge opens the door to a world of differential meanings, personal responsibilities, and social roles. Knowledge is always conditioned by the ways that human beings behave both individually and in groups, and knowledge thus continually serves to create social links and social cohesion. Naskapi knowledge is rooted in an intricate system of reciprocity that is made up of numerous combinations and complementarities. In this system, although individuals clearly belong to a female or male world, the boundaries between these worlds are continually adjusted to allow for the socio-ecological alliances essential to group survival.

Medicinal Plants and Social Recognition

The literature on Indigenous women's knowledge, while not extensive, generally concurs that, particularly in subarctic hunting societies, women are the keepers of knowledge pertaining to medicinal plants. This association was borne out in the research conducted with Naskapi elders. As part of the project aimed at restoring the Naskapi's cultural and ecological heritage, the Naskapi Development Corporation undertook to document this area of knowledge in some detail, so that the knowledge held by women elders would not be lost.

The documentation of this knowledge occurred during a two-month exercise in collective learning and knowledge transmission held in the summer of 2000 that brought together women well known for their botanical knowledge. The women were accompanied by two men, and a translator and the researchers on the team were also present. Because the village of Kawawachikamach is located in the same ecosystem as the Fort McKenzie region, many of the plants and herbs that were in use in the past are also found in the vicinity of the village. In crisscrossing the surrounding lands every day for a week, these women recreated the actions and techniques that they had used in the days before the Naskapi adopted a settled way of life. They shared and mutually validated their knowledge by retracing the steps involved in acquiring and processing these plants and herbs.[8] We categorized this information according to the four knowledge principles described above: differentiation, complementarity, transfer, and integration.

Figure 3.1 Sandra Guanish and Ann Joseph talking about medicinal plants (2000). Photograph by Nadine Trudeau.

The knowledge held by these women enables them not only to categorize the plant species in the region (conifers, deciduous trees, flowering or fruiting shrubs) and to distinguish their various parts (roots, mosses, leaves, flowers, branches, buds, berries, bark) but also to evaluate their quality, their stage in the growth cycle, and their seasonal availability. Plants and herbs are named according to their properties or the particular actions involved in processing them (see tables 3.1 and 3.2). As one woman explained:

8 It is not our intention to provide detailed information concerning the methods used to prepare specific medicines and the application of specific remedies to specific illnesses or afflictions. Such information belongs to the Naskapi people, and it is up to them to decide whether and under what circumstances to render it public.

The way we named plants referred to their appearance, their smell, their feel, and their use. Plants have different names in the spring, summer, and fall. (woman, 1999)

As this comment suggests, in speaking about plants (or parts of plants), the Naskapi use terms that capture certain nuances about the plant, including its seasonal transformations, that do not correspond to Western classifications. Attempts at translation thus run the risk of reducing the Naskapi botanical corpus to only those categories recognized by Western science.

Table 3.1 Examples of Naskapi medicinal plants

Naskapi name	English name	Scientific name
iikuta	Labrador tea	*Ledum groenlandicum*
kaakaawaasiy	Stiff clubmoss	*Lycopodium annotinum*
iyaahtikw	Black spruce	*Picea mariana*
sikaaw	Planeleaf willow	*Salix planifolia*
uskuy	Paper birch	*Betula papyrifera*
waachinaakin	Tamarack	*Larix laricina*

Source: Lévesque and Geoffroy 2001, p. 4.

Table 3.2 Examples of Naskapi medicinal plants

Naskapi name	English meaning
kaakaachiiminikisiiwaapuy	Broth made from the boiled stems of the juniper berry bush
kikiskaahtikw	Dried powdered rotten wood
minahikwaasiihtich	White spruce branches
minahikwaasiihtaapuy	Broth made from boiled white spruce branches
niipiya	Various leaves from different green herbaceous plants
sikaaw nituuhkuna	Willow medicine
waachinaakin aakupitusunaanuch	Poultice made with tamarack

Source: Lévesque and Geoffroy 2001, p. 4.

The gathering of plants is not a casual activity. In the words of one Nas-kapi elder:

Plants are very strong, like the Creator who made them. We have to be careful about how we use them. Plants are the Creator's decision. They are very important. (man, 1985)

According to one woman, plants are best gathered early in the growing season:

The best time to pick up medicine or edibles is the spring, because the smell is strong: it is filled with water and life. It is good to drink; you take off some bark with your knife and get the sap. You can do this until June, with all the trees. In the fall, you store the plants that you will use in the winter. You freeze the berries. (woman, 1999)

In addition, emphasis was placed on the relationship between human and plant life and on the need to maintain the appropriate attitude of respect:

There are particular ways to pick up the plants; each plant has to be picked in its own way and prepared in its own way. One has to be in good mood, in good dispositions, and one has to pray that the plants have good effects. Nowadays, most people are not in the right frame of mind to gather plants, so it is not done. (woman, 1999)

Once the plants have been gathered, various techniques and tools are then used to store and process them. Different parts of the same plant may require specific types of processing, such as drying, crushing, soaking, or extraction. Plants can also be combined with animal or fish parts, including fat, marrow, eggs, and blood. In addition, the same plant may be used to make several different kinds of medicines or products.[9]

Naskapi women not only understand the properties of specific plants but are also aware of the possible interactions between plants, as some combinations can be dangerous. Their processing techniques allow for the production of pills, ointments, tonics, powders, or drinks with particular

9 Although the "scientific method" is often opposed to Indigenous epistemologies, knowledge was of course gained in part through a process of observation and reasoning. This is evident in a comment made in 1999 by a Naskapi elder man: "By observing the behavior of a hurt wolf, my grandfather followed the wolf and was able to see that it was eating Labrador tea. Then he saw how fast the wolf was cured; he then deduced that Labrador tea had curative properties."

virtues that can be used for chronic or occasional health problems (fever, bronchitis, allergies, arthritis, loss of appetite, bleeding, eczema), injuries or wounds (fractures, cuts, insect bites, infections), or common health concerns (menstruation, leg fatigue, digestive problems). As one woman explained:

> No, there was no doctor [. . .] and the Indian people would use something from the tree. They use all kind of trees, and they use a rock and some part of a caribou. Like if you had pain in the back, they would heat the rock and they would put it in the back and you would sweat up, and there's another thing that would make you sweat, and there's some kind of caribou part you would boil in Labrador tea and you would drink them and put it on your chest, and there's another tree—you would scrape it and you would take and you would boil it and after you would drink it and the pain would go away. (woman, 2004)

Figure 3.2 Sandra Guanish collecting Labrador tea (2000).
Photograph by Nadine Trudeau.

In the Fort McKenzie time, girls were taught by their mothers and grandmothers how to distinguish the various plant species. But it was only when they were adults that they could acquire specialized knowledge. Knowledge was thus organized along generational divides as well as by gender. In both the male and female spheres, there was a time in life for learning and another for applying and putting into practice the knowledge acquired. Moreover, possessing this specialized knowledge was a matter of great responsibility, both social and spiritual. As plants have healing powers, the person having knowledge of healing plants also has the power to heal. Naskapi elders explained, however, that merely knowing how to use a medicine or remedy is not enough to cure someone. The person providing the care also has to demonstrate the appropriate mental attitudes:

> You have to respect the plants when you pick them up. The person who receives the medicine has to fully accept it; otherwise it will not work. Also, you have to pray. You have to speak to the medicine, tell the medicine what you want it to do, especially when it is beaver or bear. (woman, 1999)

Figure 3.3 Ruby Nattawappio crushing Labrador tea (2000).
Photograph by Nadine Trudeau.

Rituals could be performed to help prepare the healer. In addition, recounting and interpreting one's dreams often provided clues about the nature of health problems or about the treatment to be provided.

Figure 3.4 Kathleen Tooma and Ann Joseph preparing medicines (2002). Photograph by Nadine Trudeau.

During the collective learning and knowledge transmission exercise conducted in the summer of 2000, the two men had a secondary role: their involvement included cutting tree branches with axes and saws, gathering less accessible plants, and locating desired plant species. This arrangement between the men and women is illustrative of the principle of complementarity described above. Specifically, the knowledge pertaining to medicinal plants remains, as it always has, under the control of women, and the men assist them sporadically, as needed in the various stages of production. In line with the principle of knowledge transfer, however, men may also acquire such knowledge if the circumstances call for it or simply as a security measure. Most of the men who took part in the ethnographic survey, for example, reported having some knowledge of plant properties, and a few were even familiar with methods of preparing remedies. Nevertheless, it is generally held that this medicinal knowledge belongs to women and that, as the guardians of it, they have the authority to dispense it. In other words, we observe a difference in degree between possessing particular knowledge and having the ability and authority to apply it.

The rules that govern the possession, transmission, and application of knowledge are socially constructed. The fact that men recognized women as the primary holders of knowledge relating to medicinal plants illustrates the relational dimension of Naskapi knowledge, as well as the manner in which it is socially organized. In the context of our study, the reconstruction of this knowledge extended beyond the summer of 2000. In the years that followed, many additional meetings were organized with men and women in an effort to expand the body of knowledge on this subject and to ensure that the information had been fully recorded and thoroughly validated. In the course of these meetings, many stories were told about people's experiences during the Fort McKenzie time, when traditional care was the norm and plant-based remedies were routinely produced and applied. Beyond describing the illnesses or accidents that occurred, these stories provide insights into some of the reactions to certain remedies, the phases of recovery, the people concerned, and the times and places involved. On each occasion, these narratives were recounted in the presence of many women and men, which not only helped to document the knowledge but also deepened the collective understanding.

The knowledge that each person possessed was gradually set out in detail and enhanced through a process of discourse and exchange. This exercise allowed for the operation of what Pierre Lévy calls "collective intelligence" and generated a shared understanding of the knowledge, the historical events, and the everyday situations that constitute the Naskapi heritage.[10]

---

10 Lévy (1999, 13) defines collective intelligence as "a form of *universally distributed intelligence*, constantly enhanced, coordinated in real time, and resulting in the effective mobilization of skills." Collective intelligence allows human beings to forge links among bodies of knowledge, thereby producing what Lévy (2003) describes as "ecosystems of ideas." An analogy can certainly be drawn with the Naskapi, who are,

Moreover, placing an emphasis on women's voices has undoubtedly fostered a more nuanced understanding of the interactions between the knowledge spheres of men and women, as well as providing a clearer and more complete picture of the Naskapi way of life as a whole.

Conclusion

The importance of narratives in the transmission of Indigenous knowledge has been widely emphasized (Cruikshank 1998; Heine et al. 2001; Turner et al. 2008), and, over the past few decades, projects similar to the one initiated by the Naskapi Development Corporation have been undertaken all across Canada. Such projects have, however, been less common in Québec. Quite apart from its location, however, this project stands out for the reflective approach that the Naskapi adopted in working to restore their cultural and ecological heritage, for its examination of gender specificity, and for the recognition given to the social dimensions of knowledge. Although their attention was turned toward the past, the methods that the Naskapi elders developed to ensure that the voices of all persons were heard, as well as the importance they placed on sharing and circulating knowledge, have placed these elders in a position to become integral players in a rapidly evolving knowledge- and information-based society. In our view, a fundamental structural relationship exists between the manner in which Indigenous peoples produce and share knowledge and the way that knowledge is created and distributed in a knowledge society. In both cases, the key elements of explanation and mutual understanding serve to prevent the development of divisions among different knowledge systems or among the knowledge bearers themselves. On the contrary, they facilitate the discovery and application of the bodies of knowledge in question.

It may seem paradoxical that two systems of knowledge that have evolved so separately could have something in common. And yet it is probably no coincidence that the debates regarding the value of traditional knowledge—and the international claims that such knowledge deserves to be recognized—have arisen at a time of major transformation in the realm of human understanding. The advent of new information technologies has brought about a resurgence of interest in ways of knowing, as well as in the

---

in effect, attempting to reconstitute the ecosystems of ideas that at one point constituted the product of their own collective intelligence.

ways that human beings have always stored, reproduced, renewed, and transmitted information about the world that they live in and their ways of life.

Clear ties exist between the emergence of questions about the nature and utility of Indigenous knowledge and the worldwide rise of Indigenous peoples' movements. Over time, Indigenous peoples' demands to have their political, territorial, and human rights recognized have expanded to encompass the sphere of knowledge. Excluded from the places of knowledge production for too long, Indigenous peoples have gradually advanced their own intellectual traditions, epistemologies, knowledge systems, and "regimes of nature,"[11] all of which express both the complexity of their relations with the various worlds—natural, social, spiritual—with which they interact (Descola 2005). Meanwhile, other movements such as globalization and significant opening up of national borders, precursory to the major technological and communication changes that we are experiencing today, have helped to transform the ways that we produce information and knowledge. The age-old substantive, scalar, epistemological, and hierarchical barriers that stood between different bodies of knowledge are gradually eroding, which is opening the way to innovative combinations, facilitated by new communication and information technologies. The categories of knowledge (written, oral, artistic, spiritual, etc.) are increasing as a result of the new means and platforms of dissemination. The social relationships and networks that form around knowledge systems of all kinds sometimes become more important to people than the knowledge itself. Indeed, Indigenous elders have long tried to convey that knowledge is first and foremost a matter of relationships between human beings and nature.

In research both into the knowledge society and into Indigenous bodies of knowledge, emphasis is now placed on participatory, community-based, and partnered projects, as well as on the co-production of knowledge, in the form of interdisciplinary and/or intersectorial collaborations. In the field of Indigenous knowledge, collaborative initiatives of this kind have been favoured from the beginning. Indeed, our own study deliberately created a "community of learning," one that not only fostered the sharing of knowledge but also reinforced a systemic and organic understanding of Naskapi culture and heritage.

---

11 Regime of nature corresponds to types of relationships that different people have with nature. For example, in Eurocentric approach, nature is a source of resources to be exploited; alternatively, in an Indigenous context, humans are part of nature.

In reconstructing their traditional knowledge to benefit future generations, the Naskapi have reclaimed their own history. In so doing, they have reflected on their contribution not only to the ecological and cultural heritage of the Naskapi people but also to the heritage of humanity as a whole. Embedded in Naskapi traditional knowledge are teachings that transcend time, space, and culture. Given that these teachings constantly reference the surrounding environment, they are obviously grounded in the local, but they concern phenomena that are universal—gender and generational relationships, relationships between the individual and the group, the methods by which information is gathered, preserved, and passed down, means to social and cultural recognition, and modes of individual and social governance. All these rest on a system of values that is worthy of restoration and respect.

References

Berkes, Fikret. 1999. *Sacred Ecology: Traditional Ecological Knowledge and Resource Management*. Ann Arbor, MI: Taylor and Francis.

Chabot, Marcelle, and Carole Lévesque. 2001. *Indigenous Knowledge: Contribution to a Review of the Literature*. Montréal: Institut national de la recherche scientifique (Centre urbanisation culture société).

Cooke, Alan. 1976. "A History of the Naskapis of Schefferville: Preliminary Draft." Naskapi Band Council of Schefferville. Montréal.

Cruikshank, Julie. 1998. *The Social Life of Stories: Narrative and Knowledge in the Yukon Territory*. Lincoln: University of Nebraska Press.

Descola, Philippe. 2005. *Par-delà nature et culture*. Paris: Éditions Gallimard.

Desmarais, Danielle, Carole Lévesque, and Dominique Raby. 1994. "La contribution des femmes naskapies aux travaux de la vie quotidienne à l'époque de Fort McKenzie." *Recherches féministes* 7 (1): 23–42.

Ellen, Roy, Peter Parkes, and Alan Bicker, eds. 2000. *Indigenous Environmental Knowledge and Its Transformations*. London and New York: Routledge.

Graburn, Nelson. 1975. "Naskapi Family and Kinship." *Western Canadian Journal of Anthropology* 5 (2): 56–80.

Heine, Michael, Alestine Andre, Ingrid Kritsch, and Alma Cardinal. 2001. *Gwichya Gwich'in Googwandak: The History and Stories of the Gwichya Gwich'in*. Tsiigehtchic and Yellowknife: Gwich'in Social and Cultural Institute.

Leroi-Gourhan, André. 1971. *L'homme et la matière*. Paris: Albin Michel.

———. 1973. Milieu et technique. Paris: Albin Michel.

Lévesque, Carole, Catherine Lussier, Marcelle Chabot, David Toro, and Ginette Lajoie. 2001. *Traditional Knowledge: Issues, Ideas, Challenges*. Montréal:

Institut national de la recherche scientifique, Conseil Tribal Mamuitun, and Cree Regional Authority.

Lévesque, Carole, Charleen Rains, and Dominique de Juriew. 2001. "Les Naskapis: Peuple des grands espaces." In *Atlas Historique du Québec*. Vol. 5, *Le Nord. Habitants et Mutation*, edited by Gérard Duhaime, 69–84. Québec: Les Presses de l'Université Laval.

Lévesque, Carole, and Denise Geoffroy. 2001. Field notes ethnographic survey on medicinal plants. Manuscript. Montréal: Institut national de la recherche scientifique (Centre urbanisation culture société).

Lévesque, Carole, Christiane Montpetit, Isabelle Poulin, and Ginette Lajoie. 2004. *Environmental Knowledge in the Aboriginal Communities of Northern Québec: Elements of a Communication Strategy*. Montréal: Institut national de la recherche scientifique and Cree Regional Authority.

Lévesque, Carole, Denise Geoffroy, and Geneviève Polèse. 2006. *Towards a Community Sharing and Dynamic Transmission of Naskapi Ecological Knowledge*. Montréal: Institut national de la recherche scientifique and Naskapi Development Corporation.

Lévesque, Carole. 2009. "Québec Research Relating to Aboriginal Peoples in the Age of the Knowledge Society and the Knowledge Mobilization." *Inditerra* 1: 91–101.

Lévy, Pierre. 1997. *Collective Intelligence: Mankind's Emerging World in Cyberspace*. Trans. Peter Bononno. Cambridge, MA: Perseus Books.

———. 2003. "Le jeu de l'intelligence collective." *Sociétés* 79: 105–22.

Lutz, John Sutton, and Barbara Neis, eds. 2008. *Making and Moving Knowledge: Interdisciplinary and Community-Based Research in a World on the Edge*. Montréal and Kingston: McGill-Queen's University Press.

Mailhot, José. 1983. "À moins d'être son Esquimau, on est toujours le Naskapi de quelqu'un." *Recherches amérindiennes au Québec* 13(2): 85–100.

———. 1993. *Le savoir écologique traditionnel: La variabilité des systèmes de connaissances et leur étude*. Dossier-synthèse no. 4, Évaluation environnementale du projet Grande-Baleine. Montréal: Bureau de soutien de l'examen public du projet Grande-Baleine.

Menzies, Charles R., ed. 2006. *Traditional Ecological Knowledge and Natural Resource Management*. Lincoln: University of Nebraska Press.

Menzies, Charles R., and Caroline Butler. 2006. "Understanding Ecological Knowledge: Introduction." In Menzies 2006, 1–17.

Native Women's Association of Canada. 2007. "Aboriginal Women and the Convention on Biological Diversity: An Issue Paper." http://www.laa.gov.nl.ca/laa/naws/pdf/nwac-CBD.pdf.

Stevenson, Marc G. 1996. "Indigenous Knowledge in Environmental Assessment." *Arctic* 49 (3): 278–91.

Turner, Lucien M. (1894) 1979. *Indiens et Esquimaux du Québec*. Montréal: Desclez.

Turner, Nancy J., Anne Marshall, Judith C. Thompson (Edōsdi), Robin June Hood, Cameron Hill, and Eva-Ann Hill. 2008. "'Ebb and Flow': Transmitting Environmental Knowledge in a Contemporary Aboriginal Community." In Lutz and Neis 2008, 45–63.

UNESCO. 2005. *Towards Knowledge Societies*. Paris: UNESCO. http://unesdoc. unesco.org/images/0014/001418/141843e.pdf.

United Nations. 1992. *Convention on Biological Diversity*. New York: United Nations. http://www.cbd.int/doc/legal/cbd-en.pdf.

———. 2007. *United Nations Declaration on the Rights of Indigenous Peoples*. http://www.un.org/esa/socdev/unpfii/documents/DRIPS_en.pdf.

CHAPTER FOUR

Mapping, Knowledge, and Gender in the Atlantic Coast of Nicaragua

Isabel Altamirano-Jiménez and Leanna Parker

Much has been written in recent years about Indigenous knowledge—about the nature of this knowledge, the appropriate ways to study and apply it, and the epistemological foundations on which it rests. It is now well recognized that Indigenous knowledge offers insights into ecological systems that can aid in environmental protection and that plans for development cannot simply ignore a local community's rights and interests in the land. It is also abundantly clear that the knowledge and skills held by Indigenous women differ in many respects from those held by men. Gender influences patterns of access to resources, as well as the relative capacity of men and women to control and use these resources. In turn, the degree to which the knowledge specific to women is recognized and respected has an impact on women's livelihoods and overall status and well-being. However, even though the existence of gendered bodies of knowledge is well established, it is commonly assumed that the knowledge held by Indigenous women pertains to domestic matters, an assumption that not only blinds us to the variety of contexts in which gender relations are produced but also has the effect of effacing women's presence on the land (Bryant 1998; Peet and Watts 1996).

Taking as an example the lawsuit brought by the Mayangna community of Awas Tingni against the government of Nicaragua, we focus in this chapter on the creation of land use maps, with the goal of examining how the use of such maps as legal tools, in tandem with Western knowledge and conceptions of property rights, reinscribe patterns of colonial, racial, and gender inequalities. We argue that by making Indigenous women's knowledge and contributions to subsistence and market production invisible, women are effectively excluded. The Awas Tingni complaint was lodged after the Nicaraguan government unilaterally granted a concession to a logging company on lands claimed by the community as its traditional territory. The legal battle culminated in 2001, when the Inter-American Court of Human Rights decided in favour of the community.[1] The court held that, by virtue of the international human right to the enjoyment of property, Indigenous peoples have a right to the protection of their customary lands and that Nicaragua had violated that right (see Anaya and Grossman 2002, 1–2). The court further ruled that when an Indigenous community lacks legal title to their lands, proof of traditional land use and occupation is sufficient for them to obtain official recognition of their property (IACHR 2001, para. 151).

This outcome is considered to be an important legal victory not only for the Mayangna but for Indigenous peoples worldwide. The case set a legal precedent for the recognition of Indigenous property rights as a human right to be enjoyed and protected. Questions have arisen, however, about the methods by which maps used to secure legal recognition of land rights are produced. Specifically, critics have noted that such maps, which are typically based on information provided by some members of the community, reveal a bias toward the representation of the practical knowledge held by elder men. David Natcher (2001, 118) further warns that an incomplete representation of diverse Indigenous land uses can generate patterns of use that "appear historic, static and unrefined" and can seem to support the conclusion that "traditional" land use is being abandoned in favour of participation in the modern wage economy. Moreover, emphasis on masculine economic activities and Indigenous land rights as granted by the state privilege a masculine subjecthood and reinforce the power of the state in defining access to land. These critiques raise important questions about how gender is implicated in the process of securing collective land rights.

---

1 *Mayangna (Sumo) Awas Tingni Community v. Nicaragua*, Inter-Am. Ct. H. R. (ser. C) no. 79 (2001). See Inter-American Court of Human Rights (2001).

The Nature of Knowledge: Indigenous Women's Relationship with Place

In recent years, efforts have been made to incorporate gender into the management of natural resources and related policy development. Indigenous women and children have been targeted populations of climate mitigation policies (UNIFEM 2008, 8–9). A review of the literature on gender and the environment reveals two general orientations. The first advocates for liberal correctives to gender-blind perspectives that inform development policy and implementation. Criticism of this approach focuses on the fact that it tends to regard women as a homogenous category, thereby failing to take into account differences of race and ethnicity, geographic location, degree of education, and level of income. The second adopts a relational perspective that emphasizes the binary power relations between men and women that exist in particular local settings. Despite their differences, both approaches recognize that relationships to the environment are gendered. Accordingly, they acknowledge that men and women have specific interests, roles, responsibilities, and knowledge in connection with the environment.

Especially during the 1980s, writers with a broadly ecofeminist orientation theorized that there is a direct link between women's oppression and the domination of nature. From this perspective, rural women are conceived of as "caretakers" of the environment (Rodda 1991; Shiva 1988). Others, such as Karen Warren (1987) and Bina Agarwal (1992), rejected the notion that women have an innate understanding of the natural world, focusing instead on "the material practices that bring women closer to nature and which thus give them learned, practical knowledge of ecosystems" (Nightingale 2006, 165). Accordingly, the knowledge that women develop of the environment stems from the work they do to sustain a livelihood for themselves and their families. Because women do much of the household work, the tendency has been to assume that women's knowledge of the environment is exclusively related to domestic activities. Moreover, as Melissa Leach (2007, 75) points out, while a focus on natural connections between women and the environment may provide a corrective to liberal, gender-blind policies, it ended up essentializing women's roles.

More recently, the focus has shifted from women to gender. Recognizing that gender is inherently relational and is continually renegotiated through individual actions, scholars have explored the implications of the gender-environment nexus for the distribution of power between men and women. Differing degrees of access to and control over resources, as well as the gendered nature of environmental knowledge production, have meant that, especially in the context of land and resource development, men and women are not equally empowered (see, for example, Nightingale 2002). Local environmental struggles are, moreover, frequently embedded in the global political economy (Schroeder 1997; Altamirano-Jiménez 2016). Importantly, these studies acknowledge that, far from being confined to social reproduction, the household is also a site of production. Thus, knowledge held by women extends to the territory and the use of natural resources.

This approach to the intersection of gender, environment, and natural resource management is significant in that it shifts the direction and emphasis of analysis. Rather than seeing gender as structuring people's interactions with the environment, stress falls instead on how the social construction of nature and the economy produces categories of social difference, including distinctions of gender. As Shubhra Gururani (2002) suggests, for instance, forests are not simply biophysical entities but are spaces structured by the social politics of work, access, and control. Building on the insights offered by feminist theorizing on gender and space, Nightingale (2006, 166) argues that gender is better understood as a process: gender is "not constant and predetermined materially or symbolically but rather becomes salient in environmental processes through work, discourses of gender, and the performance of subjectivities." As she goes on to point out, these gendered subjectivities "are defined and contested in relation to *particular* ecological conditions" (171). Gender itself is accordingly both constituted and reinscribed in and through the discourses, practices, and policy implementation associated with specific local environments.

While the above perspectives all shed light on the intersection of gender and environment, they continue to operate within a framework that posits society and nature as two separate domains. Feminist geographers have, however, produced an important body of work that reflects on the spatiality of cultural practices, identity formation, and meaning production. They argue that because people's lives unfold in specific locations and environments that are socially constructed, we need to consider what meanings people attribute to place and the relationships they build with and within those places (Domosh and Seager 2001; Desbiens 2007). From this point of view, Indigenous women's knowledge derives not only from the specific roles, activities, and responsibilities assigned to women but also from the relationships that women establish with a particular natural and cultural landscape (McKinley 2007). In other words, not only is Indigenous women's knowledge place specific, but place is also crucial in defining subjectivities—"what it means to be a 'woman' or a 'man'" in the context of a specific location (Nightingale 2006, 171).

Place can thus be understood as an intricate web of economic, political, social, spiritual, and environmental relations that together constitute people's surroundings. Place is defined not merely by a physical location but also by a sense of belonging to that place and by the practices that shape people's livelihoods, social relationships, and identity (Harcourt and Escobar 2005, 5). Place is, in other words, a way of knowing and inhabiting the world (Coulthard 2010, 79–80). Indigenous places are produced by people's relationships to the land but also to other-than-human beings that inhabit a place, such as animals and spirits. These relationships are central to Indigenous knowledge, and, by acknowledging this centrality, we are able to move away from exclusively anthropocentric landscapes.

Indigenous peoples have developed their knowledge systems not only by living on the physical land but by establishing social and spiritual relationships with place and with the beings that inhabit it. Indigenous knowledge is experiential, holistic, and evolving, and knowing involves acknowledging and respecting relationships. As Aileen Moreton-Robinson and Maggie Walter (2009, 5) point out, in a holistic Indigenous world view, knowledge cannot exist in separation from relationships and the principles by which these relationships are governed. Similarly, Indigenous law cannot exist in separation from such relationships. Law both sustains and reflects these relationships and the pattern of creation that is the world. Law is part of a larger way of knowing the world, one that is formed by a living landscape in which time is measured by cycles, not lines, and the "space" of place is both physical and metaphysical (Moreton-Robinson and Walter 2009, 6).

Place is also fundamental to Indigenous economies and social organization. As in other societies, Indigenous women play a central role in Indigenous economies. Today, these are most often mixed economies, still largely driven by subsistence activities but incorporating some degree of participation in the market economy (in the form of wage labour, for example, or the sale of handicrafts), as needed to sustain the social organization. Besides being an economic activity, Indigenous economic practices are an expression of who people are collectively and culturally (Kuokkanen 2011, 219). In the Atlantic

Coast region of Nicaragua, Mayangna women have a rich knowledge of diverse medicinal and edible plants and also depend on the forest in carrying out their daily responsibilities, which include cooking, feeding livestock, gift giving, and cultivating plants. Whereas men tend to make use of an extended area, but chiefly for the purpose of hunting and trapping, women generally make more localized use of the land but depend on its natural biodiversity to provide constant and reliable support for their families. Women contribute to their families and communities in indispensable ways. They look after their extended family, they grow rice, beans, cassava, and corn, as well as looking after the livestock they have in their yards. Women also collect, conserve, and commercialize edible plants and produce that account for an important percentage of their dietary requirements.

The Mayangna women who live in the Awas Tingni community often participate in hunting as well, another important subsistence activity. Entire families travel for days looking for deer and wild boar. Travelling through the Awas Tingni territory on hunting expeditions reinforces relations not only among community members but also with their ancestors and the spirits that inhabit the mountains and control wildlife. Disrespecting these spirits puts the well-being of the community at risk. Thus, hunting is better conceptualized as a collective enterprise that relies on the work of both men and women. As is the case for other Indigenous peoples, access to their territory and resources is crucial to the ability of Mayangna women to sustain themselves and their families and to maintain their relationships with spirits, animals, and the supranatural forces intrinsic to place. As Sámi political scientist Rauna Kuokkanen (2011, 219) notes, these relationships are "premised on an ethos of reciprocity in which people reciprocate not only with one another but also with the land and the spirit world."

Like Indigenous men, women can be considered "local specialists" who possess knowledge of the environment, of human interactions with animals and with the spirit world, and of their customs and cultural heritage. Indigenous women's roles and experiences as mothers, wives, members of their communities, and economic producers constitute specific sites of their knowledge. As Moreton-Robinson and Walter (2009, 6) suggest, even though individual experiences differ, the "worldview and reality of being an Indigenous woman is intertwined with lived experience." As they go on to point out, all Indigenous women understand the "intersecting oppressions of race and gender and the subsequent power relations that flow from these into the social, political, historical, and material conditions of our lives" (6). Contemporary Indigenous territories offer one means through which we can understand these experiences and the many specific ways of being both Indigenous and a woman. At the same time, these territories provide an opportunity to explore the power relations that naturalize oppression and asymmetries in how knowledge is conceived of. By looking at mapping and the knowledge it excludes, we hope to make such gendered asymmetries visible.

Mapping Indigenous Knowledge

Because territorial rights, as well as conflicts over the use of the associated natural resources, are among the most pressing issues for Indigenous peoples, it is crucial that we consider how power and knowledge shape the processes through which territorial rights are secured and, in the process, gender inequalities reinscribed. The legal protection of Indigenous lands has opened the door to new economic opportunities, but it has also contributed to the reconceptualization of Indigenous land tenure. As we have seen, "land" is not merely a geophysical entity: it is also socially constructed space and, as such, both creates and reflects gendered distinctions. Typically, however, the methods used to secure Indigenous rights to land operate on the assumption that information is gender neutral, with the result that no systematic effort is made to ensure that women have an equal part in the process. Rather, their participation is incidental and informal. In this way, Indigenous women's voices are silenced and their knowledge discounted, even though the rhetoric surrounding the protection of Indigenous rights and ways of life frequently emphasizes the central role of women in Indigenous livelihoods.

Maps are increasingly used for the purposes of securing Indigenous land rights. J. B. Harley (1988, 278) observes that "maps are never value-free images." Rather, as a form of discourse, they are inherently ideological and represent a specific understanding of the world. As a number of scholars have suggested, however, maps can also work to redress this imbalance. In colonial contexts, the capacity of mapping to render power visible can yield profound insights about settler-Indigenous relations and may even contribute to a shift in power toward Indigenous peoples and other marginalized groups. In recent decades, mapping has accordingly become a key strategy in efforts to document Indigenous land title and to resolve disputes between Indigenous peoples. For example, Matthew Sparke (1998) illustrates how the Gitxsan and Wet'suwet'en used maps based on oral history to describe their traditional territory and to counter the maps placed into evidence by the Crown. Similarly, Nancy Lee Peluso (1995) discusses "counter-mapping" in Indonesia as a response to government forest planning that ignored the customary forest rights of Indigenous peoples. By appropriating the techniques of the state, the Indigenous peoples were able to legitimate, in the eyes of the state, their customary claims to forest resources and to defend their territory from further encroachment.

By creating their own maps, Indigenous peoples can also reinsert people into the landscape, thereby challenging efforts on the part of the state to depict the land in question as "empty" or "unused" and hence to claim that plans for resource development will have no significant human impact. As Peluso (1995, 386–87) argues:

> Maps can be used to pose alternatives to the languages and images of power and become a medium of empowerment or protest. Alternative maps, or "counter-maps" as I call them here, greatly increase the power of people living in a mapped area to control representations of themselves and their claims to resources. . . . Counter-maps thus have the potential for challenging the omissions of human settlements from forest maps, for contesting the homogenization of space on political, zoning, or property maps, for altering the categories of land and forest management, and for expressing social relationships in space rather than depicting abstract space in itself.

Indigenous peoples can, in short, use the techniques of the state to reassert their claims to the land and protect the resources on which they depend. This has given rise to what Joel Wainwright and Joe Bryan (2009) call the "legal-cartographic" strategy, in which maps are used as a legal tool to claim territorial rights. In many cases, including that of Awas Tingni, Indigenous peoples have employed this strategy to defend their lands and resources. Likewise, in Canada, the courts have established and repeatedly reaffirmed the government's duty to consult and accommodate when resource development projects or other plans for land use might infringe upon the rights of Indigenous peoples. Among many Indigenous communities, and increasingly government and industry, land use studies have become the standard means to describe and attempt to mitigate land use conflicts between Indigenous communities and resource developers.

Although the legal-cartographic approach has produced some victories for Indigenous communities, it is not without its drawbacks. In the context of Aboriginal rights in Canada, Natcher (2001) has questioned the value of land use studies on the grounds of their methodological limitations as well as the cultural misrepresentations that tend to inhere in them. As Anthony Stocks (2003) argues, researchers have focused almost exclusively on gathering and preserving traditional knowledge without thinking about or working toward the recognition and protection of Indigenous land rights. Importantly, Peluso (1995) has noted land use mapping has created new ideas of Indigenous territoriality. As she suggests, in connection with this new understanding of territory, one must ask whether tradition has been reinvented in a way that undermines customary laws, practices, and patterns of resource distribution and how the involvement of external experts has altered Indigenous peoples' access to and control over resources (393). Similarly, Wainwright and Bryan (2009, 161) point out that although maps have become a popular instrument for settling land claims, they do not guarantee justice, first, because those who participate in the process of creating maps are not necessarily able to read them in the way that judges and other legal authorities will and, second, because not everyone in the community is given equal authority to participate in mapping. In particular, Indigenous women tend to be wholly or partially excluded from the process, as they "are often not seen as bearers of the sort of geographical knowledge that should be mapped to define the community's territory." Rather, this authority is generally awarded to elder males.

Land use studies, in Canada and elsewhere, have indeed focused for the most part on subsistence activities that are assumed to be the responsibility of men—namely, hunting, fishing, and trapping. In maps solicited by Western law, Indigenous land uses are understood as a set of practices that are culturally regulated and which are performed in specific ways. The focus on "man the hunter" obscures the fact that Indigenous economic practices are organized by an interdependent gender division of labour (Frink 2007; Bodenhorn 1990. Staples and Natcher (2015, 148) warn that when women's activities are not recorded on land use maps, information about "nested activities"—the chain of activities performed by women to guarantee the survival and social reproduction of the household—is lost. Moreover, as Caroline Desbiens (2007) has demonstrated, maps that neglect women's knowledge obviously produce a skewed portrait of the interdependence of Indigenous men's and women's activities. Although the need for a more inclusive portrait of gender roles in Indigenous economies has been recognized, women are not often interviewed during the collection of information to be represented in the maps, even when their activities on the land are related to subsistence production.

As Natcher (2001, 118) argues, this omission can have serious consequences for women's livelihoods. If a map records only men's areas of activity on the land, certain areas may appear to be used quite sporadically are in fact used fairly consistently by women. Thus, land management and planning decisions may be made on the basis of maps that present an incomplete, and hence distorted, picture of Indigenous land use. For example, whereas the cultivation of large fields—a typically "male" activity—is usually captured on maps, home gardens, often managed by women, may not be recognized as part of agricultural activities. Similarly, areas in between gardens or adjacent areas of bush where women gather or extract uncultivated resources may be defined as "pristine" or "unused" in order to justify the appropriation of the land for new uses.

As Desbiens (2007, 362) reminds us, the division of labour—far from reflecting differences grounded in biological sex—is a function of the constructed division of space on the land, which in turns serves to shape gender roles. In the West, spatial frameworks create a division between public and private spheres, and specific forms of labour are then assigned to each of these spheres, with men generally operating within the public sphere, while women are relegated to the private sphere. In Indigenous societies, these spheres are not quite so rigidly separated, in practice, men and women cross the gender barriers to overcome unforeseen obstacles, such as resource scarcity, illness or injury, or death, in order to ensure the survival of their families. Land use studies typically focus on activities performed in the "public" sphere (hunting, fishing, and trapping), and women are excluded as a result. Problematically, these economic activities are emphasized on the grounds that they are the most traditional and closer to nature than those of non-Indigenous peoples, reproducing an ahistorical and idealized conception of Indigenous peoples' identity.

Related to this gender issue is a broader problem around the representation of land and resources. The focus of most land use studies falls on the productive dimension of Indigenous land, that is, on how the resources available on the land are used to sustain the community. In other words, land and resources are primarily perceived in economic terms—an approach to land and resources that is more Western than Indigenous. Conventional land use planning and resource management accordingly focuses predominantly on the physical landscape, thereby largely ignoring legal, social, and cultural features. Kinship ties and other interpersonal relationships, exchange networks, principles of reciprocity, and linkages between landscape and the spirit world are all central to Indigenous economies and social organization, yet such intangibles are difficult to depict and interpret, with the result that they are rarely factored into conventional development planning and modelling. From the perspective of Western resource management, land is a resource, not a place embedded in social relations and imbued with dynamic meanings. By privileging an economic view of territory as a source of productivity, however, mapping skews our understanding of how Indigenous peoples relate to their territory and its resources. Even though songs, sand paintings, and other Indigenous records have been accepted as evidence of Indigenous land rights, their admission is contingent upon experts' ability to represent them in cartographic form.

This reconfiguration of Indigenous peoples' relationship to territory can be even more problematic for Indigenous women, who have already seen their rights and their place on the land eroded through colonialism. While Indigenous practices around access to land and allocation of resources and exchange networks were organized around gendered lines, in Indigenous societies both men and women were provided with opportunities to fulfill their responsibilities and gain status and recognition. The process of colonization imposed conceptions of property and the nuclear family, based on hierarchical and patriarchal assumptions. In this view, women are consigned to a subordinate role in property ownership, economic exchange, and resource management. As a result, Indigenous women suffered even more from colonial reconfigurations than did men. To the extent that land use studies reproduce this Western understanding of land and resources, they continue the process of the exclusion of women from the land that began with colonization. Although in some communities of the Atlantic Coast Indigenous women sketched their use of their land, these records remained subordinate to what was required by law.

In Latin America, international conservation organizations and financial institutions such as the World Bank have insisted on the value of using maps to stabilize property regimes. Since the early 2000s, Indigenous communities in the region have resorted to mapping in order to gain title to their lands and prevent them from further fragmentation (Llancaqueo

Toledo 2005). The discourses of ethno-development employed by the World Bank's International Development Association and the International Monetary Fund are particularly interesting, as they link the titling of Indigenous and black communities' lands to private investment in and development of these lands (Hoekema and Assies 1999; for an example, see World Bank 2009). From the perspective of these international organizations, the issue is not about recognizing Indigenous territorial rights but about recognizing a relation to property that is compatible with economic development (Altamirano-Jiménez 2016). As Wainwright and Bryan (2009, 156) note, "When indigenous communities and their allies produce maps and lawsuits, they do so under conditions not of their choosing. These struggles unfold within an already-mapped world where one cannot elect to live outside of sovereignty, territory, or the law."

Awas Tingni Versus Nicaragua: Producing "Differential Empowerment"

If as Wainwright and Bryan suggest, Indigenous communities pursuing legal recognition of their title must adhere to Western law and spatial understandings of the world, what patterns of colonial, gender, and racialized inequalities are reproduced? What Wainwright and Bryan (2009, 161) call "differential empowerment" refers to the symptomatic inequities that are reinscribed through the cartography legal approach. Before initiating this discussion some historical context is required.

The Atlantic coast of Nicaragua has had a history of land conflicts. The origins of these conflicts can be found in the imperial competition developed between Spain and England. The Spaniards colonized the Pacific and the British the Atlantic coast, effectively creating two different geographic regions that barely interacted with one another. On the Atlantic coast, the English established a relationship of commercial and political cooperation with the Miskito people. The appointment of Jeremy I, the first Miskito King, in 1687 consolidated Miskito dominance over other Indigenous peoples, including the Mayangna, and guaranteed that the British would have unrestricted access to natural resources and slaves of the region. The forced African migration as well as intermarriage between Indigenous people and Black Caribs resulted in the existence of ethnic groups that consistently rejected the mono-cultural Mestizo society that was the project of the Nicaraguan state (Tompson 2004, 21). In the 1970s, the encroachment of Mestizo peasants on Indigenous lands fuelled new conflicts that were addressed by titling land for a few Miskito and Mayangna communities (Instituto de Estudios Políticos para América Latina y África 1986). According to the Nicaraguan state, the Atlantic coast was inhabited by "savage tribes" that could not govern themselves and needed to be reconquered (Pérez Baltodano 2003, 397). As Gordon, Gurdian, and Hale have argued, Indigenous communities on the Atlantic coast have revolted against the dispossession of their lands and the assimilationist state project (2003).

The conflictive relationship between the Nicaraguan state and the Indigenous communities was further exacerbated by the Sandinista Revolution in the early 1980s. The revolutionary movement, concerned with overthrowing the Somoza regime and ending oppressive class relationships, undermined the relevance of Indigenous identity. The economic problems that precipitated the fall of the Somoza dictatorship in the Pacific region ultimately reached the Atlantic coast as industrial agriculture and cattle-ranching displaced thousands of poor Mestizo peasants, who then invaded Indigenous lands (Gordon, Gurdian, and Hale 2003, 375). The Sandinista government's nationalist approach to fighting American imperialism clashed with an emergent Indigenous nationalist consciousness that emphasized conceptions of territory and self-determination (Hale 1994).

Seeking to create an economically and culturally unified nation, the Sandinistas pursued policies that trampled on the rights and customs of the Indigenous peoples living in the Atlantic coast region. Resentment and discontent created the conditions for recruiting Miskito militia and forming the "contra revolution," a movement against the Sandinistas, financed by the United States. In 1981, armed conflict erupted, with guerrilla groups fighting against government forces. The civil war lasted almost ten years, from 1980 to 1989, and influenced the creation of two Autonomous Indigenous Regions on the Atlantic coast of Nicaragua, the North Atlantic Autonomous Region (NAAR) and the South Atlantic Autonomous Region (SAAR). These two regions represent approximately forty-two percent of the national territory and contain important natural resources, including marine resources and major forests (Kaimovitz 2002). In 1987, the Sandinista government enacted the law *Autonomy Statute for the Regions of the Atlantic Coast of Nicaragua*. In addition to dividing the Atlantic coast into two autonomous regions, the statute recognized the rights of the Indigenous peoples living in the region to retain their cultural identity and, in particular, to benefit from their natural resources and practice their traditional subsistence activities.[2]

After the electoral defeat of the Sandinistas in 1990, Miskito leaders, who represented the majority of the Indigenous population and were committed to advancing Miskito land rights, were elected to political offices in the government of the North Atlantic Autonomous Region, the region in which the Awas Tingni community is located. Although the rights of Indigenous peoples were constitutionally recognized, subsequent national governments consistently undermined the territorial rights and political basis of the autonomous regions on the grounds that these were "national lands." The Mayangna, who represent only a very small fraction of the Indigenous population of the region, were even more vulnerable than others.

The Awas Tingni community consists of approximately 150 families, who hold the land communally. In 1995, the community learned that the Nicaraguan government was planning to grant a logging license to a Korean lumber company, SOLCARSA, on 63,000 hectares of the community's land. Although the Autonomy Statute provided protection for all Indigenous communities in the Atlantic Coast, the government argued that the members of the Awas Tingni community neither held title to their land nor were making use of it. The government further contended that because the local village was built in the 1940s, Awas Tingni was a "new" community and hence could not claim ancestral rights to the territory. The Mayangna's customary practice of creating new villages once the population of the mother community had grown too large or faced specific challenges thus became the target of government attacks—claiming the Mayangna's "new community" could not be considered ancestral. The government's arguments also misrepresented Mayangna subsistence practices—agriculture, logging, fishing, and hunting—as not being traditional enough. In the Awas Tingni community,

---

2 For example, section VII of the preamble to the statute stipulates that the granting of autonomy "makes possible the effective exercise of the right of the Communities of the Atlantic Coast to participate in working out how to make use of the region's natural resources and how to reinvest the benefits from these in the Atlantic Coast and the nation, thereby creating the material basis for the survival and development of the cultural expressions": *Autonomy Statute for the Regions of the Atlantic Coast of Nicaragua* (Law No. 28), http://calpi.nativeweb.org/doc_3.html. The rights of the Indigenous peoples of the Atlantic Coast region were further affirmed in Nicaragua's Constitution, also promulgated in 1987.

each family farm includes several crop fields, each of about 1.5 hectares, on which they cultivate plantain, beans, rice, corn, and bananas using the slash-and-burn method. In this method, the land is cultivated until the soil is exhausted, at which point it is allowed to lie fallow for up to five years in order to replenish its nutrients. Although this agricultural technique has been praised for maintaining healthy ecosystems, the Nicaragua government represented it as unsustainable.

Seeking to protect their rights, Awas Tingni decided to pursue the cartographic legal approach by taking their case to the Inter-American Court of Human Rights. In addition to an ethnographic study, participatory mapping was used to establish the Awas Tingni community's long-standing relationship to and use of their lands (see Anaya and Macdonald 1995). The Mayangna community produced a map in order to legally document their occupancy and use of the land from time immemorial. As noted earlier, in order to be considered a legal tool, such a map and the legal case itself needed to adhere to Western law and cartographic understandings of connections to the land. Because as a form of property Indigenous land title is equated with economic uses of the land, the tendency is to represent the economic practices that are considered to be closer to nature based on the information provided by those considered most knowledgeable, often elder men. Since Indigenous women's access to land has been mediated by their relationship to men, ongoing unequal access to land touches on the core structure of this cartographic legal approach. This unevenness is intertwined with patriarchal ideologies that extend beyond Indigenous communities.

These cartographic representations supported the claims that the Mayangna are an Indigenous people and that the Nicaraguan state had violated their rights to property established by their customary use and occupancy of that territory. However, this understanding of property replicated a patriarchal understanding of man, the breadwinner, which reproduced Mayangna women as housewives, whose contributions to their household and community's economies have no value. In its decision, the Inter-American Court of Human Rights referred to the American Convention on Human Rights (OAS 1969), to which Nicaragua is a signatory. Parties to the convention are obliged by article 1 to "respect the rights and freedoms recognized herein and to ensure to all persons subject to their jurisdiction the free and full exercise of those rights and freedoms." In other words, it is not enough that the rights of Indigenous peoples are recognized in Nicaragua's Constitution and in the Autonomy Statute. As a party to the convention, the government of Nicaragua must also take steps to ensure Indigenous groups are able to make effective use of these rights—which, the court argued, it had not.

Specifically, the court found that Nicaragua had violated article 21 (1) of the American Convention on Human Rights, which states that "everyone has the right to the use and enjoyment of his property." Importantly, the court established that "property" includes the communal property of Indigenous peoples, as defined by their customary use, arguing that "possession of the land should suffice for indigenous communities lacking real title to property of the land to obtain official recognition of that property" (IACHR 2001, para. 151). As a remedy, the court ordered the government of Nicaragua to use the map to proceed with demarcation and titling of Awas Tingni territory. Furthermore, the court recommended that the Nicaraguan state develop procedures to guarantee property rights not only for Indigenous communities but also for black communities in the region. Property rights do not refer to ownership of the land itself but to the performance of specific activities on the land. As such, the titling of property rights redefined Mayangna's relationship to their land by assigning them a bundle of rights to act on the land. Although, in 2008, the Nicaraguan state did grant a title to the Awas Tingni community, titling cannot be completed until their territory has been fully demarcated, and demarcation cannot proceed until overlapping claims to land use are resolved.

As noted by Wainwright and Bryan, although the Court decision has been considered a victory, it has also reproduced structural inequities that extend both within and beyond indigenous communities" (2009, 161). By delineating relationships between people and places, maps contribute to the representation of specific understandings of community, valued land uses, and rights. Under the guise of securing Indigenous land rights, the titling of Mayangna landholding has created the conditions for the dispossession of this people's lands and resources and for the appropriation of women's invisible labour. For this reason, it is not enough for Indigenous peoples to create their own maps of their territory—that is, their place—when such representations are structured through laws, norms, institutions, and knowledge that are not Indigenous. As shown earlier, reducing territory, or place, to a set of economic activities and notions of property rights erases the Indigenous ontological framework that sustains relationships with place and knowledge.

In this regard, Paul Nadasdy (2002, 242) argues that, as a socially constructed concept, "property" reflects the set of norms and gendered values embodied in the national state. By accepting the notion of property rights, Mayangna communities authorize judges, government institutions, and bureaucrats to impose those norms and values upon them, thereby foreclosing the possibilities of envisioning alternative ways of being in the world. In other words, the communities are forced to play by the rules of the state. Moreover, by accepting the notion of property rights, Indigenous communities must accept the fact that it is the state that extends this right to Indigenous peoples. This situation raises questions about whether Indigenous rights to communal property can be protected if Nicaragua's domestic law does not provide for communal land ownership (Pasqualucci 2009, 65).[3]

As can be seen in the case of the Awas Tingni in Nicaragua, the cartographic legal approach can have a number of unintended consequences. The emphasis on the priority criterion as the basis for recognizing Indigenous title underlines cultural practices and lifestyles that are claimed to be more ancient, more traditional, and different facilitating overly static interpretations of Indigenous peoples histories and relations to the land. By selectively engaging with certain aspects of Indigenous peoples' identity and cultures, both the law and cartography combine to envision a new socio-spatial order for Indigenous communities.

CONCLUSION

The practice of creating and using maps as legal tools to secure Indigenous land rights is an important site to explore how power relations and hegemonic conceptions of the world are reproduced and contested. The analysis

---

3 The concept of property is enshrined in Nicaragua's Family Code (1987), according to which all property brought into or acquired during marriage is jointly held. In the event of separation or divorce, all property and income are divided equally between the spouses, and, in case of death, half remains with the surviving spouse. At the same time, customary practices can prevent a widow from inheriting her husband's property. In a study of gender and land tenure in Bolivia, for example, Lastarria-Cornhiel et al. (2003) note that, when a husband dies, all of the couple's property is sometimes passed directly to his heirs, without taking the widow into account. Further research is needed to determine whether Mayangna women face similar situations or, more generally, into what happens when customary practices surrounding personal property conflict with state law.

of the Awas Tingni case shows that the legal efficacy of maps largely depends on their capacity to represent Indigenous uses of their land in terms of cultural survival. Thus, Indigenous land rights must be protected to guarantee the collective survival of the Mayangna people. Although this case set an international legal precedent for Indigenous peoples around the world by establishing that the benefits of property is a human right, it also raises questions about the potential for human rights to secure a meaningful future for Indigenous peoples for several reasons. First, the use and enjoyment of Indigenous property rights emphasizing "traditional," unchanged economic practices. Indigenous communities are not isolated from the market economy and some would likely want to respond to initiatives to exploit their resources in however sustainable ways. Second, neither international law nor cartography are neutral, both are shaped by Western knowledge, actors and values. Moreover, although Indigenous land and body are inseparable, absent in the cartographic legal approach is how Indigenous women have walked and continue to walk on the land. This situation shadows the celebratory potential of maps as tools to empower Indigenous communities. Who is empowered when racial and gender hierarchies are reproduced is not an irrelevant question and it forces us to think about how Indigenous rights are driven by governmental rationalities.

If Indigenous mapping is to have the potential to benefit Indigenous peoples, maps must be constructed in ways that challenge Western concepts and norms implicit in current approaches. Rather than produce maps that defer to Western frameworks, Indigenous mapping must be used to build Indigenous peoples' capacity to articulate and revitalize their legal orders. Indigenous laws, knowledge, allocation of resources, and relations to land are not, nor were they ever, static. If Indigenous maps are to reflect Indigenous knowledge and histories, they must be able to represent different ways of inhabiting the world. Given that colonialism and land dispossession disempower Indigenous men and women to differing degrees, Indigenous maps need to place women back at the centre of their geographies and represent the epistemologies shaping peoples' interactions with territory and the non-human world. Not only are Indigenous relationships and obligations to the land and the non-human world critical to an accurate portrayal of Indigenous ontologies, but they serve to challenge Western conceptions of land and natural resources that exist exclusively to be exploited.

Research for this chapter was funded by a Killam Cornerstone Grant from the University of Alberta.

References

Agarwal, Bina. 1994. *A Field of One's Own: Gender and Land Rights in South Asia*. Cambridge: Cambridge University Press.

Altamirano-Jiménez, Isabel. 2016. "How Do Real Indigenous Forest Dwellers Live? Neo-liberal Conservation in Oaxaca, Mexico." *Atlantis*, forthcoming.

Anaya, S. James, and Claudio Grossman. 2002. "The Case of Awas Tingni v. Nicaragua: A New Step in the International Law of Indigenous Peoples." *Arizona Journal of International and Comparative Law* 19 (1): 1–15.

Anaya, S. James, and Theodore Macdonald. 1995. "Demarcating Indigenous Territories in Nicaragua: The Case of Awas Tingni." *Cultural Survival Quarterly* 19 (3): 69–73.

Bodenhorn, Barbara. 1990. "I Am Not the Great Hunter, My Wife Is": Inupiat and Anthropological Models of Gender." *Études/Inuit/Studies* 14 (1–2): 55–74.

Bryant, Raymond L. 1998. "Power, Knowledge, and Political Ecology in the Third World: A Review." *Progress in Physical Geography* 22, no. 1: 79–94.

Chapin, Mac, Zachary Lamb, and Bill Threlkeld. 2005. "Mapping Indigenous Lands." *Annual Review of Anthropology* 34: 619–38.

Coulthard, Glen. 2010. "Place Against Empire: Understanding Indigenous Anti-Colonialism." *Affinities: A Journal of Radical Theory, Culture, and Action* 4 (2): 79–83.

Desbiens, Caroline. 2007. "Speaking the Land: Exploring Women's Historical Geographies in Northern Québec." *Canadian Geographer* 51 (3): 360–72.

Domosh, Mona and Joni Seager. 2001. *Putting Women in Place: Feminist Geographers Make Sense of the World*. New York: Guilford Press.

Frink, Lisa. 2007. "Storage and Status in Precolonial and Colonial Coastal Western Alaska." *Current Anthropology* 48 (3): 349–74.

Gordon, Edmund T., Galio C. Gurdian, and Charles R. Hale. 2003. "Rights, Resources and the Social Memory of Struggle: Reflections on a Study of Indigenous and Black Community Land Rights on Nicaragua's Atlantic Coast." *Human Organization* 62 (4): 369–81.

Gururani, Shubhra. 2002. "Forests of Pleasure and Pain: Gendered Practices of Labor and Livelihood in the Forests of Kumaon Himalayas, India." *Gender, Place and Culture* 9 (3): 229–43.

Harcourt, Wendy, and Arturo Escobar, eds. 2005. *Women and the Politics of Place*. Bloomfield, CT: Kumarian Press.

Harley, J. B. 1988. "Maps, Knowledge, and Power." In *The Iconography of Landscape*, edited by Denis Cosgrove and Stephen J. Daniels, 277–312. Cambridge: Cambridge University Press.

Hoekema, André, and Willem Assies. 1999. "El manejo de los recursos: Entre la autonomía y la cogestión." In *El reto de la diversidad: Pueblos indigénas y reforma del estado en América Latina*, edited by Willem Assies, Gemma van der Haar, and André Hoekema, 415–42. Zamora, Michoacán: El Colegio de Michoacán.

IACHR (Inter-American Court of Human Rights). 2001. *Final Judgment in the Case of the Mayangna (Sumo) Awas Tingni Community v. Nicaragua*, 31 August 2001. Reprinted in *Arizona Journal of International and Comparative Law* 19 (1) (2002): 395–456.

Instituto de Estudios Políticos para América Latina y África. 1986. *Los miskitos*. Managua: IEPALA Editorial.

Kaimovitz, David. 2002. "Resources, Abundance, and Competition in the Bosawas Biosphere Reserve, Nicaragua." In *Conserving the Peace: Resources, Livelihoods, and Security*, edited by Richard Matthew, Mark Halle, and Jason Switzer, 171–198. Winnipeg, MB: International Institute for Sustainable Development and World Conservation Union.

Kuokkanen, Rauna. 2011. "Indigenous Economies, Theories of Subsistence, and Women: Exploring the Social Economy Model for Indigenous Goverance." *American Indian Quarterly* 35 (2): 215–40.

Lastarria-Cornhiel, Susana, Sonia Agurto, Jennifer Brown, and Sara Elisa Rosales. 2003. "Joint Titling in Nicaragua, Indonesia, and Honduras: Rapid Appraisal Synthesis." Land Tenure Center, University of Wisconsin–Madison. http://minds.wisconsin.edu/hand- le/1793/22043.

Leach, Melissa. 2007. "Earth Mother Myths and Other Ecofeminist Fables: How a Strategic Notion Rose and Fell." *Development and Change* 38 (1): 67–85.

Llancaqueo Toledo, Víctor. 2005. "Políticas indígenas y derechos territoriales en América Latina: 1990–2004 ¿Las fronteras indígenas de la globalización?" In *Pueblos indígenas, estada y democracia*, edited by Pablo Dávalos, 67–102. Buenos Aires: CLACSO.

McKinley, Elizabeth. 2007. "Postcolonialism, Indigenous Students, and Science Education." In *Handbook of Research on Science Education*, [electronic resource] edited by Sandra K. Abell and Norman G. Lederman, 199–226. Mahwah, NJ: Erlbaum.

Moreton-Robinson, Aileen, and Maggie Walter. 2009. "Indigenous Methodologies in Social Research." In *Social Research Methods*, edited by Maggie Walter, 1–18. Melbourne: Oxford University Press Australia.

Nadasdy, Paul. 2002. "'Property' and Aboriginal Land Claims in the Canadian Subarctic: Some Theoretical Considerations." *American Anthropologist* 104 (1): 247–61.

Natcher, David C. 2001. "Land Use Research and the Duty to Consult: A Misrepresentation of the Aboriginal Landscape." *Land Use Policy* 18: 113–22.

Nightingale, Andrea J. 2002. "Participating or Just Sitting In? The Dynamics of Gender and Caste in Community Forestry." *Journal of Forestry and Livelihoods* 2: 17–24.

———. 2006. "The Nature of Gender: Work, Gender, and Environment." *Environment and Planning D: Society and Space* 24 (2): 165–85.

OAS (Organization of American States). 1969. *American Convention on Human Rights "Pact of San Jose, Costa Rica."* http://www.oas.org/dil/treaties_B-32_American_Convention_on_Human_Rights.htm

Parlee, Brenda, Fikret Berkes, and Tetl'it Gwich'in Renewable Resources Council. 2005. "Health of the Land, Health of the People: Case Study on Gwich'in Berry Harvesting in Northern Canada." *Eco Health* 2: 127–37.

Pasqualucci, Jo M. 2009. "International Land Rights: A Critique of the Jurisprudence of the Interamerican Court of Human Rights in Light of the Declaration on the Rights of Indigenous Peoples." *Wisconsin International Law Review* 27: 51–98.

Peet, Richard, and Michael Watts. 1996. "Liberation Ecology: Development, Sustainability, and Environment in an Age of Market Triumphalism." In *Liberation Ecologies: Environment, Development, Social Movements*, edited by Richard Peet and Michael Watts, 1–45. New York: Routledge.

Peluso, Nancy Lee. 1995. "Whose Woods Are These? Counter-Mapping Forest Territories in Kalimantan, Indonesia." *Antipode* 27 (4): 383–406.

Rodda, Anabel. 1991. *Women and the Environment*. London: Zed Books.

Schroeder, Richard A. 1997. "'Re-Claiming' Land in the Gambia: Gendered Property Rights and Environmental Intervention." *Annals of the Association of American Geographers* 87: 487–508.

Shiva, Vandana. 1988. *Staying Alive: Women, Ecology, and Development*. London: Zed Books.

Sparke, Matthew. 1998. "A Map That Roared and an Original Atlas: Canada, Cartography, and the Narration of Nation." *Annals of the Association of American Geographers* 88 (3): 463–95.

Staples, Kiri and David Natcher. 2015. "Gender, Critical Mass, and Natural Resource Co-Management in the Yukon." *The Northern Review* 41: 139–55.

Stocks, Anthony. 2003. "Mapping Dreams in Nicaragua's Bosawas Reserve." *Human Organization* 62 (4): 344–56.

Tompson, Doug. 2004. "'Useful Laborers' and 'Savage Hordes': Hispanic Central American Views of Afro-Indigenous People in the Nineteenth Century." *Transforming Anthropology* 12(1-2): 21–29.

UNIFEM (United Nations Development Fund for Women). 2008. *Concept Paper on Climate Change and Gender*. New York: United Nations.

Wainwright, Joel, and Joe Bryan. 2009. "Cartography, Territory, Property: Post-Colonial Reflections on Indigenous Counter-Mapping in Nicaragua and Belize." *Cultural Geographies* 16: 153–78.

Warren, Karen J. 1987. "Feminism and Ecology: Making Connections." *Environmental Ethics* 9 (1): 3–20.

World Bank. 2009. "Indigenous Peoples' Land Demarcation and Titling." http://go.worldbank.org/NISUSI0HA0

CHAPTER FIVE

Métis Women's Environmental Knowledge and the Recognition of Métis Rights

Nathalie Kermoal

Picking plants for food and medicine was and still is part of our lifestyle. We have [. . .] studied plants and their medicinal uses for generations. We have [. . .] preserved the knowledge of traditional plants as an intellectual right given to us by our ancestors. As technology advances, and industry moves further north, we are beginning to lose control of the very land on which our medicines grow. (Richardson 2003, pt. 1, 1).

These words of Métis elder Rose Richardson, of Meadow Lake, Saskatch-ewan, illustrate the deep attachment of the Métis to their land in western Canada, their extensive knowledge of this environment, and their concern for the future in the face of ongoing resource exploration and development. In 2004, in its Haida Nation and Taku River Tlingit decisions, the Supreme Court of Canada established the duty of government to consult and accom-modate Aboriginal peoples whose rights or title may be infringed upon by proposed resource development. These decisions hinged on section 35(1) of the Constitution Act, 1982, which recognizes and affirms "the existing aboriginal and treaty rights" of Canada's Aboriginal peoples, who are defined in section 35(2) as "the Indian, Inuit and Métis peoples."[1]

The Constitution Act did not explicitly define what constitutes Aboriginal rights. In R. v. Van der Peet, however, the Supreme Court determined that, in order to be considered an Aboriginal right, "an activity must be an element of a practice, custom or tradition integral to the distinctive culture of the aboriginal group claiming the right" ([1996] 2 SCR 507 at 509). The Van der Peet decision further recognized that, owing to historical differences between the Métis and other Aboriginal groups, the "manner in which the aboriginal rights of other aboriginal peoples are defined is not necessarily determinative of the manner in which the aboriginal rights of the Métis are defined" (510). In the context of Métis rights, the key legal decision to date is R. v. Powley ([2003] 2 SCR 207), with reference to a dispute that arose after a Métis father and son were charged with illegally killing a moose. In its decision, the Supreme Court not only recognized the Métis right to hunt for food but also laid out ten criteria—the Powley test—for establishing the existence of a Métis right.[2] In connection with one of these criteria, the Court stated: "In addition to demographic evidence, proof of shared customs, traditions, and a collective identity is required to demonstrate the existence of a Métis community that can support a claim to site-specific aboriginal rights" (para. 23). The decision further stipulated that "the test for Métis practices should focus on identifying those practices, customs and traditions that are integral to the Métis community's distinctive existence and relationship to the land" (para. 37).

It was within this legal context that the Supreme Court's decisions in the Haida Nation and Taku River Tlingit cases were taken. To date, however, the implementation of the Crown's duty to consult and accommodate has been

---

1 The two cases in question—Haida Nation v. British Columbia (Minister of Forests), [2004] 3 SCR 511, and Taku River Tlingit First Nation v. British Columbia (Project Assessment Director), [2004] 3 SCR 550—pertained to First Nations whose rights had not been recognized by treaty. The duty to consult was further elaborated the following year in Mikisew Cree First Nation v. Canada (Minister of Canadian Heritage), [2005] 3 SCR 288, a case that involved a signatory of Treaty 8. For discussion, see Newman 2009.

2 The Powley test is an adaptation of the principles laid out in R. v. Van der Peet for determining what constitutes an Aboriginal right in the case of First Nations and Inuit.

uneven, especially with regard to the Métis (see Teillet 2008). Saskatchewan, Manitoba, and Ontario have developed consultation guidelines that explicitly include the Métis, as do the federal guidelines (Canada 2011). At the opposite end of the spectrum, British Columbia refuses to recognize a legal obligation to consult with Métis people "as the Province is of the view that no Métis community is capable of successfully asserting site specific Section 35 rights in B.C." (British Columbia 2010, 9). Somewhat ironically, Alberta—the only province in Canada to have granted a legal land base to the Métis (Alberta 2000)—has yet to develop consultation procedures for use with Métis communities (see Conroy and Hansen 2015). At least in part, this delay reflects the fact that, in Alberta, "responsibility for carrying out consultations with Aboriginal peoples has in most cases been delegated to industry and incorporated into the environmental assessment process" (Métis Nation of Alberta 2009, 1).

Even though consultation processes, including those that surround environmental impact assessments, typically stress the need to recognize and respect traditional ecological knowledge, Métis contributions to that knowledge remain relatively unexplored, as indeed does the question of whether the label "Indigenous knowledge" can adequately capture Métis ways of knowing (Chrétien and Murphy 2009, 1). Given the historical bias of ethnographic research toward men, the knowledge held by Métis women is especially apt to be ignored and/or marginalized—knowledge that is essential to fulfilling the need to identify "those practices, customs and traditions that are integral to the Métis community's distinctive existence and relationship to the land," as well as many of the other criteria laid out in the Powley test. The neglect of Métis women's knowledge is, of course, illustrative of a broader trend. Relatively little research in Canada has been devoted to Indigenous women's knowledge of the environment and their roles and responsibilities with regard to the harvesting of resources, stewardship of the land, and governance of the land, and their perspectives are typically undervalued, if not missing entirely, in land claims and resource and land use plans. Despite the recognition that both men and women are involved in multiple activities on the land and that these activities are often complementary, most of the work performed by women remains poorly documented and hence poorly understood.

Especially given that access to and control over resources lie at the heart of Indigenous concerns about the recognition of their rights, an urgent need exists for gender-sensitive research into traditional land use. In an article written in 1999, Paul Nadasdy observed (1999, 1) that "the widespread recognition that something called 'traditional ecological knowledge' even exists represents, in itself, an important first step toward the full participation of aboriginal communities in the management of land and resources." But this recognition is only a first step. Writing about water policy in Australia, Linda Wirf, April Campbell, and Naomi Rea (2008, 511) point out that failing to pay attention to women's environmental knowledge can lead to the "potential breakdown of carefully synchronized environmental management strategies that depend on the implicit links between men's and women's complementary and dialogical knowledges and practices." Indeed, effective environmental consultation requires a holistic approach, which demands that we bring women's knowledge and activities into the centre of inquiry, rather than allowing them to remain at the periphery.

In an effort to offset this gender eclipse, I focus in this chapter on Métis women's knowledge of the land, with particular attention to the medical expertise of Métis women in western Canada. In so doing, I hope to demonstrate the range and depth of the traditional knowledge Métis women have of their environment and thus render visible their complex connection to the land. In turn, by shedding light on the ways in which Métis women conceptualize their relationship to the land and how these relationships may shift over time, I seek to deepen our understanding of Métis identity and the importance of territory to that identity. As Linda Tuhiwai Smith (1999, 7) points out, "Research is one of the ways in which the underlying code of imperialism and colonialism is both regulated and realized." In what follows, I hope to illustrate the importance of what she calls "researching back" (7)—that is, using research to challenge dominant historical narratives that have tended to write Indigenous peoples, including the Métis, out of existence.

Colonial Paradigms and Subjugated Knowledges

The authors of a Statistics Canada article on the cultural activities of the Métis define cultural continuity as "the connection that individuals feel with their cultural past, as well as their projections of that culture into the future" (Kumar and Janz 2010, 63). Noting that research on cultural continuity has so far focused primarily on First Nations, they list a number of factors—"Aboriginal language knowledge, land claims, self-government, availability of cultural facilities, and the provision of culturally appropriate education, health, police and fire services"—that contribute to cultural continuity among First Nations (63). Seeking to identify factors that generate cultural continuity among the Métis, the authors examine participation in traditional harvesting activities (hunting, fishing, trapping, and gathering plants) and the consumption of traditional foods, engagement in Métis arts and crafts and other cultural activities, as well as membership in a Métis organization, a commitment to spiritual practices, and the knowledge of an Aboriginal language.

Like Aboriginal women elsewhere, Métis women in western Canada contribute in many ways to the ongoing transmission of knowledge on which cultural continuity depends.[3] They continue to engage in the practices taught to them by their mothers, grandmothers, and aunts, while in turn teaching their own daughters, granddaughters, and nieces. At the same time, partly in response to the pressures of colonization and industrialization, Métis women have also participated in the creation of new knowledge. "Traditional" cultures are often wrongly assumed to be static, as if tradition were something immutable, when, in reality, all cultures continually innovate. As Marlene Brant Castellano (2000, 24) observes, "a constant testing of knowledge in the context of current reality creates the applications that make timeless truths relevant to each generation."

Whereas early European explorers often depended for their survival on the knowledge held by Aboriginal guides, settler-colonists embarked on a process of delegitimizing Aboriginal knowledge. As Linda Tuhiwai Smith (1999, 26) points out, European colonizers "established systems of rule and forms of social relations" that structured their interaction with those colonized, whether in Canada or elsewhere. The colonial imposition of "order," whereby Indigenous peoples' reality was reconstituted within Western frames of reference (political, legal, economic, social, ideological), created

---

3 I use "Métis" to refer to the peoples who descend from the historic Métis Nation and therefore share a culture and a history. From its beginnings in the Red River settlement, the Métis homeland came to extend across Manitoba, Saskatchewan, Alberta, and into parts of British Columbia, the Northwest Territories, Ontario, as well as south into Montana and North Dakota. Historically, the Métis spoke many Indigenous languages—such as Cree or Ojibwe or other local Aboriginal languages— but they were associated in particular with the Michif language, a mixture of French and Cree. The Prairie Métis people also used Michif-Cree and Bungee (consisting of Gaelic and Cree mixed with French and Saulteaux).

a cultural disorder that disconnected people from their land, their languages, their knowledge, and their histories. In the case of the Métis, their political marginalization at the hands of the Canadian state has further contributed to the suppression of cultural knowledge.

Western epistemologies continue to dominate and define the boundaries of legitimate knowledge. In this view, traditional knowledge "is assumed to be qualitative, intuitive, holistic, and oral" and is held to be the antithesis of scientific knowledge, which "is seen as quantitative, analytical, reduction-ist, and literate" (Nadasdy 1999, 2; see also Lévesque 2004). Even when the values of traditional knowledge are recognized (i.e. Indigenous ontologies and related ethics), researchers are prone to analyze and classify it. As Julie Cruikshank (1998, 50) aptly puts it, traditional knowledge "continues to be presented as an object for science rather than a system of knowledge that could inform science." As an object, traditional knowledge can, moreover, be repurposed. In the context of environmental impact assessments, for example, traditional knowledge is selected, framed, and prioritized by the development project under review, which also imposes geographic bound-aries and sets timelines. This, in turn, shapes what can or should be studied, and, by extension, what will be left out (Usher [2000] 2003, 44).

The discourse surrounding traditional knowledge is thus intimately con-cerned with power. Michel Foucault argues that power cannot be dissociated from knowledge. The possession of knowledge confers the power to control, but the power to control confers the ability to know—to gather knowledge, to dictate its relative value, to determine who has access to it, and to use it to exercise power more efficiently. In other words, relations of power generate what Foucault calls regimes of truth, forms of discourse whereby knowledge is variously legitimated or subjugated by those who hold power.[4] Pierre Bourdieu's notion of "legitimate" language adds another dimension to the relationship between knowledge and power. Bourdieu (1991, 45) argues that "the official language is bound up with the state, both in its genesis and in its social uses. It is in the process of state formation that the conditions are created for the constitution of a unified linguistic market, dominated by the official language." To participate in processes of negotiations or

---

4 For a useful introduction to Foucault's ideas on the nexus of knowledge and power, see, especially, "Truth and Power," in Foucault (1980). See also Arun Agrawal's "The Politics of Indigenous Knowledge" (2005).

consultations, as Nadasdy (2003, 5) points out, Aboriginal peoples have no choice but to conform "to the very particular forms and formalities of the official linguistic fields of wildlife management, Canadian property law, and so forth."

Thus, while Indigenous peoples may be given the opportunity to speak, this does not mean that what they say will be valued, or even that it will necessarily be understood. Gayatri Spivak ([1988] 1994) questions whether the subaltern can ever speak—a question that applies doubly to women, given that, in colonial historiography, "the ideological construction of gender keeps the male dominant" (82). "If, in the context of colonial production," she argues, "the subaltern has no history and cannot speak, the subaltern as female is even more deeply in shadow" (82–83). Unsurprisingly, given the deeply patriarchal structures of the Canadian state, Aboriginal women have occupied only a marginal role in political negotiations (and that only quite recently), and their perspectives are largely missing in land use studies, environmental monitoring, and wildlife management.

As Gerdine Van Woudenberg (2004, 82) argues, the persistence of the colonial portrayal of Aboriginal women as landless and consigned to domestic space further serves to perpetuate the subordination of female to male. The structures of power in a patriarchal colonial environment have created what Foucault terms "subjugated knowledges"—"a whole set of knowledges that have been disqualified as inadequate to their task or insufficiently elaborated: naive knowledges, located low down on the hierarchy, beneath the required level of cognition or scientificity" (1980, 82).[5] Vrinda Dalmiya and Linda Alcoff (1993) argue that, within Western societies, legitimate knowledge has been constructed so as to deny epistemological validity to the traditional knowledge held by women. Thus, for instance, knowledge about childbearing and child rearing or about herbal medicines is generally dismissed as "old wives' tales," which, because perceived as unscientific, fail to receive "the honorific status of knowledge" (217). It is therefore important to unravel the subjugated, or "disqualified," knowledge that arises out of

---

5 Foucault elaborates his concept of an "insurrection" of subjugated knowledges in "Two Lectures" (Foucault 1980, 78–108; see esp. 81–84). For a critique from a feminist perspective, see Sawicki (1991). Foucault, she writes, "never spoke of 'male domination' per se; he usually spoke of power as if it subjugated everyone equally" (49).

the experience of oppression, to turn our attention to "relations not always visible" (Gordon 2006, 431).

Van Woudenberg (2004, 82) raises a number of thought-provoking questions about the position of Aboriginal women not only as participants in negotiations surrounding Aboriginal rights and title but also as historical actors with agency. As we have seen, in Canada, it falls to the courts (especially the Supreme Court) to define precisely what constitutes Aboriginal rights and by whom these rights can be claimed. Van Woudenberg argues that, because the relevant legal decisions have primarily focused on hunting and fishing, these activities have come to be regarded as fundamental to Aboriginal cultures, while other activities on the land, notably those in which women engage, are relegated to a secondary position, as if to imply that Aboriginal people themselves regard women's activities as accessory to men's. In the context of Métis rights, the Powley case, which turned on subsistence hunting, is an apt illustration. As Van Woudenberg (2004, 81) warns, "The silence surrounding women's traditional relations with the land could easily be used to disinherit them legally in the present."[6] Political participation is an essential component of access to, allocation of, and control over resources. Métis women may (and do) perceive their relationship to the land as essential to community well-being. Yet, even though Métis women have sometimes provided valuable information about traditional knowledge in connection with legal proceedings, their own activities continue to be virtually invisible in the courts as well as in the realm of research, including land use studies.

Knowledge may also be rendered invisible because it exists in marginalized spaces. In the West, "legitimate" sites of knowledge are almost entirely public, perhaps because the public sphere is also the male sphere. As Van Woudenberg suggests, the colonial projection of a fundamentally Western equation, that of women with domestic space, onto Aboriginal cultures has had the effect of erasing women from sites of knowledge in which they do not "belong." Similar to the public sphere, the "wilderness" was, and still is, coded male. As a result, places where women hunt and fish, harvest berries, and pick medicinal plants (as well as those where they traditionally gave

---

6 "[...] le « silence » entourant les relations traditionnelles des femmes à la terre pourrait bien servir à les déshériter légalement dans le présent" (81). The translation is mine.

birth) have been ignored. Women have therefore been similarly effaced from the bodies of discourse surrounding these activities and thus from the legal frameworks and the spiritual traditions associated with them. In part, then, the neglect of Aboriginal women's knowledge may reflect the fact that it often exists in places where non-Aboriginal people do not expect to find it.

Among Aboriginal peoples, place is inseparably intertwined with cultural identity and sense of self. Writing on Western Apache language and culture, Keith Basso (1990, 133) argues that "conceptions of the land work in specific ways to influence Apaches' conceptions of themselves (and vice versa)," with the two then working together "to influence patterns of social action." As he further observes, "Knowledge of places is therefore closely linked to knowledge of the self, to grasping one's position in the larger scheme of things, including one's own community, and to securing a confident sense of who one is as a person" (1996, 34). This knowledge is conveyed in place names and through stories about specific locations on the land, and this naming and storytelling serve to fuse past and present. Whereas Western histories seek to reconstruct the sequence of past events, "what matters most to Apaches is *where* events occurred, not when" (31). History—or what Basso aptly calls "the country of the past" (32)—is not a matter of relics. Rather, "the place-maker's main objective is to speak the past into being, to summon it with words and give it dramatic form, to *produce* experience, forging ancestral worlds in which others can participate and readily lose themselves" (32).

This perspective is by no means unique to the Western Apache—nor has this intimate relationship to the land ever been the sole preserve of men. Rather than reinforce colonial conceptions of gender, in which men's activities on the land somehow become more essential than women's, we need to understand how Aboriginal women perceived their connection to the land and to their cultural heritage. In this context, it becomes all the more important to examine Métis women's ways of knowing the land as well as their ways of speaking it—of giving voice to the experiences through which their relationship to the land is continually renewed and made present.

"Our Land is Our Life"

Words such as *displacement, dispossession*, and *migration* are often used to describe the experiences of the Métis people after the events of 1869–70 at Red River, in present-day Manitoba. The events were triggered by the Hudson's Bay Company's transfer of the vast northwest territory of Rupert's

Land to the Canadian government without prior consultation with the peoples who lived on these lands. Concerned, the Métis, through a provisional government led by Louis Riel, negotiated terms for entering Confederation. As a result of these negotiations, the province of Manitoba was created by the Manitoba Act (1870). Section 31 of the Manitoba Act promised the Métis 1.4 million acres of land, to be redeemed in the form of scrip—government-issued certificates good for land or a cash equivalent. Because this system operated by doling out individual parcels of land (for which the Métis were obliged to compete with white settlers), it effectively denied the Métis a collective land base. Over a period of roughly fifty years, moreover, the Métis lost most of the land promised to them, chiefly at the hands of white speculators who cheated individuals and families out of their scrip.[7]

After 1870, the Métis were made to feel strangers in their own land. From the late nineteenth century onward, landless Métis moved from one locale to another across the Prairie provinces, endeavouring to eke out a livelihood. Some families moved further west while others relocated in other areas in Manitoba. Many new Métis communities were founded, but even these were not immune to actions on the part of government, and the Métis themselves were often the target of racial discrimination. Early in the twentieth century, for example, a number of Métis families founded a community at Ste-Madeleine, in western Manitoba. As was often the case, the community was located on lands that were not especially well suited to agriculture. All the same, after Parliament passed the Prairie Farm Rehabilitation Act in 1935, which was intended to encourage drought-stricken white farmers of the Depression era to remain on the prairies and continue to farm, the Métis from Ste-Madeleine—perceived as "squatters"—were forced to relocate, and their community was burned (see Zeilig and Zeilig 1987). While the events at Ste-Madeleine are perhaps an especially egregious example, they are part of a well-recognized pattern of dispossession.

Yet despite this history of displacement, Métis people have maintained a very strong connection to the land and, more generally, to the Northwest, carrying with them knowledge systems integral to their culture. In "Métis and Feminist," Emma LaRocque (2007, 57) speaks of the experiences of her

---

7 On the scrip system, see Tough and McGregor (2007, esp. 36–43). In "I Still Call Australia Home," Aileen Moreton-Robinson (2003) offers a thoughtful exploration of dispossession and Indigenous concepts of belonging and place.

people, the Apeetowgusanuk (or "half-sons" in Cree), and their deep emotional attachment to the land:

My parents, aunts and uncles all spoke of "scrip" and how Apeetowgusanuk lost and were continuing to lose beloved domains of lands either through scrip or simply through urban, industrial and farming encroachments. Legally, we did not own any land but in those years we could still definitely live on, from and with the land, for morally, it was our land. My grandparents occupied, used and loved this land long before Confederation, and my father was born before Alberta became a province. My parents' generation made a living from the many resources of the land, including hunting and trapping, as well as wage labour, wherever such could be found.

According to Métis elder Lucy Desjarlais Whiteman, "Women never stopped talking about the lost lands. They were more bitter than the men who were told there was more land and they believed that" (quoted in Shilling 1983, 90–91). The ontological relationship that Métis people have with the land is still very much at the centre of their political and collective aspirations. Historically, the Métis way of life depended on the existence of open spaces— territory across which they could travel freely, hunting, fishing, and gathering plants. The encroachment of settlers gradually reduced this mobility. For women healers, limitations on mobility required modifications to recipes for medicines, the ingredients for which might originally have been scattered over a wide area. In *Our Knowledge Is Not Primitive: Decolonizing Botanical Anishinaabe Teachings*, Wendy Makoons Geniusz (2009, 119–20) speaks of the need to modernize recipes by substituting new products and of using new technologies—such as "iron knives, pots, and axes" and in the twentieth century "blenders, supermarket bags, and pocketknives—to gather botanical materials and manufacture medicines (119).

The elders interviewed for *In the Words of Our Ancestors: Métis Health and Healing* (Métis Centre 2008) testify to the central role that Métis women played in the well-being of their communities. Métis mothers and grandmothers were teachers and role models, and they remained so even beyond the grave, as the knowledge they shared was stored in the memory of their children, grandchildren, and great-grandchildren. This knowledge belongs to the future as well as to the past: the elders often emphasized that traditional knowledge, while rooted in ancient stories and oral histories, is current, contemporary, and sustainable. All the same, many elders and community members throughout western Canada are worried about the future. Further fragmentation of the land is occurring as a result of development, while pollution, environmental change, and the simple destruction of open spaces have led to the relative disappearance of certain plant species, as well as to reductions in the availability of fish and game. In addition, pharmaceutical companies have begun to take a proprietary interest in medicinal plants. As elder Rose Richardson pointed out in the comment that opens this chapter, in the face of resource development, the Métis sense that they are losing control over their traditional lands and, by extension, over the knowledge associated with the plants that grow on those lands. She went out to say that "in many cases the information taken from our people has become patented or copyrighted without giving recognition to our people and to our ancestors" (Richardson 2003, pt. 1, 1). As Ikechi Mgbeoji (2006, ix) argues biopiracy thrives "in a cultural milieu in which non-Western forms of knowledge are systematically marginalized and devalued as 'folk knowledge.'" The appropriation and the privatization of plants—through patents—continues to favour the dominant narrative of Western epistemology by not crediting the intellectual contributions of Indigenous people.

A poll conducted in 2002 by the National Aboriginal Health Organization revealed that 80 percent of the eight hundred Métis who participated in the survey felt that the revitalization of Aboriginal traditions was essential to improving current health care. And yet roughly 60 percent said that they did not know where to find traditional remedies or did not have access to traditional healers (Edge and McCallum 2006, 86–87). In 2006, the Aboriginal Peoples Survey discovered that, on average, fewer than three out of ten Métis (29 percent) had gathered wild plants during the previous twelve months, with the proportion declining from a high of 35 percent among people aged forty-five to fifty-four to 24 percent among people aged fifteen to nineteen (Kumar and Janz 2010, 64 and chart 1).[8] These numbers suggest that Métis today may be at risk of losing their connection to the land.

The fact that roughly 70 percent of Canada's Métis now live in urban areas helps to explain in part this disconnect with the land (Canada 2013, 8).

---

8 Among Métis living in rural areas, the proportion rose to 41 percent (Kumar and Janz 2010, 64). Although the survey indicated that men and women were equally likely to report having gathered plants, it did not ask whether the plants were intended for food or for medicinal purposes.

However, other factors have also been at play. The elders who contributed to *In the Words of Our Ancestors* speak of many losses their people have experienced in the wake of colonization. Common themes were

> loss of Aboriginal identity; loss of Aboriginal languages; death of family members from infectious diseases; loss of access to land and resources; loss of access to hunting, fishing and trapping; loss of traditional teachings; experiences with violence and abuse; loss of parenting skills; influences of religion and/or churches; experiences of attending Residential School; or of relocation or displacement from ancestral lands. (Métis Centre 2008, 14–15)

The elders also emphasized the importance of regaining and revitalizing traditional teachings for the benefit of families and communities. Speaking about traditional medicine, elder Norman Fleury commented,

> For those that want to know, it is a teaching. Some of our people have been so far removed from that. Our grandmother was a medicine woman. But now we are so far removed from it, all they know now is peppermint tea. They don't know the other medicines, but they'll talk about it. This will be a good start to try to teach it again. (Métis Centre 2008, 42)

Acknowledging the emotional and spiritual aspects of healing, he also underscored the need for a commitment to understanding traditional medicine as an integrated system of knowledge: "Now I have to say to myself, how interested am I to retrieve some of those medicines, those traditional herbs, and who is going to put them in proper perspective, or is it just a story?" (Métis Centre 2008, 44). From the perspective of gender, one might wonder how the loss of knowledge identified by Fleury has affected Métis women and their connection to the land, as well as their status within their communities and their ability to sustain traditional values.

In a study on berry harvesting among Gwich'in women, Brenda Parlee and her colleagues argue that berry picking connects these women "to their mental, emotional, physical, and spiritual selves, to each other and to the land" (Parlee, Berkes, and the Teetl'it Gwich'in Renewable Resources Council 2005, 132). The women who took part in the study perceived berries as having both nutritional and medicinal value (132), and they also spoke of "the benefits of going out on the land with family and friends and working together" (133). As the research evolved, other important elements became apparent, such as a strong sense of cultural continuity and stewardship of the land. For many of the women, the practice of berry picking was a legacy passed on from generation to generation. They would go back to the same berry patches "to remember and respect their mothers and grandmothers who were there before them," and they expressed the hope that their children and grandchildren "will continue to go to these places and remember them there also" (133). These women also perceived themselves as stewards of the land, maintaining cabin sites and trails to specific berry patches, and felt a strong pride of ownership. Through berry harvesting, Gwich'in women participate in the governance of the land. A few "suggested that their berry patches should be protected under the Gwich'in land use plan or other Gwich'in laws to ensure that their children and future generations would be able to harvest berries in those places," and they were also concerned about the impact of climate change (134). In short, the study demonstrated how women's relationship to the land is bound up with values that are integral to the well-being not only of their families and communities but also of the environment.

Although Métis women's experiences may differ in their details from those of Gwich'in women, research such as this can provide valuable insights into how women situate themselves in their relation to the land and the world. It can also help us to grasp the scale at which the women's knowledge of the environment is produced and to understand activities such as berry picking and plant picking as practices bound by rules and laws. As John Briggs and Joanne Sharpe (2004, 667) point out, by focusing on the deeper ways of knowing embedded in such activities, one is able to understand "the worldview of the people involved, such as understanding of social justice, gender relations, familial responsibilities, and so on." While berry picking might easily be dismissed as supplementary food gathering, in the Gwich'in world it is an activity that opens a window onto social, cultural, legal, economic, and spiritual relationships.

LII MICHIN: THE MEDICAL KNOWLEDGE OF MÉTIS WOMEN

Knowledge of medicine was accumulated over centuries by the Aboriginal peoples of North America on the basis of observation and experimentation. An overemphasis on the role of the "medicine man" has, however, obscured the extent to which women were involved in family and community health. Until fairly recently, this effacement of Aboriginal women's medical knowledge extended even to histories of midwifery (Lux 2001, 97). Attempting to insert Aboriginal women back into history, Kristin Burnett (2011, 157) argues that, even as the settlement of the Prairie West in the latter part of the nineteenth century worked to create a social order that marginalized Aboriginal women, newly arriving European-Canadian women "took advantage of the obstetrical expertise of Aboriginal women," relying on them "to aid them as midwives, caregivers, and healers." Similarly, Maureen Lux (2001, 97) observes that "until the 1920s, immigrant women on homesteads were rarely attended in childbirth by a physician" and that, even when a doctor was available, fees were high. In addition, given that physicians—who were, of course, overwhelmingly male—were "not necessarily seen as competent" to deliver babies, women often preferred to rely on the expertise of an Aboriginal midwife (97). As Burnett (2011, 160) explains, the practice of obstetrics was not held in especially high regard within the emerging Western medical profession, and physicians were thus apt to have had relatively little obstetrical training. Moreover, aside from those who might earlier have acquired some knowledge of nursing or midwifery, European-Canadian women living on Prairie homesteads typically had little or no experience with the delivery of babies—in contrast to Aboriginal midwives, who "underwent significant apprenticeship and training, which usually began at a young age" (160; see also Burnett 2010).[9] What Burnett and Lux describe for First Nations women applies equally to Métis women's medical knowledge.

"One of the most damaging legacies of the colonial project in western Canada," writes Burnett (2011, 158), "has been the discursive erasure of Aboriginal women from the landscape after the 1870s." Since the pioneering work of Jennifer Brown (1980) and Sylvia Van Kirk (1980), considerable emphasis has been placed on defining the historical roles of Aboriginal women during the fur trade era. During roughly the same period, interest in the field of Métis studies and Métis history has grown and diversified considerably. To date, researchers have been concerned mainly with the

---

9 As settlement progressed, however, efforts were made to suppress the activities of Aboriginal midwives and healers. Such was the case for Métis midwife and healer Marie Rose Delorme Smith. As her daughter, Mary Hélène (Smith) Parfitt, recalled, "Marie Rose had put in many years of midwifery and the doctors were disgruntled at not being called to deliver the babies. Soon Marie Rose had a letter from officials in Edmonton telling her that she must desist from this practice" (quoted in Carpenter 1977, 149). Similarly, Lux (2001, 96) notes that "on reserves where medical missionaries had established hospitals, Native midwives were seen as unwelcome competition."

Red River resistance and the central figure of Louis Riel or with the reasons that the Métis left the province of Manitoba after 1870 (see, for example, Sprague 1988; Flanagan 1991; Ens 1996; Bumsted 2001). Attention has also focused on issues surrounding Métis identity and Métis rights (for example, Wilson and Mallet 2008; Andersen 2014). Studies of Métis women are still relatively rare, however (see Payment 1990; Racette 2004; Kermoal 2006; St-Onge 2008; Iseke-Barnes 2009; Macdougall 2010; Andersen, 2011), and rarer still are those that discuss the specific roles that Métis women played in maintaining and passing on their values in relation to the land and its resources (Adese, 2014). This discursive erasure necessitates the process of "researching back" that Linda Tuhiwai Smith (1999, 7) proposes.

Although it is impossible, at this point, to trace specific lines of transmission, Métis women built upon a large corpus of medical knowledge inherited from their First Nations ancestors, and with that knowledge came many obligations. As David Newhouse (2004, 151) observes, "When a person comes into a relationship with certain knowledge, he or she is not only transformed by it, but must assume responsibility for it." Métis medical knowledge—*lii michin*, "the medicines"—was often passed on from mother to daughter, grandmother to granddaughter, auntie to niece, or a woman might acquire such knowledge from a respected elder in the community. Women cared for and gave medical advice to men, as well as women and children, and their activities were integral to the health and well-being of the community. Since illnesses are part of everyday life, women's knowledge and skills were indispensable.

Expertise in medicine was primarily associated with "grandmothers" (*nokoms*) because they were no longer occupied with raising their children—even though they often took care of grand-children—and no longer fell under the taboos surrounding menstruation (Niethammer 1977, 146). Many of these women became respected midwives, although not all women proved to be suited to midwifery: the test was often the first delivery of a baby. In an interview, Elsie (Hourie) Bear explains that older women tried to teach her "because they wanted it to go on from generation to generation [...] and I went with my grandmother and the first time she took me, I ran away. I didn't want no part of that" (quoted in Kermoal 2006, 145). Most women were, however, adept in the use of homemade remedies. Métis author and elder Maria Campbell (2011) remembers that, in her family, herbs and medicines were stored in cotton bags that were hung from the rafters of the cellar. "Although our nokoms did most of the doctoring," she writes, "every mother had her own stash of medicines used for croups, coughs, fevers and any number of childhood illnesses." For more serious illnesses, however, a woman who had earned a reputation as a healer would be consulted.

The names of some of these women have come down to us. The mother of Victoria Belcourt Callihoo (1861–1966) was a recognized healer at the time of the great buffalo hunts, who cared for the sick and the injured and whose expertise was greatly valued (MacEwan 1995, 191). Callihoo's contemporary, Marie Rose Delorme Smith (1861–1960), who lived most of her life in the Pincher Creek area of southern Alberta, said nothing about her role as a healer in her written reminiscences, but family members recall that she "was known as a 'medicine woman' to many First Nations people, who reportedly travelled for miles to seek her remedies" (MacKinnon 2012, 75; see also Carpenter 1977, 149). Born in 1868, Elise Vivier Boyer, of Fort Ellice (in present-day Manitoba), was another well-known midwife and traditional healer. Known locally as "Mrs. Cha-Cha"—after the nickname of her husband, Norbert Boyer, whom people called "Cat" (*cha'-cha'*)—she was renowned for treating tuberculosis and women's miscarriages and hemorrhages (Fleury and Barkwell 2009, 1). Elder Norman Fleury's grandmother was also a healer, from whom he learned much about traditional medicine:

> My grandma, she taught us all these things to respect with, because she lost her mother when she was younger, but she learned, she had medicine people that helped her to learn, *lii michin*, to learn medicine. [. . .] My grandma brought all of us kids all into this world. There was nobody else. They never saw a doctor, not once. Even miscarriages, she gave them medicines, stuff like that. She also talked to me about when you prepare medicines, the importance of preparing medicines. (Métis Centre 2008, 43)

Although Métis healers sometimes travelled many miles to gather the plants they needed, this was not always the case. Recalling her childhood, Maria Campbell (2011) writes, "Our drug store was half a mile up the road in a meadow called Omisimaw Puskiwa (oldest sister prairie) where yarrow, plantain, wild roses, fireweed, asters, nettles and pigweed could be found in great abundance. Some of it was just medicine and some of it like fireweed, nettles and pigweed was medicine and food." Indeed, as she goes on to say, food was itself a source of medicine:

I have since come to understand that most everything we ate in those days was medicinal, including the moose and other wild animals. Moose, for example, eat willow and poplar branches all full of medicine. They eat water plantain and dig down deep in the water to eat the water lily and roots, both of which are very important ingredients in some cancer medicines. Bears eat berry and the roots of many plants, making their fat, especially, highly prized by medicine people.

As she suggests, her Métis ancestors were well aware of the way that nutrients are transmitted from animals to human beings and that a healthy diet affords protection against illness.

Every plant was thoroughly studied and experimented so that its qualities were fully understood. For that reason, it was not uncommon for the same plant to serve multiple purposes. For example, according to Lawrence Barkwell (2009, 1), in the fall, usually after the first frost, the Métis would gather the seeds of a shrub known as wolf willow (*Elaeagnus commutate*, also called silver willow, buffalo willow, rosary bush, or silverberry) and use them to make rosaries, bracelets, and necklaces. The bark was used in weaving blankets, clothing, and baskets, while the berries were used in making soap but could also be eaten or used as an ingredient in other foods. In addition, the plant had medicinal properties:

> The fruit of the Wolf Willow is a rich source of vitamins and a source of fatty acids. It is rich in vitamins A, C and E. The fruit of the Wolf Willow is being investigated as a food that reduces the incidence of cancer and may even halt or reverse the growth of some cancers. A decoction of the bark mixed with oil is used as a salve for children with frostbite. A decoction of Wolf Willow and sumac roots has been used for syphilis; however, this mixture is quite poisonous and usually causes sterility. (Barkwell 2009, 2)

Wolf willow illustrates the range of knowledge that could accumulate around a single plant.

The grandmothers knew the curative powers of each and every plant. They relied mainly on the land around them to find wild plants and roots that function as painkillers, digestive aids, and anti-inflammatory agents. These were part of a large pharmacopoeia that is still in use today. This knowledge has yet to be systematically documented, but a sense of its range can be gleaned, for example, from the words of respected Métis elder and healer Rose Richardson:

As a child, when we went picking berries, my mother always got us to pick yarrow in case we got stung. Yarrow was used to counteract bee stings and to regulate our sleep. Balsam bark or tamarack were used as a herbal tea to cure ulcers. Since their belief was that ulcers was caused by a bacteria, balsam bark and tamarack are considered to be antibacterial and anti-fungal. Rat root was used to keep your throat clear, to keep your throat clear of infection and to stop coughing. It was also used to prevent tooth, a toothache, and had many other medicinal values. (Richardson 2003, pt. 2, 1)

As elder Madeline Bird writes in *Living Kindness* (1991, 71):

I could talk about so many things and how they can be used. I don't always know the name, especially the white man's name, for things in nature, but when I see them out there I know right away which ones are good and which ones are dangerous. That's the most important to know, because it would be terrible to poison or kill someone when you are really trying to cure them. That's why it's best to learn from somebody who really knows, like the elders.

Healers knew which plants or roots were safe and which were not, as well as which plants could be safely combined with others. For elder François King from Fort Resolution, "There are hardly any poisons if you know the right kind of medicines to use. There are two roots that look the same and one of them is poison, but if you know medicine you know which one is good" (Beaulieu 1987, 68).

Plants and roots had to be harvested carefully. Some plants had to be picked at a specific time of day or during a full moon to ensure that they would not be spoiled or their healing powers reduced (Assiniwi 1988, 18; Anderson 2011, 151). Others were best harvested two days after a rain or during the full moon, as elder Rose Fleury, of Duck Lake, Saskatchewan, learned from her grandmother (Anderson 2011, 149). Certain roots had to be picked in the fall, after the leaves of the plant had completely fallen, while others were harvested in the spring. Rose Fleury recalled how her grandmother taught her the correct way to pick medicinal plants:

She would point at the thing. I had to dig away from the bottom. She said, "If you break the root it won't work as strong. Shake it, don't pull on it!" And then we would put it in the little cotton. You couldn't put it in a plastic bag or a paper bag. She always had a little cotton rag and she would tear it into squares. "And don't take the flower off," she would tell me. "Leave it there." It would dry in there and then she would know what kind of medicine it was. (Quoted in Anderson 2011, 151)

Once harvested, herbs, plants, barks, and roots were usually dried, sometimes pickled, and then prepared as herbal tea, decoctions, or powders. In addition, women made ointments by mixing plants or roots with animal fat, fish bones, or oil. Healers understood which plants could be prepared in what way without losing their medicinal properties and in what form a medicine was best administered. As Maria Campbell (2011) recalls, "We drank wild rose hip tea every morning all winter long cause we needed the vitamin C and as I learned from my aunty, wild rose hips do not lose their vitamin content with boiling or cooking." Medicinal herbs and plants also formed part of the repertoire of midwives. After the birth of a child, the midwife would often prepare an infusion of red ash, using the inner bark of the tree, to help expel the placenta and prevent infection. Herbal tea made with mint and raspberry was used as an analgesic. If a woman was in fragile health, the midwife might recommend an herbal tea—the ingredients in which were known only to midwives—to delay another birth (see Kermoal 2006).

Women were, in short, the repositories of knowledge relating to the medicinal properties of plants. Auguste Vermette (1891–1986) recalled that his mother had all kinds of roots stored in small bags, which she kept in a larger bag ("son sac à tout mett'e"). She did not need to mark the names of the plants because she knew what they were, and she also knew exactly where to find them (Létourneau 1973; see also Ferland 2000, 19). According to Jock Carpenter (1977, 39), women who were accustomed to life on the trail "filled a buckskin bag with pouches of herbs, tea drinks, and poultices," used for treating minor accidents and illnesses, and "Mother Delorme" (as Marie Rose Delorme Smith was known) evidently had such a medicine bag. In some families, the medicine bag was passed on from one generation to the next. For instance, Justine Beaudry Bellerose (1878–1948), who farmed with her husband in St. Albert (not far from Edmonton), inherited her medicine bag from her mother, Lucie Breland Beaudry (Iseke-Barnes 2009, 97).

Learning about medicine and plants, as well as providing services for the good of the family and the community, meant not only knowing the land, especially the local resources, but also understanding how to manage these resources. Rose Richardson recalled that, when she was young, the elders would come to see my mother and to borrow me to be their guide to find medicinal plants. Some plants were so sensitive that they would become transparent. [. . .] They would hide from certain people, or they would simply relocate if they were not respected. One-tenth of the medicinal plants in each area could be picked to make sure that there was always plants left to propagate. Plants were not picked during the flowering season unless the whole plant was used for medicine. (Richardson 2003, pt. 2, 1)

As Richardson suggests, plants, like people, respond to the treatment they receive. She went on to say that "land has to be set aside to preserve these medicines and to allow them to grow in their natural environment" (pt. 2, 2). Grandmothers also shared their knowledge with other Métis healers. They exchanged knowledge "through dialogue, prayers, and gifts" (quoted in Anderson 2011, 152).

While they were in the bush to gather medicines, women often visited sites linked to particular stories or spiritual beliefs. For elder Maria Campbell, "these women"—the grandmothers she knew as a child—"were all deeply spiritual rather than religious" (Anderson 2011, xvi). Campbell remembers going to a place called Old Lady Lake when she was young. As Maria Campbell (quoted in Anderson 2011, 153) explains:

This lake was called Nōtokēw Sākahikan, "Old Lady Lake." It stands out in her memory because the children were taught to be quiet and reverent when visiting there. Even though there was a beautiful beach, they were not allowed to swim. In speaking to her father many years later, Maria realized that the reason they called it Nōtokēw Sākahikan was because it was a place where the old ladies would pick medicines and, in particular, medicines that they would use in their work with birth and death. Midwives harvested their medicines from this lake, as did those who needed medicines that could "absorb the smell of death."

Far from deriving solely from the material properties of the plant, the power of medicines depended on the attitude with which they were harvested. Furthermore, women would talk to the plants "to ask for both a spiritual as well as a physical healing for oneself and one's patient" (Siisip Geniusz 2015, 22). This understanding of the complex relations between humans and non-humans is characteristic of Indigenous worldviews. As Rose Richardson puts it:

Being spiritually in tune with your own body and the plants just became a way of life for us. For example, stinging nettle is used for many purposes, including the treatment of arthritis. When you are using nettle for healing, it will not sting you. Nettle is whipped on to the aching joints to relieve pain. We never questioned how it happens, you just know it works, and you show gratitude. (Richardson 2003, pt. 2, 1)

The theme of gratitude was echoed by Norman Fleury, who recalled how his grandmother taught him about the need to offer respect to the land when picking medicinal plants: "And when you picked up this medicine, you prayed, and you put tobacco, and it was a spiritual significance and we gave thanks because it was going to heal somebody. So you took and you put back, and those are the kind of things that I learned as a young boy" (Fleury 2003, pt. 3, 3). As he explained on another occasion, at one time, the Métis used tobacco as an offering, as did many First Nations. "Grandma used to use it," he said, "because you know why? It was a Cree woman that taught her those medicines, so that's what she used to do, my grandmother" (Métis Centre 2008, 43).

These offerings were made to keep balance in the world. The stories taught to Métis children likewise reminded them of the importance of loving and respecting the land and of acknowledging the interrelatedness of all life. In the words of Maria Campbell (2007), "The stories taught us that we had to observe all the protocols and to never ever forget that there is always reciprocity, meaning you give an offering to receive an offering." There were, she says, two kinds of stories: *ahtyokaywina*, or sacred stories, about the origins of life, as well as *tahp acimowina*, or family histories (Anderson 2011, xv). Campbell (2010) remembers that her great-grandmother, who knew both kinds of stories, "was respected for her ability not only in our community but also far away." But there were other stories as well, such as those told by "hunters, trappers and gatherers who knew the land intimately and could recount the history and stories of all the places on the land as well as their own adventures on it" (Campbell 2010). These stories underscore the importance of place—or what Keith Basso (1990, 134) has described as a "moral relationship with the land." As he demonstrates, embedded in stories about places are social and moral lessons, such that—as one Apache woman, Mrs. Annie Peaches, put it—"The land makes people live right" (100).

This relationship with the land was expressed in many ways besides stories. Women were healers, but they were also seamstresses, and they reproduced what they saw in nature as designs on the clothing and other items they made both for their families and as commodities. As Sherry Racette (2004, 160) notes, throughout the nineteenth and twentieth centuries, Métis women "continued subsistence production for their own needs while simultaneously producing for a market." Although, for their floral art, they could choose between Indigenous and imported goods, to this day they still favour "quills, hide, sinew, natural fibres and dyes" (251). Moreover, imported materials were not always available. Thus, for example, the Métis artist Madeleine Bouvier Laferte, born in 1862, developed moose-hair tufting "as a creative solution to the critical shortage of silk and beads during the First World War" (257). For some women, artistic production and medicine went hand in hand. Elizabeth "Betsey" Houle, born in 1874, was described by her granddaughter as a "real herb doctor" who also did porcupine quillwork and whose knowledge of plants was employed to produce both medicines and dyes (258). Women also stress the healing and therapeutic power of beadwork (Racette 2004, 274). Through their own healing, and by choosing in some instances to bead plants and flowers that have curing powers, they are transferring the medicine onto the clothing. By beading the plants used to heal members of the community, they are mapping the territory on leather or fabric as a way of affirming their Métis identity and their role in society.

Métis women's knowledge of the land is multidimensional since the traditional knowledge pertaining to the use of plants, rhizomes, and berries has many more layers than what is seen on the surface. Most importantly, it is concerned with Indigenous ontologies that stress the interconnectedness of all beings (humans and non-humans). It has spiritual, economic, cultural, environmental, medicinal, and political purposes and meanings. Since it is an evolving knowledge, it also speaks to the innovations of individuals and communities. The land-based practices and activities of these women were adapted to an ever-changing environment, just as stories are constantly retold, and new interpretations layered onto older ones. In some cases, customary practices simply persisted alongside newer ones. The arrival of Western doctors, for example, roughly coincided with the arrival of unfamiliar infectious diseases, such as smallpox, measles, polio, tuberculosis, typhoid, and diphtheria, for which Aboriginal healers knew no cure. This fact did not, however, lead to the abandonment of natural remedies, as these were known to be effective against certain ailments. Other times, circumstances—such as a shortage of silk thread or lack of access to a particular plant—demanded the creation of new knowledge (the technique of moose-hair tufting, a revised recipe). Acknowledging this flexibility, this responsiveness to change, is integral to a clear understanding of Métis cultural continuity and Métis conceptions of stewardship of the land.

Further research will assist us in grasping the impact of reduced access to the land on Métis women's lives, on their knowledge, and on their sense of empowerment within their communities. The encroachment of settlers on Métis lands, followed by public and private land policies, restrictions on hunting, attendance at residential schools, and the twin forces of urbanization and industrialization, have obviously conspired to undermine connections to the land and weaken Métis cultural continuity. Other factors are perhaps less obvious: the loss of the Michif language, the participation of both women and men in wage economies, the loss of dietary traditions through the introduction of new food products, and an inability to sustain traditional approaches to stewardship of the resources found on the land. As Nancy Turner and Katherine Turner (2008, 103) note, the cumulative effect of these factors is powerful, and ways need to be found "to retain and reinforce the knowledge and practices still held by individuals and communities, to reverse some of the negative influences on cultural retention, and to develop new, relevant, and effective ways to revitalize languages, cultures, and ethnobotanical knowledge within contemporary contexts."

The work of Métis artist Christi Belcourt exemplifies the many ways in which knowledge—in this case botanical knowledge—is revitalized. Her floral art in beadwork style is firmly grounded in her Métis ancestral history. She actively listens to elders and gathers scientific information regarding the plants she harvests and paints on canvas (Baird 2010). Belcourt's paintings can be said to serve a dual purpose: they preserve knowledge shared by elders, while they also provide a tool for teaching younger generations about plants and their properties, thus ultimately reconnecting them with the land (Belcourt 2007). Indeed, as Métis artist Leanne L'Hirondelle (2003, 3) recognizes, Belcourt's art "speaks of a deep attachment to the land and living things."

Conclusion

Historically, the federal government (and by extension the provinces) never recognized the collective rights of the Métis through the signing of treaties, as it did in the case of First Nations in western Canada. This refusal to acknowledge the rights of the Métis as a distinct community ended in 2003, when the Powley decision recognized and affirmed the constitutional right of the Métis to engage in subsistence hunting. The process of determining the scope and the nature of Métis rights is ongoing, however, and, to move toward reconciliation, government, industry, and the Métis will have to work together. For the Métis, moving forward means that, as far as development is concerned, consultation and ultimately accommodation must happen.

Since the Haida Nation and Taku River Tlingit decisions in 2004, provincial governments (with the notable exception of British Columbia) accept, in principle, that the duty to consult applies to the Métis, although, in the case of Alberta, provincial consultation guidelines pertaining to the Métis are a long time in coming. The stakes are high for Métis communities. As we have seen, the issues extend beyond the impact of mining or petroleum projects. At the heart of Métis concerns are access to territory, control over resources, and the preservation of knowledge. Métis communities in western Canada often lack both the financial means and the human resources required for effective participation in all stages of the consultation process. Capacity building is therefore an issue. In addition, the Métis recognize the necessity of documenting the knowledge, practices, and land uses that will in turn allow them to think about the revitalization and sustainable development of their distinct culture.

At the Working Forum on the Duty to Consult, held in Edmonton in October 2009, the Métis participants agreed on the need to undertake holistic studies that consider not only the environmental impact of development but also the economic and social impact (Cosco 2009, 10). To this multidimensional framework, we must add a gendered component, so as to ensure that the perspectives and knowledge of Métis women are fully incorporated into the process. Nearly a decade ago, the Native Women's Association of Canada (2007, 4) argued that "Aboriginal women must have sufficient capacity to ensure meaningful and effective participation at any legislative, administrative and policy regime affecting Indigenous and traditional knowledge." Gender plays a critical role in determining who does what and who controls what in any given community. As historian and activist Andrea Smith reminds us, a critical interrogation of heteropatriarchy must be at the core of nation building, sovereignty, and social change (see Smith 2008, 255–72). The inclusion of women's voices in the future definition of Métis rights will expand that definition to encompass rights pertaining to the protection of sacred sites, to water and food safety, and to the protection of natural habitats, as well as the right to continue to access *all* the resources of the land, including plant life. Only through active participation, however, can Métis women take ownership of the processes of consultation and negotiation through which the collective identity of the Métis will be affirmed and their rights to the land defined.

I would like to thank the three anonymous readers engaged by Athabasca University Press as well as my colleagues Sarah Carter and Chris Andersen for their very constructive criticisms on earlier drafts of this chapter.

References

Adese, Jennifer. 2014. "Spirit Gifting: Ecological Knowing in Métis Life Narratives." *Decolonization, Indigeneity, Education and Society* 3 (3): 46–66.

Agrawal, Arun. 2005. "The Politics of Indigenous Knowledge." *Australian Academic and Research Libraries* 36 (2): 71–81.

Alberta. 2000. *Metis Settlements Act*. RSA 2000, c. M-14. http://www.qp.alberta.ca/documents/Acts/M14.pdf.

Andersen, Chris. 2014. *"Métis": Race, Recognition, and the Struggle for Indigenous Peoplehood*. Vancouver: University of British Columbia Press.

Anderson, Kim. 2011. *Life Stages and Native Women: Memory, Teachings and Story Medicine*. Winnipeg: University of Manitoba Press.

Assiniwi, Bernard. 1988. *La médecine des Indiens d'Amérique*. Montréal: Guérin Littérature.

Barkwell, Lawrence J. 2009. "Wolf Willow (*chalef changeant*)." Louis Riel Institute, Winnipeg. Virtual Museum of Métis History and Culture, Gabriel Dumont Institute of Native Studies and Applied Research. http://www.metismuseum.ca/resource.php/11389.

Basso, Keith. 1990. *Western Apache Language and Culture: Essays in Linguistic Anthropology*. Tucson: University of Arizona Press.

———. 1996. *Wisdom Sits in Places: Landscape and Language Among the Western Apache*. Albuquerque: University of New Mexico Press.

Beaulieu, Gail, ed. 1987. *That's the Way We Lived: An Oral History of the Fort Resolution Elders*. Yellowknife: Department of Culture and Communications, Government of the Northwest Territories.

Belcourt, Christi. 2007. *Medicines to Help Us: Traditional Métis Plant Use—Study Prints and Resource Guide*. With an essay by Rose Richardson. Saskatoon: Gabriel Dumont Institute.

Bird, Madeline, with Agnes Sutherland. 1991. *Living Kindness: The Memoirs of Métis Elder Madeline Bird*. Yellowknife: Outcrop.

Bourdieu, Pierre. 1991. *Language and Symbolic Power*. Edited by John Thompson. Translated by Gino Raymond and Matthew Adamson. Cambridge: Polity Press.

Briggs, John, and Joanne Sharp. 2004. "Indigenous Knowledges and Development: A Postcolonial Caution." *Third World Quarterly* 25 (4): 661–76.

British Columbia. 2010. *Updated Procedures for Meeting Legal Obligations When Consulting First Nations: Interim*. Victoria: Province of British Columbia.

Brown, Jennifer S. H. 1980. *Strangers in Blood: Fur Trade Company Families in Indian Country*. Vancouver: University of British Columbia Press.

Bumsted, J. M. 2001. *Louis Riel v. Canada: The Making of a Rebel*. Winnipeg: Great Plains Publications.

Burnett, Kristin. 2010. *Taking Medicine: Women's Healing Work and Colonial Contact in Southern Alberta, 1880–1930*. Vancouver: University of British Columbia Press.

———. 2011. "Obscured Obstetrics: Indigenous Midwives in Western Canada." In *Recollecting: Lives of Aboriginal Women of the Canadian Northwest and Borderlands*, edited by Sarah Carter and Patricia A. McCormack, 157–71. Edmonton: Athabasca University Press.

Campbell, Maria. 2007. "Could That Really Be Kokom in the Mirror?" *Eagle Feather News*, January, 5.

———. 2010. "Storytellers Were Held in High Esteem." *Eagle Feather News*, February, 6.

———. 2011. "Nokoms Had Their Own Stash of Medicines." *Eagle Feather News*, February, 5.

Canada. 2011. *Aboriginal Consultation and Accommodation: Updated Guidelines for Federal Officials to Fulfill the Duty to Consult*. Ottawa: Department of Aboriginal Affairs and Northern Development Canada. http://www.aadnc-aandc.gc.ca/DAM/DAM-INTER-HQ/STAGING/texte-text/intgui_1100100014665_eng.pdf.

———. 2013. *Aboriginal Demographics from the 2011 National Household Survey*. Ottawa: Department of Aboriginal Affairs and Northern Development Canada. https://www.aadnc-aandc.gc.ca/eng/1370438978311/1370439050610.

Carpenter, Jock. 1977. *Fifty Dollar Bride: Mary Rose Smith—a Chronicle of Métis Life in the 19th Century*. Sydney: Gray's Publishing.

Castellano, Marlene Brant. 2000. "Updating Aboriginal Traditions of Knowledge." In *Indigenous Knowledges in a Global Context*, edited by George

J. Sefa Dei, Budd L. Hall, and Dorothy Golding Rosenberg, 21–36. Toronto: University of Toronto Press.

Chrétien, Annette, and Brenda Murphy. 2009. *"Duty to Consult," Environmental Impacts, and Métis Indigenous Knowledge*. Ottawa: Aboriginal Policy Research Series.

Conroy, Meaghan, and Rebecca Hansen. 2015. "Métis Excluded from Consultation on Provincially Regulated Projects in Alberta." *Canadian Bar Association E-News*. August. http://www.cba.org/CBA/newsletters-enews/2015/08-e.aspx.

Cosco, Gina, ed. 2009. *Working Forum on the Duty to Consult: Now What? Synthesis*. Edmonton: Faculty of Native Studies and School of Energy and the Environment, University of Alberta.

Cruikshank, Julie. 1998. *The Social Life of Stories: Narratives and Knowledge in the Yukon Territory*. Vancouver: University of British Columbia Press.

Dalmiya, Vrinda, and Linda Alcoff. 1993. "Are 'Old Wives' Tales' Justified?" In *Feminist Epistemologies*, edited by Linda Alcoff and Elizabeth Potter, 217–44. New York and London: Routledge.

Edge, Lois, and Tom McCallum. 2006. "Métis Identity: Sharing Traditional Knowledge and Healing Practices at Métis Elders' Gatherings." *Pimatisiwin: A Journal of Indigenous and Aboriginal Community Health* 4 (2): 83–115.

Ens, Gerhard. 1996. *Homeland to Hinterland: The Changing World of the Red River Métis in the Nineteenth Century*. Toronto: University of Toronto Press.

Ferland, Marcien, ed. 2000. *Au temps de la Prairie: L'histoire des Métis de l'Ouest canadien racontée par Auguste Vermette, neveu de Louis Riel*. Saint-Boniface: Les Éditions du Blé, 2000.

Flanagan, Thomas. 1991. *Métis Lands in Manitoba*. Calgary: University of Calgary Press.

Fleury, Norman. 2003. Remarks Made During the Métis in the 21st Century Conference, Saskatoon, 18–20 June. Virtual Museum of Métis History and Culture, Gabriel Dumont Institute of Native Studies and Applied Research. http://www.metismuseum.ca/browse/index.php/858 (parts 1 to 4).

Fleury, Norman, and Lawrence Barkwell. 2009. "Elise Vivier Boyer (1868–1976)." Virtual Museum of Métis History and Culture, Gabriel Dumont Institute of Native Studies and Applied Research. http://www.metismuseum.ca/resource.php/11387.

Foucault, Michel. 1980. *Power/Knowledge: Selected Interviews and Other Writings, 1972–1977*. Edited by Colin Gordon. Translated by Colin Gordon, Leo Marshall, John Mepham, and Kate Soper. New York: Pantheon.

Gordon, Linda. 2006. "Internal Colonialism and Gender." In *Haunted by Empire: Geographies of Intimacy in North American History*, edited by Ann Laura Stoller, 427–51. Durham, NC: Duke University Press.

Iseke-Barnes, Judy. 2009. "Grandmothers of the Métis Nation: A Living History with Dorothy Chartrand." *Native Studies Review* 18 (2): 69–104.

Kermoal, Nathalie. 2006. *Un passé métis au féminin*. Québec: Les Éditions GID.

Kumar, Mohan B., and Teresa Janz. 2010. "An Exploration of Cultural Activities of Métis in Canada." Component of Statistics Canada Catalogue no. 11-008-X. *Canadian Social Trends*, 63–69. Ottawa: Statistics Canada.

LaRocque, Emma. 2007. "Métis and Feminist: Ethical Reflections on Feminism, Human Rights and Decolonization." In *Making Space for Indigenous Feminism*, edited by Joyce Green, 53–71. Winnipeg: Fernwood Publishing.

Létourneau, Henri. 1973. Entrevue avec Auguste Vermette et Elzire Vermette (née Carrière) réalisée par Henri Létourneau, 8 March. Centre du patrimoine, Société historique de Saint-Boniface, BS 01150.

Lévesque, Carole. 2004. "Indigenous Knowledge: Questions, Issues and Challenges." In *The Handing Down of Culture, Smaller Societies, and Globalization*, edited by Jean-Paul Baillargeon, 161–70. Toronto: Grubstreet Books.

L'Hirondelle, Leanne. 2003. Remarks made during the Métis in the 21st Century Conference, Saskatoon, 18–20 June. Virtual Museum of Métis History and Culture, Gabriel Dumont Institute of Native Studies and Applied Research, http://www.metismuseum.ca/browse/index.php/858.

Lux, Maureen. 2001. *Medicine That Walks: Disease, Medicine, and Canadian Plains Native People, 1880–1940*. Toronto: University of Toronto Press.

Macdougall, Brenda. 2010. *One of the Family: Metis Culture in Nineteenth-Century Northwestern Saskatchewan*. Vancouver: University of British Columbia Press.

MacEwan, Grant. 1995. "Victoria Callihoo: Granny." In *Mighty Women: Stories of Western Canadian Pioneers*, 190–99. Toronto: Greystone.

MacKinnon, Doris Jeanne. 2012. *The Identities of Marie Rose Delorme Smith: Portrait of a Métis Woman, 1861–1960*. Regina: Canadians Plains Research Center.

Makoons Geniusz, Wendy. 2009. *Our Knowledge Is Not Primitive: Decolonizing Botanical Anishinaabe Teachings*. Syracuse, N.Y.: Syracuse University Press.

Métis Centre. 2008. *In the Words of Our Ancestors: Métis Health and Healing*. Ottawa: National Aboriginal Health Organization.

Métis Nation of Alberta. 2009. *Policy Guidelines Regarding the Duty to Consult and Accommodate Métis Aboriginal Rights and Interests in Alberta*. Edmonton: Métis Nation of Alberta.

Mgbeoji, Ikechi. 2006. *Global Biopiracy: Patents, Plants, and Indigenous Knowledge*. Vancouver: University of British Columbia Press.

Moreton-Robinson, Aileen. 2003. "I Still Call Australia Home: Indigenous Belonging and Place in a White Postcolonizing Society." In *Uprooting/ Regrounding: Questions of Home and Migration*, edited by Sarah Ahmed, Claudia Castañeda, Anne-Marie Fortier, and Mimi Sheller, 23–40. Oxford: Berg.

Nadasdy, Paul. 1999. "The Politics of TEK: Power and the 'Integration' of Knowledge." *Arctic Anthropology* 32 (1–2): 1–18.

———. 2003. *Hunters and Bureaucrats: Power, Knowledge, and Aboriginal-State Relations in the Southwest Yukon*. Vancouver: University of British Columbia Press.

Native Women's Association of Canada. 2007. "Aboriginal Women and the Convention on Biological Diversity." Ottawa: Native Women's Association of Canada.

Newman, Dwight G. 2009. *The Duty to Consult: New Relationships with Aboriginal Peoples*. Saskatoon: Purich Publishing.

Newhouse, David. 2004. "Indigenous Knowledge in a Multicultural World." *Native Studies Review* 15 (2): 139–54.

Niethammer, Carolyn. 1977. *Daughters of the Earth: The Lives and Legends of American Indian Women*. New York: Collier Books.

Parlee, Brenda, Fikret Berkes, and the Teetl'it Gwich'in Renewable Resources Council. 2005. "Health of the Land, Health of the People: A Case Study on Gwich'in Berry Harvesting in Northern Canada." *Ecohealth* 2: 127–37.

Payment, Diane Paulette. 1990. *"The Free People—Otipemisiwak": Batoche, Saskatchewan, 1870–1930*. Ottawa: National Historic Parks and Sites, Canadian Parks Service.

Racette, Sherry Farrell. 2004. "Sewing Ourselves Together: Clothing, Decorative Arts and the Expression of Métis and Half Breed Identity." PhD diss., Interdisciplinary Doctoral Program, University of Manitoba.

Richardson, Rose. 2003. Remarks made during the Métis in the 21st Century Conference, Saskatoon, 18–20 June. Virtual Museum of Métis History and Culture, Gabriel Dumont Institute of Native Studies and Applied Research. http://www.metismuseum.ca/browse/index.php/858 (parts 1 and 2).

Saskatchewan. 2010. *First Nation and Métis Consultation Policy Framework*. Regina: Government of Saskatchewan.

Sawicki, Jana. 1991. *Disciplining Foucault: Feminism, Power, and the Body*. New York: Routledge.

Shilling, Rita. 1983. *Gabriel's Children*. Saskatoon: Saskatoon Métis Society, Local 11.

Siisip Geniusz, Mary. 2015. *Plants Have So Much to Give Us, All We Have to Do Is Ask: Anishinaabe Botanical Teachings*. Minneapolis: University of Minnesota Press.

Smith, Andrea. 2008. *Native Americans and the Christian Right: The Gendered Politics of Unlikely Alliances*. Durham, NC: Duke University Press.

Smith, Linda Tuhiwai. 1999. *Decolonizing Methodologies: Research and Indigenous Peoples*. London: Zed Books / Dunedin: University of Otaga Press.

Spivak, Gayatri. [1988]. 1995. "Can the Subaltern Speak?" In *Colonial Discourse and Post-Colonial Theory: A Reader*, edited by Patrick Williams and Laura Chrisman (New York: Columbia University Press, 1994), 66–111.

Sprague, Douglas. 1988. *Canada and the Métis, 1869–1885*. Waterloo: Wilfrid Laurier University Press.

St-Onge, Nicole. 2008. "Memories of Métis Women of Saint-Eustache, Manitoba, 1910–1980." *Native Studies Review* 17 (2): 45–68.

Teillet, Jean. 2008. "Federal and Provincial Crown Obligations to the Métis." In Wilson and Mallet, 71–93. Toronto: Irwin Law.

Tough, Frank, and Erin McGregor. 2007. "'The Rights to the Land May Be Transferred': Archival Records as Colonial Text—a Narrative of Métis Scrip." In *Natives and Settler—Now and Then: Historical Issues and Current Perspectives on Treaties and Land Claims in Canada*, edited by Paul W. DePasquale, 33–63. Edmonton: University of Alberta Press.

Turner, Nancy J., and Katherine L. Turner. 2008. "'Where Our Women Used to Get Food': Cumulative Effects and Loss of Ethnobotanical Knowledge and Practice—Case Study from Coastal British Columbia." *Botany* 86 (2): 103–15.

Usher, Peter J. [2000] 2003. "Traditional Ecological Knowledge in Environmental Assessment and Management." In *Natural Resources and Aboriginal People in Canada: Readings, Cases, and Commentary*, edited by Robert B. Anderson and Robert M. Bone, 30–47. Concord, ON: Captus Press.

Van Kirk, Sylvia. 1980. *"Many Tender Ties": Women in Fur-Trade Society, 1670–1870*. Winnipeg: Watson and Dwyer.

Van Woudenberg, Gerdine. 2004. "'Des femmes et de la territorialité': Début d'un dialogue sur la nature sexuée des droits autochtones." *Recherches amérindiennes au Québec* 34 (3): 75–86.

Wilson, Frederica, and Melanie Mallet, eds. 2008. *Métis-Crown Relations: Rights, Identity, Jurisdiction, and Governance*. Toronto: Irwin Law.

Wirf, Linda, April Campbell, and Naomi Rea. 2008. "Implications of Gendered Environmental Knowledge in Water Allocation Processes in Central Australia." *Gender, Place and Culture* 15 (5): 505–18.

Zeilig, Ken, and Victoria Zeilig. 1987. *Ste. Madeleine: Community Without a Town—Métis Elders in Interview*. Winnipeg: Pemmican Publications.

CHAPTER SIX

Community-Based Research and Métis Women's Knowledge in Northwestern Saskatchewan

Kathy L. Hodgson-Smith and Nathalie Kermoal

The Métis in western Canada have a long history of sustainable entrepreneurial economies based on knowledge systems closely tied to their traditional territories. However, Métis Indigenous knowledge has not been sufficiently studied as a knowledge base despite the fact that Canada's environmental legislative regime speaks to the importance of Indigenous knowledge in addressing global environment crises, developing sustainable lifestyles, and protecting global biodiversity.[1] Métis experience, knowledge, and effective economic and environmental stewardship over natural resources is seldom the focus of studies and is hardly ever given appropriate consideration in land and resource management or in conservation strategies and policy (Kermoal 2016; Khumar and Janz 2010; Chrétien and Murphy 2009).

---

1 Knowledge linked to medicine and health is highly sought after by bio-prospectors and biotechnology, pharmaceutical, and human health care industries. Traditional knowledge is often at the core of new ideas in these industries. However, the Aboriginal people who contribute such knowledge rarely receive the benefit for these contributions but rather are much more likely to find themselves stripped of access to and use of such knowledge as a result of intellectual property regimes. For more details on Indigenous peoples and biopiracy, see Ikechi Mgbeoji (2006).

Although historians have noted the diversity of Métis communities across western Canada (Payment 1990; Ens 1996; St. Onge 2004; Foster 2006; Macdougall 2010), no comprehensive analysis of Métis land use patterns and conservation practices, whether historical or contemporary, has been conducted. To overcome such a dearth of information as well as to support a Métis land claim, in 2000, the Métis Nation of Saskatchewan undertook a land use and occupancy mapping study in the Northwestern region of Saskatchewan. Métis traditional knowledge remains a fairly unexplored area of research (Chrétien and Murphy 2009), and an even bigger gap exists when it comes to Métis women's knowledge. Especially in the area of resource management, as well as in relation to land claims, women's traditional knowledge and responsibilities have often been neglected or even overlooked entirely (see Chapter 5 of this book). And yet, in the northwestern region of Saskatchewan and elsewhere, Métis women have played and continue to play a significant role in the preservation and development of the Métis as a unique and vibrant Aboriginal people. Despite encroachments on their land, the Métis of Northwest Saskatchewan continue to sustain their identity through their relationship to the land. The Métis refer to the land as "their life" since it supports the basic social, political, and economic benefits that are crucial to their way of being and to their way of thinking.

In 2000, in order to redress this dearth of information as well as to support a Métis land claim, the Métis Nation of Saskatchewan undertook a land use and occupancy mapping study in the region of northwestern Saskatchewan. In this chapter, we present the preliminary results of this community-based research project. The Métis communities in the region include La Loche, Buffalo Narrows, Île-à-la-Crosse, Jans Bay, Cole Bay, Beauval, Pinehouse, Sapawgamik, Patuanak, Michele Village, St. George's Hill, Bay Creek, Garson Lake, Ducharme Lake, Black Point, Turnor Lake, and Green Lake. Photos and interviews collected during the research project bring to the fore valuable insights into Métis women's knowledge of the land. As we hope to demonstrate, Métis women have maintained an intimate relationship with the land and their traditional territories, especially as hunters, fishers, and food providers, and they are concerned about conservation and the safeguarding of traditional knowledge as an expression of and a means of sustaining the Métis way of life. Although they are underrepresented on management boards, maintenance of their stewardship of the land remains a major goal at a time when traditional Métis territories are coveted by large-scale development projects.

Historically, Northwestern Saskatchewan was known as the English River District, an area that linked the Churchill River and Hudson Bay with the Mackenzie and Athabasca river systems and served as a central point of commercial trade and transport in fur trade history (Macdougall 2010). The Methye Portage, an 18-kilometre divide that separated the Hudson Bay and Mackenzie River drainage systems, was a strategic location in the fur trade and helped influence the development of western Canada. By 1776, Montréal traders were active in the Athabasca country, and the Methye Portage and the trading posts along the Green Lake–Île-à-la-Crosse–Portage La Loche transport corridor served as a vital nexus in the Canadian fur trade (Macdougall 2010). The importance of the fur trade, and especially the transportation through this region, meant that the skills of the local Métis were in high demand. They were boatmen, traders, interpreters, and provisioners, and they became an essential element of fur trade success. The trade economy involved entire families: "men, women and children all worked for the Hudson's Bay Company's sphere of influence in a variety of capacities: as servants, unpaid labourers, freemen, and . . . as free traders" (Macdougall 2010, 242). By the mid-nineteenth century, the concentration of French- and Michif-speaking Métis was so significant that Île-à-la-Crosse was selected in 1846 as the site of the first Oblate mission outside of the Red River settlement. Many of these "first generation families," as Brenda Macdougall refers to them, would marry within their community and spawn a second generation (2006, 445). With time the population increased. The first census in the area, in 1881, reveals a population of 251 people in the communities of Île-à-la-Crosse, Portage La Loche, and Green Lake, with 84 percent being defined as either French breed or English breed and 74 percent relating their place of birth as the Northwest Territories (Parker and Tough 2005, 43, 46, 60, and 63). By 1891, the population in these three communities had increased to 695 people, with 90 percent being born in the communities (Parker and Tough 2005, 97 and 121) and, by 1901, the Métis population was enumerated at 97 percent (Parker and Tough 2005, 163 and 193). According to Macdougall:

> Metis society emerged and gained strength because of its connection to
> indigenous worldviews that were predicated on the children's ancestral
> connection to the lands of their female connections. Over time, the
> region itself was transformed into a Metis homeland not only by virtue

of the children's occupation of the territory, but also through their relationship with the Cree and Dene women and fur trader men from whom they were descended. The Metis, like their Indian and fur trader relations, lived in a social world based on reciprocal sharing, respectful behavior between family members, and an understanding of the differences between themselves and outsiders. The Metis of the area were part of the economic structure of the fur trade, facilitating its success by embodying the principles of family loyalty, accountability, and responsibility. (2010, 45)

These former centres of economic and religious activities were the forerunners of today's Métis communities in the region.

The treaty and scrip commissioners came into the area in 1906 and in 1907, in an effort to extinguish the Aboriginal title to these lands.[2] According to Tough and McGregor (2007a, 1), "In September of 1906, Treaty and Scrip Commissioner J. A. McKenna took scrip applications at the Northwest Saskatchewan communities of Green Lake, Isle à la Crosse, La Loche River, La Loche Mission, and Portage La Loche. Commissioner McKenna did not have time to visit all of the Métis communities and Indian Bands in the Treaty Ten region that year." Commissioner T. Borthwick visited the remaining communities a year later. Overall, in 1906, "more people in the Treaty Ten region took scrip than joined treaty" (Tough and McGregor 2007a, 1). The Federal Justice Department maintained a legal opinion, which stated that any interest Métis had to their traditional territories by way of Aboriginal title claims was effectively extinguished by scrip. The effect of the scrip process on Métis Aboriginal title remains to this day an unanswered legal question (Tough and McGregor 2007b; Tough and Dorion 1993).

For the first time in the history of the region, scrip and treaty "drew a line in the northwest" and "divided treaty and non-treaty people geopolitically and legally" (Macdougall 2010, 247). With time, the Métis of Northwest Saskatchewan became increasingly frustrated by the implementation of

---

2 The 1998 Court of Queen's Bench decision in *R. v. Morin and Daigneault* ([1996] 3 C.N.L.R. 157 (Sask Prov Ct.); aff [1998] 1 C.N.L.R. 182 (Sask.QB)) upheld that the effect of scrip on Aboriginal title was a separate question from its effect on resource use, holding that the Métis Aboriginal right to hunt and fish and gather for food was not extinguished. The question of Aboriginal title was not decided. It should be noted, however, that in these court actions, Métis women provided invaluable information regarding traditional knowledge to the court.

provincial laws and policy, which interfered with their constitutional rights to maintain their traditions and practices. Throughout the twentieth century, government regulations imposed seasonal restrictions on hunting and fishing, and trappers had to obtain licenses and list the animals they caught. While the goal of these government regulations was to conserve fur or fish stocks, the consequences of the fur blocks and the quotas limited trapping or fishing seasons and the amount of animals trapped or fished. For instance, in the 1940s, Saskatchewan and Manitoba introduced registered trapline programs, "which gave trappers the right to trap in a registered area, provided the trapper conserved stock. Provincial governments also implemented aid programs to help Métis trappers" (Young, Paquin, and Préfontaine 2003, 9). Such regulations pushed the Métis to look for other sources of employment to survive. Overall, they had to fight to preserve a way of life.

In March 1994, the Métis of Northwest Saskatchewan launched a land claim—*Métis Nation of Saskatchewan v. Saskatchewan and Canada* (Q.B. No. 619 of 1994, Judicial Centre of Saskatoon)—in the Court of Queen's Bench seeking three major declarations in relation to their traditional territories, which they claim encompass much of Northwestern Saskatchewan: Aboriginal title to the lands and resources in the claim area; Aboriginal hunting, fishing, and gathering rights; and the right of self-government.

In 1998, in preparation for the litigation, the Métis entered into a partnership with historical geographer Frank Tough, of the University of Alberta, to conduct broad-based research on their historic land use practices and patterns in the region. Tough and the community together developed research questions, and a Métis traditional land use and occupancy mapping program which was implemented in 2000. In addition, in 2003, the partners were successful in obtaining funding from the Community-University Research Alliance (CURA) program of the Social Sciences and Humanities Research Council of Canada for a five-year project titled "Otipimsuak—the Free People: Métis Land and Society in Northwest Saskatchewan." The CURA project involved the Northwest Saskatchewan Métis Council, the Métis Nation in Saskatchewan, and researchers from the University of Alberta and the University of Saskatchewan.[3] The land use study determined that

---

3 Clement Chartier, president of the Métis National Council and a resident of Northwest Saskatchewan, and Frank Tough served as the principal investigators on this project. Kathy Hodgson-Smith, who, at the time, was the research director for the

the traditional territory of the Métis of Northwest Saskatchewan extended across the Alberta border along the southern shores of Lake Athabasca and into the central parts of Alberta. It also included Frobisher Lake, in west-central Saskatchewan, with its intricate web of islands that are essentially non-navigable to the visitor.

The collaboration between Tough and members of the Northwest Saskatchewan Métis communities revealed the Métis multidimensional geographic knowledge of the region that can be defined as "knowledge in action" since practical skills are mixed with stories and place names. Being on the land is not just a way of life but also a way of being and a way of "speaking the land." As French geographer Béatrice Collignon argues in *Knowing Places: The Inuinnait, Landscapes and the Environment* (2006), land is extremely important in the construction of identity for Aboriginal peoples since physical landscapes transform into "memoryscapes," inhabited by human beings, animals, and spirits of all kinds.

During a meeting organized in the summer of 1999 between Métis leaders and the Métis citizens of Northwest Saskatchewan in Île-à-la-Crosse, Métis elders from the different communities spoke at length about their deep attachment to the land. They also shared their worries about the future, especially around issues of land and resource use and management, and the interference with subsistence and commercial livelihoods, including fishing, hunting, trapping, and gathering. One of the most significant issues they saw was the increasing number of youth who were growing toward dependence on alcohol and drugs. They felt that the youth faced these issues as a result of the loss of relationship with their historic lands, and the lifestyles that had sustained their families for generations. The young people were losing access to their rightful cultural inheritance and identity in relation to their traditional lands and resources now being governed by non-Aboriginal governments. They were losing access to their language and the traditional knowledge that embodies the Métis way of life. They

Northwest Saskatchewan Métis Council, oversaw the design and implementation of the research, and also worked with a team of researchers who recorded the interviews. These interviews have since been summarized, but they have not yet been fully transcribed. We are grateful to the families who participated in this research, who also provided the photographs that appear in this chapter and gave their permission to reproduce them here. Nathalie Kermoal was a collaborator on Dr. Frank Tough's CURA-SSHRC Grant *Otipimsuak: Métis Land and Society in Northwest Saskatchewan*.

raised further concerns with the encroachment of extractions industries in sensitive environmental areas, the clear-cutting of forests, the negative impact on some species of animals and plants, the contamination of lakes and rivers, and the erratic behaviour of game and fish populations and the significant changes in weather patterns.

They spoke to the fact that the land was not being cared for, as it should be. While governments held constitutional jurisdiction over lands and resources of the area, the stewardship necessary for conservation and preservation of the lands and resources for future generations was perceived as absent. The Métis elders of Northwestern Saskatchewan are echoing the same concerns as elders in other Métis communities across the Northwest (Métis Centre 2008). For them, an important aspect of the solution to the issues facing the young people is to rebuild a stronger caring relationship between the youth and their traditional lands, based upon Métis indigenous knowledge. The young people are to be given a greater understanding of the history of the region and the role of the Métis, and are to become re-engaged as the proper stewards of their traditional land and the resources.

Based on the concerns raised by the elders, the Métis community conducted the study. A list of potential Métis interviewees was drawn up beginning with the elders and senior traditional resource users. The study area was determined to be the general area of the 1906 scrip commission. A questionnaire was then developed to determine the content of the study, and interviews were digitally audio and visually recorded.

During each interview a map was produced which captured the territory and the general nature of the use of the land and resources by species (plant, fish, animal), by season, and at what point in time (year) and for what purpose (see figure 6.1). Sacred sites (medicinal, cultural, burial) were located as well. Historic and contemporary photographs capturing cultural practices of Métis traditional resource users and knowledge holders were collected and scanned. It should be noted that the community members brought the photographs on a voluntary basis. Then, a second round of interviews was done based on the photographs. In addition, working with the Northern Saskatchewan Trappers Association, a series of interviews were conducted with trappers (men and women) on the effect of government actions on trapping and traditional lifestyles and knowledge associated with trapping. A genealogical study was also undertaken as well as a specific study on the work and knowledge of Métis women.

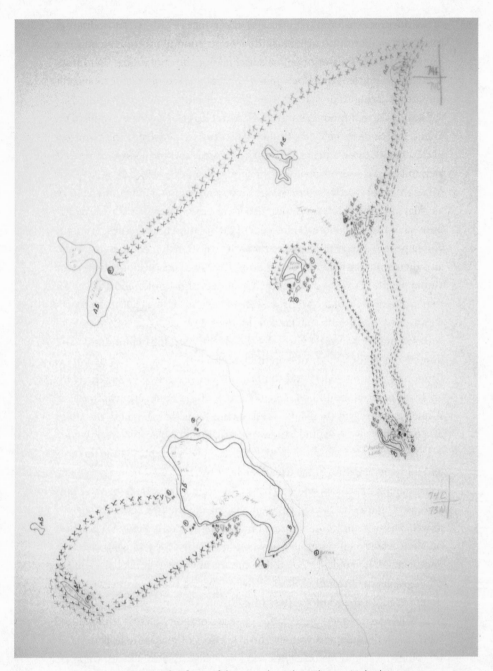

Figure 6.1 An example of one of the maps based on Eleanor Moberly's interview.

The documentation of the lives and experiences of the Métis traditional knowledge holders provided the entire Métis community with a common strength, a shared history, and an enriched hope for the future. The information gathered was presented to the community, where researchers made oral presentations of the information gathered and the maps were placed on the wall of the community centre for Métis citizens to review and discuss. Traditional knowledge holders told their stories to the crowd. These stories, told in Michif, Cree, and Dene languages, were recorded in an effort to hold them for future generations.

The traditional land use and occupancy mapping study was conducted in four languages: Michif, Cree, Dene, and English.[4] A Michif and Cree translator was engaged and one of the students involved in the project served as a Dene translator and interviewer. Interviews were conducted in the language of choice of the interviewee and later translated and transcribed. Many of the elders interviewed spoke all four of the languages and in addition spoke

---

4 Mapping was a challenge as the modern maps provided by the provincial government used in preparation of the personal maps of traditional use were often identified by place names that were unfamiliar to the Métis resource users. Names of lakes, streams, particular hunting and fishing territories, the location of settlement and burial grounds were mostly identified by Michif, Cree, or Dene names and not known by the names more recently assigned by governments. For example, the Métis Nation region of Northwest Saskatchewan which encompasses the communities of Buffalo Narrows, Michele Village, Black Point, St. George's Hill, Turnor Lake, Garson Lake, Bear Creek, La Loche, and Ducharme is called the Clearwater Clear Lake Métis Region. This is one of the twelve regions in the governance structure of the Métis Nation-Saskatchewan. The map of Saskatchewan, as drawn by the provincial government, identifies this lake, known by the Métis as Clear Lake, as Peter Pond Lake. Traditionally, specific sites and waterways were often named after families from the area. For example in the community of Buffalo Narrows, the main channel joining the now named Churchill Lake and Peter Pond Lake is known as the Keizie Channel, named after the Keizie family. The province has named this channel the Kisis Channel. The Métis community has raised this naming issue with the government; however, to date, their concern has not been addressed. With many of the traditional resource users, orientation to maps of particular territories often took a lot of time and often required a translator. The elderly traditional knowledge holder was intimately familiar with their traditional territories and had never relied upon government maps that took an aerial view and showed these new place names and elevation levels. The study was undertaken on map scales of 1:200,000 to maintain privacy of particular use areas and to allow for a more general discussion of use and occupancy.

French, learned in the Residential School or in conversing with the Roman Catholic priests and nuns. As well, many of the Métis families from Northwest Saskatchewan were French Métis.

Métis Women's Knowledge of Waterways, Land, and Resources

While much research on the Métis has focused mainly on hunting practices, Frank Tough (2000, 3) documents that "the importance of fish has been under-appreciated as early research grappled with the relative merits of buffalo hunting and agriculture," adding that "freshwater fish has always been an integral part of the Métis way of life." What Tough describes for Manitoba can apply to Saskatchewan since water is very central to the region. The summaries of the interviews indicate that women and children have always been part of the daily navigation of the waters and still are, as is illustrated in figures 6.2. They participated in the fishing industry and prepared the fish taken for subsistence purposes.

Many of the women interviewed, now mothers, grew up on the same waterways and trails as their ancestors. Looking at the maps, women discussed traditional ways of fishing and hunting, talked about the appropriate time of day to fish or hunt moose or caribou, the appropriate means by which to attract various species to be taken (see figure 6.3). They know moose calls and how to listen to the loon for information as to animal movement. They know where the animals will be during any given season and when they move to new areas.

As well, they know how to fish with nets and line, how to snare an animal, how to skin it to protect the meat, and how to keep it clean and free from infestation and contamination. For instance, each year an annual sucker harvest takes place at Sucker Creek, Saskatchewan. The families all come together for one or two days. The creek is teeming with suckers during the spawning season. This is the only season when suckers are edible. The women set up camp alongside the creek, setting up tables and smokehouses and pails for storage of the sucker fishheads. The men and children gather the fish from the creek with nets or by hand, standing in the bubbling creek where the fish are moving along, layered up to two or three feet deep. The heads are removed and used to make sucker head soup. The filets are cleaned, with the skin still on, and smoked flesh side down. The filets are then frozen and when needed they are fried in a frying pan to warm them up. The entire year's harvest is taken in one or two days during the spring.

Figure 6.2 Hanson and Pederson families water activities, Buffalo Narrows.

Figure 6.3 Mary and John Hanson with caribou on lake. Photo courtesy of Mary J. Hanson.

Women handle firearms, traps, and filleting knives. Since they are responsible for the preservation of food, they smoke meat and fish immediately after the kill to preserve it. The meat is cut into strips and the fish is filleted and hung from wooden racks over a fire (see figure 6.4, 6.5, and 6.6). Dry meat and smoked fish continue to be eaten as delicacies today. Hunting, fishing, trapping, and gathering serve as the means of feeding the family.

Through their testimonies, women revealed that they learned the knowledge from their mothers and grandmothers, and they want to pass it down to their children and grandchildren. Early on, as children, they learned the limits of their family territory as well as limits of the territory of neighbouring families. The family returns to their own territory on a cyclical basis each season. Territorial integrity is an essential part of maintaining control over conservation of species and habitats. Respect for territory is crucial to keeping outsiders out and limiting the capacity of individual families to have negative impacts on species populations. The family territory becomes an essential identifier, provides a sense of belonging and responsibility and cultural identity. Marriage and adoption are two ways in which kinship is expanded and territory is shared.

Figure 6.4
Drying meat on the land.
Photo courtesy of Cecile
Morin.

Figure 6.5
Cecile and Alfred
Morin family drying
meat today.

Figure 6.6
Cecile Morin preparing
meat for a cultural
gathering.

Figure 6.7 Eleanor Moberly at camp with grandchildren.

Camps are set up at various sites along the routes through the territory. In the past, semi-permanent dwellings were established: tents with a wood stove and chimney. This practice is still used today (see figure 6.7). The women cook over a stone fireplace created in situ from local resources. Tarps are stretched out over the top of the tents to keep the rain and branches from falling directly on the tents. When large families or a group of families engage in the seasonal cycle of hunting or fishing, tarps are typically hung above the tents on an angle, and arranged in an overlapping method extending from one tent to another, creating an adjoined ceiling over the village of tents and forming walkways in between. During the Palmbere Days festival, held annually at Palmbere Lake, such a scene is common.

In winter while in the bush, individuals keep warm by using a feather robe, or a goose or duck feather blanket, made by the women (see figure 6.8). These robes are all that is needed for bedding even in winter. Some of the territories of Métis families extend more than 200 kilometres in distance; the men often leave for the seasonal hunt with only a feather robe. The women pluck and prepare the feathers for use in the blankets, sewing and decorating the blanket covers. The blankets are sometimes stored and transported in a cloth bag.

Firewood is gathered as needed from the forest floor and from harvesting trees along the way. Knowing which tree makes the best firewood for the particular activity and season is part of the traditional knowledge. The women also gather wild berries, mushrooms, and duck eggs. They know where and during what time of year each activity is appropriate. They know which species of animals and plants are essential to sustain their way of life and their overall health as human beings. They know when and where to gather and harvest and how to prepare the resources for sustenance. Some of this knowledge is gained from personal experience and some is the knowledge that has been passed on from one generation and one family to another over many years.

Figure 6.8 Eleanor Moberly plucking birds.

Apart from providing food, Métis women process animal hides to make them usable in the production of various types of clothing. In Northwest Saskatchewan, moose hide is the hide most predominantly used in the production of clothing. Caribou hide is also prepared and used. The animal is skinned at the time of the kill and the hide is typically stored in ice water until the following spring. The hide is retrieved and brought back to camp. The hides are then stretched onto large frames and tanned by hand, removing all hair and flesh (see figures 6.9 and 6.10).

Figure 6.9 Mary Hanson tanning hide with a young boy.
Figure 6.10 Eleanor Moberly tanning a moose hide, Turnor Lake.

The hide is then smoked. Once tanned, the hide is used for clothing, typically decorated with beadwork and fur. Knowledge of how to smoke a hide includes the knowledge of particular wood, bark and needles/leaves, heat, duration, and weather suitable for the tanning process. This knowledge is gained and changed through experience as it continues to be passed from one generation to the next. As times change, the skinning of the flesh from the hide often requires adaptation of old knowledge with new technologies, by way of tools and methods. Tanning hides is premised upon the knowledge of the particular animal hide, the appropriate time to prepare the hide and the ability to make or find necessary tools and the recipes to prepare the mixtures that are used to treat and prepare the hides for cleaning. Knowledge of the various trees that are used to smoke the hides is essential (see figure 6.11). This is true of smoking of fish and meat also.

Figure 6.11 Cecile Morin smoking a hide.

Moccasins, gauntlet gloves, and jackets are the most common clothing items. Beadwork designs are regional and familial (see figure 6.12). The Métis beadwork patterns include flowers, eagles, thunderbirds, and geometric shapes. Women become known for their particular beadwork patterns. Clothing is also trimmed with rabbit, beaver, fox, and other fur. Gauntlets are commonly decorated with beaver fur.

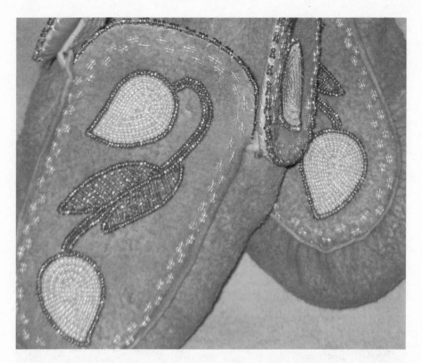

Figure 6.12 Beadwork and moccassins made by Albertine Herman, La Loche.

MÉTIS WOMEN AS STEWARDS OF THE LAND

Certain knowledge holders serve the whole community and are essentially the elders of the elders. Some act as resources for the whole community, while others inform their own "students" or take on "students" as required to ensure their knowledge is not lost. These "students" are sometimes sons and daughters and sometimes from the extended family. Traditional knowledge holders often hold specific kinds of knowledge; some are known by members through the public service they provide or the specific role they hold in the cultural community. For Karen Anderson (2011, 145), "as teachers of the youngest children, then, elders taught them to be contributing members of their societies, and they did this through formal, non-formal, and informal education."

According to the interviewees, while individual persons hold knowledge, customary Métis law governs the sharing and access to much of the knowledge. Oftentimes the knowledge is protected or has limited access because it is held and expressed in the Michif, Cree, or Dene language. Other knowledge is demonstrated in situ and held by particular families in relation to a specific tract of land or ecosystem. Other knowledge is shared during a ceremony. These safeguards provide a cultural barrier to unauthorized use of the knowledge.

The old ways of doing things are always under review and modification. As territories become more affected by development, such as forestry and mining, traditional knowledge–based conservation and agricultural practices once used and relied upon are interrupted. Roads are built and areas that had remained largely unaffected by human actions except for small family-sized economic activity, are now subject to significant change. Reforestation initiatives are often undertaken. The women have reported at annual trapper and fishermen conventions their observations of the success of these initiatives and the ultimate impact on the animals and plant resources.

One medicine person discussed the return to the family's traditional territory to get plants associated with medicinal uses. Often one child—a grandchild, niece, or nephew—shows an interest and a predilection for medicinal knowledge, and that child is selected for the passing down of such knowledge. The medicine person will then return to the traditional territory over several years during appropriate seasons for the gathering of plants and roots used for this purpose. Scheduling around school timetables, the young person is taken to the territory. Here the process for finding and gathering the plant or root, and its agricultural care, is taught, along with the teaching of ceremonies that accompany its access and use. As traditional territories are appropriated and regulated by licensing and permit arrangements, Métis access is negatively affected. Alternative sources of the plants must be found or determined through traditional methods such as prayer, ceremony, or through research and experimentation. In this way, traditional knowledge is adapted over time, continuously being developed and created.

The women reported being taught their skills from their mothers and grandmothers, although many women also recounted their own research inquiries, studies, and findings. Medicinal knowledge is premised on being able to identify properly and classify appropriate trees, plants, and roots; on knowing the specific territory where they grow; on knowing the routes to these territories; and on managing the continued wellness of the environment and region to sustain access to these resources. Medicinal knowledge also involves the knowledge of cultural ceremonies to ensure that the proper spiritual respect entwined in the relationship is shown. To teach the concepts underlying these relationships many stories, such as those about Wesakachak, capture the values that must be honoured. These stories are told in Cree, Michif, or Dene. Wesakachak is a mythological character whose foolish and heroic adventures allow children and adults alike a chance to learn the values and teachings of the culture. The stories speak of the natural world and the medicines that are available on the land. According to Maria Campbell, Wesakachak stories "taught the young how to live 'a good life' and reminded the old to stay on that path. The stories were multilayered with knowledge and teachings interwoven into each of them" (Anderson 2011, xvii).

The stewardship of the land is central to the women's worldview. Some of the women have been hunting, fishing, trapping, and gathering with their husbands in their traditional territory for several decades. One of the women had observed an area that had been logged over and had been sub-sequently subject to a reforestation scheme. She compared the success of this forest's rejuvenation with respect to particular plant and animal species with one that had been burned out by forest fire. She commented on the underbrush, the plant species that returned after the burn, which attracted birds, smaller rodents, and then those species upon which these plants and animals depended in the food chain. She reported how the logging process, by contrast, removed all of the underbrush and essentially devastated the area of essential plants and ultimately affected the animal species. She had made these observations over about a thirty-year period. Her knowledge has implications for human and animal well-being.

Women are essential fact finders and resource managers since they are alert to fish disorders and disease, to changing climate situations, and to the varying plant and animal species populations. As stewards of the land, they were and continue to be part of the discussion within the Métis community on conservation and protection of vulnerable populations, the culling of predators, and the teaching of spiritual traditions related to life on the land.

Métis Women's Knowledge Expresses a Way of Life

In the Métis communities of Northwest Saskatchewan, the youth popu-lation is growing rapidly.[5] Grandparents raise many Métis youth, at least

5 Data from the National Household Survey (NHS) show that "1,400,685 people had an Aboriginal identity in 2011, representing 4.3% of the total Canadian popula-tion. Aboriginal youth under the age of 25 represent almost half of the Aboriginal

from the formative years to age 11.[6] The general consensus is that if the way of life of the Métis is to be preserved and the traditional knowledge which is so critical to the advancement of Métis culture is to be passed on to the younger generation, then continuing efforts will have to be made to invest in this regard. The study confirmed that the traditional knowledge is typically passed on in the context of social relationships. The learning context is often part of the day-to-day life when the family is gathering food or materials. While community Elders play an important role, kinship ties also play a significant part in the transmission of traditional knowledge. Gender is a significant element of this transmission as girls help their mothers, aunts, or grandmothers, and the boys are typically in the company of their fathers, uncles and grandfathers. According to Mililani Trask (n.d., n.p.),

> In Indigenous societies, reciprocity is the way things work—in society, within the family and extended family frameworks, and in the relation-ships between human kind and the rest of God's creation. Reciprocity is not defined or limited by the language of the market economy because it implies that more is owed than financial payment, when goods and services exchange hands. Reciprocity is the way of balance—planting precedes harvesting, sowing precedes reaping. In most Indigenous societies there is a common understanding (sometimes referred to as the "original instructions"), that humankind's role in the world is to be the guardians of the creation. Indigenous peoples know that if we care for, nurture, and protect the earth, it will feed, clothe and shelter us.[7]

---

population in Canada" (Statistics Canada 2013, 4). Jeremy Hull's study *Aboriginal Youth in the Labour Market*, notes that "between 2001 and 2026 more than 600,000 Aboriginal youth will turn 15, including more than 100,000 in each of British Columbia, Alberta, Saskatchewan, Manitoba, and Ontario. This growth represents a massive influx into the working-age population, particularly in Saskatchewan, where it is projected that by 2026, fully 36 percent of the population aged 15 to 29 will be Aboriginal" (Hull 2008, 41).

6 Aboriginal children under the age of 15 are more likely than their non-Aboriginal counterparts to live with their grandparents without either of their parents present. The 2006 census showed that 3 percent of First Nations children were living with their grandparents, as were 2 percent of Inuit children and 2 percent of Métis children. The proportion of non-Aboriginal children under the age of 15 years that lived solely with their grandparents was 0.4 percent (Statistics Canada 2010, 9).

7 As Trask notes, gender is a sociological construct that encompasses economic, social, and cultural distinctions between women and men, arising from their unique

In the study area, as part of the reciprocity process, Métis youth camps are organized and take place on the land, with family members teaching all aspects of the hunt, including the conservation ethics around the taking of wildlife and other resources, the hunting techniques, the way to cut and preserve meat, to value sharing the resource, to use the hide and to live off the land during the appropriate season for the hunt. Youth of both genders are taught how to build and maintain shelters and how to create a home. They learn to care for one another, their families, the land, the animals and the fish as a way of life. Family members join the youth over the course of the camp.

They are taught to build a fire, to use snare wire, to use a shotgun and a rifle as well as to kill and how to make use of the hunt or the catch for food. They are instructed how to prepare the meat or fish for a meal, how not to waste, and how to preserve for the future. They gather mushrooms and other edible vegetation. They are told the stories of the families and the communities around the campfire. The men often play the fiddle and the women tell of the history and train the young in the wildlife diet and lifestyle.

The women organize and guide these teaching opportunities, typically with their husbands (see figure 6.13). The camps are often done with the assistance of the eldest siblings who demonstrate for the younger ones the core teaching of respect, reciprocity, and stewardship. They are taught basic

---

roles, authority, and cultural place. Indigenous peoples and societies delineate these roles. The pathway to "meaning" is through the expression of these unique roles through cultural protocols and in response to basic survival needs of the Indigenous society. She further discusses the fundamental value of the gift economy underlying the relationships that underpin Indigenous societies, and the reciprocity, a give and take, that infers the essential recognition of the value of mutual sharing, within the family and extended family networks, across societies and with the rest of human kind and the Creator. This essential value permeates the Indigenous view of their relationship to the land and the obligation as stewards to care for, nurture and protect the earth: Indigenous societies serve the earth and the lands provide. In this view, women have specific and highly specialized knowledge, have developed expertise and knowledge specific to the local environment, ecosystems, plants, animals and their uses, and contribute to the well-being of their families and communities through their key role in a gift economy. "The gift economy is diametrically opposed to the market economy. The Gift Economy is collective, the market economy favours individualism. The Gift Economy thrives when there is a bounty to be given. The market economy increases the price and fiscal value of items that are rare commodities. The values, activities, and outcomes of these diametrically opposed economy systems also conflict" (n.d., n.p.).

survival skills. They attend on the lakes by boat and canoe and in the bush on skidoos (snowmobiles) and on foot.

The elders teach the young people as an act of love for them as individuals, for their families and for the community. Teaching is an expression of love for the Métis way of life and the land. The elders always say: "our land is our life." The young people are taught the skills that underlie the relationship they have with the land. The sharing of meat and hides, the collaboration in caring for the children, are all part of the healthy Métis community. Everyone has a role to play in the well-being of others. These aspects of life are part of the pride and the sense of belonging, being in control of one's life. Certain young people are singled out for particular skills such as medicine.

Figure 6.13 A class from the Cecile and Alfred Morin Métis Culture Camp for youth.

When a large community gathering is planned, such as Palmbere Days, fish and firewood are gathered and distributed among the families as part of the cultural celebration. In an extended family gathering the food is hunted, trapped, or harvested in the family context, and the children and grandchildren are taught how to prepare the fish for meals and for preservation. In the nuclear family context, the meat and fish gathered as part of the subsistence practices are cut and wrapped and distributed among family members, the sick and the elderly, and then among other families. The women make the decisions regarding the distribution of the meat and fish.

Within the kinship system there exists also a cultural practice, which provides for "experts" from within the Métis community. The advice and guidance of these people are sought when certain activities are undertaken. As well, families typically join one another during cultural festivals and to take part in the hunting or trapping in both commercial and subsistence settings (see figures 6.14 and 6.15). Intermarriage of families provides for opportunity to share and learn the knowledge held and developed during the previous season from each other.

Knowledge of the environment is shared during cultural festivals and general social interactions at community meetings and events. When meat or fish is shared, conversations are often about the state of fish stocks and changes in the landscape and local environment. Discussions of weather conditions are shared and discussed. As each family will hold a particular set of knowledge of their particular territory, the sharing of a family meal will provide ample opportunity for the sharing of essential knowledge among family members. This knowledge is then shared in a reciprocal way with other families during larger community events.

Festivals provide opportunity for sharing and learning together. Métis women often compete in animal calling, log sawing, hauling, and other cultural competitions. This builds skills and provides for teaching and learning in a social context and for sharing joy and laughter in the shared culture context. Métis traditional territories extend outside of provincial boundaries and families cover extensive territories, ranging as far as 300 kilometres in width. As such, the knowledge shared covers considerable distances and a diversity of topics.

Métis women continue to practice their traditional knowledge as a way of life. They may be employed in professional and other jobs and many have now settled into the villages and settlement areas close to church and school. Some continue, with their husbands, to trap and live off the land. However, at every opportunity, they report their return to the land to carry on whatever practices that time and access will allow. As in the past, many families spend all available time on the land. Some families are limited to spending holiday times together to practice, learn, teach, and share the knowledge.

Some families, however, have made and continue to draw their entire annual income from traditional lifestyles. While commercial fisheries are governed by quotas and by local community conservation and cooperative boards, trapping remains a way of life for many, although the level of income

Figure 6.14 The Morin family on the land.

Figure 6.15 The Morin family at Potato Point family gravesite.

from trapping is extremely low. The protest against fur harvests by environmental protection groups has had negative effects on the small sustainable economic Métis family unit, who attempt to maintain traditional cultural trapping practices. In 2000, one family reported that the source of their entire annual income of $6,000 was from trapping.

In contrast to government compensation given to farming or other economies when governments interfere with access to lands and resources typically relied upon, traditional economies such as trapping are often destroyed without provision of any compensation or accommodation to the trapper. When lands are taken up for roads, agriculture, forestry, or mining, this is often done without consultation, accommodation, or consideration of trappers and traditional resource users. The Métis report showing up on their trap lines to find a single trap strapped to a single tree, with all other trees removed pursuant to a license or permit. The establishment of the Primrose Lake Air Weapons Range caused the Métis to lose access to an entire fur block without compensation or accommodation. The Métis showed up to attend to their business to find themselves blocked from entry onto these lands. Since that time, co-management agreements have been reached with First Nations. The Métis have been blocked from bringing their claim forward through established tribunal processes. Métis women and men are typically part of trapper associations, which attempt to influence government regulation and policy. Few women, if any, sit on management boards or conservation committees. No federal or provincial infrastructures ensure that Métis women, or any women for that matter, are engaged in any conservation or land and resource management regime in Saskatchewan.

As in the past, Métis women often draw an income from making items of clothing for sale. In the nineteenth century, Métis women developed their own floral beaded style and started to make large quantities of objects that were then sold or exchanged. Through their talent, they played an important economic role within the Western Canadian Métis Nation and ensured the survival of their families, which allowed them to express their identity as individuals and as a community (Racette 2004; Kermoal 2007). Women's beadwork, while a source of pride for a family and for the Métis community as a whole, remains undervalued as an economy. Mass-produced moccasins, often made without proper intellectual property recognition, can be bought at a fraction of the price which would, in fairness, be paid to a woman who has hand-tanned the hide used in this clothing.

As well, the great contribution of women continues to be done through volunteer work, leadership, and through their continued involvement in cultural activities such as the annual Michif language festival hosted by the local school at Île-à-la-Crosse. Métis women have also made a significant contribution to the struggle for constitutional recognition of Métis Aboriginal rights by testifying in courts about the knowledge that lies at the heart of Métis identity and culture. The loss of access to traditional lands and resources is at the core of the Métis struggle to maintain their way of life.

CONCLUSION

Northwest Saskatchewan Métis women's specialized environmental and traditional knowledge of lands and resources in their ancestral territories has gone unrecognized and has been undervalued and underutilized. Research involving Métis women's knowledge should be culturally and geographically situated and understood through a lens that acknowledges the political and socioeconomic history of the particular Métis community, values, practices, language, kinship, and extended family ties. A continued denial of access to and control over traditional territories and resources found in Northwest Saskatchewan would mean a significant loss to the culture of the Métis as a whole, to the Métis family, and to the standing of Métis women in the broader community. The protection of biodiversity and the recognition of the inevitable interrelationship between biodiversity and control over resources lie at the heart of the ultimate challenge of ensuring real space and authority for the ongoing maintenance of the unique culture of the Métis people. The Indigenous knowledge of Métis women, as evidenced in this chapter, contributes in a very significant way to the distinct, vibrant, and unique culture of the Métis people as well as the effort to pursue the stewardship of the land.

Métis women in northwestern Saskatchewan have historically practiced and continue to practice the rich traditional knowledge and skills that will maintain the Métis culture and way of life into the future. As the Métis Nation continues to struggle for recognition of their inherent right to self-determination and to govern their traditional lands and resources, Métis women play an important leadership role in maintaining the link between the past and the future. Their leadership can be understood within the context of the extended family, local community, nation-building, the gift economy, and the governance of the land. Maintenance of Métis women's relationships with their traditional lands is the key to maintenance and preservation of the distinct Métis culture, Métis Indigenous knowledge, sustainable resource management practices, and the unique and special knowledge associated with the Métis way of life in that area.

References

Anderson, Kim. 2011. *Life Stages and Native Women: Memory, Teachings and Story Medicine*. Winnipeg: University of Manitoba Press.

Aboriginal Affairs and Northern Development Canada. 2006. "Fact Sheet: 2006 Census Aboriginal Demographics." http://www.ainc-inac.gc.ca/ai/mr/is/cad-eng.asp.

Chrétien, Annette, and Brenda Murphy. 2009. "'Duty to Consult', Environmental Impacts, and Métis Indigenous Knowledge." Ottawa: Aboriginal Policy Research Series.

Collignon, Béatrice. 2006. *Knowing Places: The Inuinnait, Landscapes and the Environment*. Edmonton: Canadian Circumpolar Institute Press.

Ens, Gerhard J. 1996. *Homeland to Hinterland: The Changing World of the Red River Métis in the Nineteenth Century*. Toronto: University of Toronto Press.

Foster, Martha Harroun. 2006. *We Know Who We Are: Métis Identity in a Montana Community*. Norman: University of Oklahoma Press.

Hull, Jeremy. 2008. "Aboriginal Youth in the Canadian Labour Market." In "Hope or Heartbreak: Aboriginal Youth and Canada's Future." *Horizons* 10 (1): 40–44. Ottawa: Government of Canada.

Kermoal, Nathalie. 2007. "Floral Beadwork: A Métis Cultural Heritage to Rediscover." *Encyclopedia of French Cultural Heritage in America*. Québec: Laval University. http://www.ameriquefrancaise.org/en/article-476/.

Kumar, Mohan B., and Teresa, Janz. 2010. "An Exploration of Cultural Activities of Métis in Canada." Component of Statistics Canada Catalogue no. 11-008-X, *Canadian Social Trends*, 63–69.

Macdougall, Brenda. 2010. *One of the Family: Metis Culture in Nineteenth-Century Northwestern Saskatchewan*. Vancouver: University of British Columbia Press.

———. 2006. "Wahtookowin: Family and Cultural Identity in Northwestern Saskatchewan Metis Communities." *Canadian Historical Review* 87: 431–62.

Métis Centre. 2008. *In the Words of Our Ancestors: Métis Health and Healing*. Ottawa: National Aboriginal Health Organization.

Mgbeoji, Ikechi. 2006. *Global Biopiracy: Patents, Plants, and Indigenous Knowledge*. Ithaca: Cornell University Press.

Parker, Leanna, and Frank Tough. 2005. "Population Estimates and Censuses of Northwest Saskatchewan, 1823–1901." Report no. 4. Edmonton: School of Native Studies.

Payment, Diane. 1990. *Les Gens Libres—Otipemisiwak: Batoche, Saskatchewan, 1870–1930*. Ottawa: Lieux et parcs historiques nationaux, Services des parcs.

Racette, Sherry Farrell. 2004. "Sewing Ourselves Together: Clothing, Decorative Arts and the Expression of Métis and Half Breed Identity." PhD dissertation, Interdisciplinary Doctoral Program, University of Manitoba.

Statistics Canada. 2013. "Aboriginal Peoples in Canada: First Nations People, Métis and Inuit." Ottawa: Ministry of Industry. http://www12.statcan.gc.ca/nhs-enm/2011/as-sa/99-011-x/99-011-x2011001-eng.pdf.

———. 2010. "Aboriginal Statistics at a Glance." Ottawa: Ministry of Industry. http://www.statcan.gc.ca/pub/89-645-x/89-645-x2010001-eng.htm.

St-Onge, Nicole. 2004. *Saint-Laurent, Manitoba: Evolving Métis Identities, 1850–1914*. Regina: Canadian Plains Research Center.

Statement of Claim (no. 619) submitted March 1, 1994, to the Court of Queen's Bench in the City of Saskatoon.

Tough, Frank. 2000. "'The Storehouses of the Good God': Aboriginal Peoples and Freshwater Fisheries in Manitoba." *Manitoba History* 39 (Spring/Summer): 2–14.

Tough, Frank, and Leah Dorion. 1993. "'The Claims of the Half-Breeds . . . Have Been Finally Closed': A Study of Treaty Ten and Treaty Five Adhesion Scrip." Ottawa: Royal Commission on Aboriginal Peoples.

Tough, Frank, and Erin McGregor. 2007a. "Métis Scrip: Treaty Ten Scrip Commission Commemorative Analysis." Edmonton: Matrix.

———. 2007b. "'The Rights to the Land May Be Transferred': Archival Records as Colonial Text—A Narrative of Métis Scrip." In *Natives and Settlers—Now and Then: Historical Issues and Current Perspectives on Treaties and Land Claims in Canada*, edited by Paul W. DePasquale, pp. 33–63. Edmonton: University of Alberta Press.

Trask, Mililani. n.d. "Indigenous Women and Traditional Knowledge: Reciprocity Is the Way of Balance." http://www.gift-economy.com/womenand/womenand_indigenous.html.

Young, Patrick, Todd Paquin, and Darren R. Préfontaine. 2003. *Métis Trappers and Hide Working*. Saskatoon: Gabriel Dumont Institute.

CHAPTER SEVEN

Gender and the Social Dimensions of Changing Caribou Populations in the Western Arctic

Brenda Parlee and Kristine Wray

Just before dinnertime in a small Arctic village, a group of men riding snow-mobiles returns after a long day of hunting miles away. They had gone in search of caribou to feed their families. Their arrival is cause for jubilation, for the hunt has been successful. Attached to the snowmobiles are sleds now laden with meat, which is carried into the houses of those in the party and spread out on kitchen floors. We sit by the wood stove in one of the houses, listening to the stories of the women, who are excitedly anticipating several days of drying the meat together by the fire. They will laugh and tell stories about previous hunting expeditions, on which they sometimes joined their husbands, brothers, fathers, and grandfathers.

The chapter is a synthesis of insights garnered from more than five years of research among the Inuvialuit, Gwich'in, and Sahtú communities of the Northwest Territories on the social dimensions of caribou population change. The caribou in question are barren ground caribou, specifically, those of the Porcupine, Cape Bathurst, Bluenose West, and Bluenose East herds that migrate across portions of Canada's western Arctic region (see map 7.1). Since at least the early 1990s, these herds have, on the whole, been declining in numbers—part of a pattern of population change evident in many parts of the circumpolar Arctic. This decrease in numbers is to some degree natural: as biologists have established, populations of barren ground caribou undergo cyclic variations, peaking every forty to seventy years. Concerns have been raised, however, about how far the current decline in population numbers—which has been quite dramatic in the case of some herds—is the result of global warming and other anthropogenic changes to the environment (see, for example, Vors and Boyce 2009).

For the Inuvialuit, Gwich'in, and Sahtú communities of the Northwest Territories, periodic reductions in caribou numbers are nothing surprising. Oral histories tell of the comings and goings of caribou, movements that are as much about changes in population as they are about seasonal migrations. In the past, however, outside observers attributed declines in caribou numbers to alleged overhunting—"wanton slaughter"—on the part of Aboriginal peoples (for discussion, see Campbell 2004; Usher 2004). Even though conclusive evidence of such wholesale destruction was always lacking, federal government campaigns against hunting were set in motion over the years, and the consequent reduction of caribou in the diet of Aboriginal peoples had significant implications for their health. Particularly since land claims were settled in the 1980s and 1990s, inaugurating an era of co-management, outright bans on hunting have given way to less draconian approaches, such as quota systems. All the same, the tendency to disregard the socioeconomic and cultural implications of hunting regulations remains.

As is well documented, Indigenous peoples have their own ways of coping with scarcity. Despite the history of government intervention in caribou management, contemporary Arctic communities retain many of their customary mechanisms for adjusting to variations in the food supply. In addition to traditional knowledge and skills, these approaches turn on flexibility, both social and tactical, and an underlying ethic of mutual support. Nuttall et al. (2005, 669) describe five cultural practices that enable Indigenous peoples to cope with changes in the variability of resources:

- Mobility of hunting groups; seasonal settlements; group size flexibility with grouping and regrouping of self-supporting economic units

- Flexibility of seasonal cycles of harvest and resource use, backed up by oral traditions to provide group memory

- Detailed local environmental knowledge (traditional knowledge) and related skill sets for harvesting, navigating, and food processing

- Sharing mechanisms and social networks for mutual support and risk minimization; high social value attached to sharing and generosity
- Inter-community trade along networks and trading partnerships, to deal with regional differences in resource availability

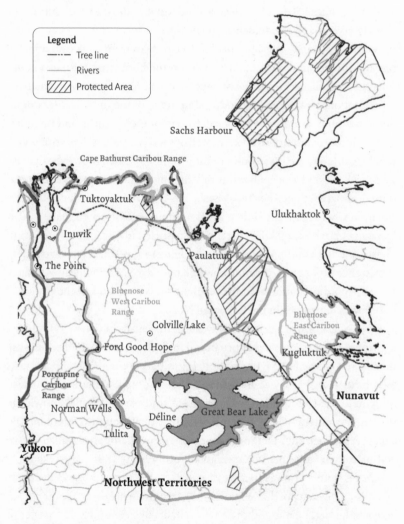

Map 7.1 Approximate ranges of the Cape Bathurst, Bluenose West, Bluenose East, and Porcupine caribou herds. Source: Map drawn by Kelsey Jansen, 2013, adapted from Northwest Territories, Environment and Natural Resources 2011, 6 (figure 1).

A host of other factors influences how, when, and where hunting takes place, or whether it takes place at all. These factors include caribou population levels at a given time, whether hunting is generally carried out communally or by individual households, the structure of these households (the number of unmarried males, for example), and the degree of participation in the wage economy (Nuttall et al. 2005; Berman and Kofinas 2004; Kruse et al. 2004).

As is now widely recognized, much of the information we have about the cultural practices surrounding hunting derives from a male-dominated research model, in which the focus falls on the hunt itself, with less attention paid to other aspects of community life. "Man the hunter" has been the archetype created and reproduced in much of the historical ethnography about human-animal relations in the circumpolar world, and its effects persist in contemporary contexts as well. As Karla Jessen Williamson points out, "Most literature on peoples of the Arctic was written by males whose writings have yet to be analyzed through non-patriarchal and non-colonial frames of perception. The strong male bias about the Arctic has led into a situation where relatively little is known about Arctic women's roles" (Williamson et al. 2004, 188). By entrenching a disregard of women as agents in household and community decision making and as active participants in subsistence economies, the reproduction of this bias in management policy has narrowed our understanding of the place of caribou in the lives and livelihoods of peoples in the Canadian North.

This neglect of women is to some extent the legacy of a male-dominated anthropological tradition that privileged Indigenous men, whether because they were assumed to be the authorities or because male anthropologists found men more easily approachable (Parlee 2013). Gender bias may also be symptomatic of a larger problem in the study of traditional knowledge systems. As others have noted, the persistent tendency is to fragment and decontextualize traditional knowledge, abstracting it from its original source and place, typically to serve the agenda of the state (Ellis 2005; Nadasdy 2003). The implication is that we discount, rather than embrace, the complexity and diversity of the relationships that exist in northerly communities between human beings and the environment. By listening to the voices of women, we aim to arrive at a richer understanding of the social dimensions of caribou population change in the western Arctic. More specifically, we examine questions of agency. What role do women play in the comings and goings of caribou? In consequence of their knowledge and responsibilities, what perspectives do they bring to bear on issues of caribou scarcity? And what part do women play in both household and regional responses to caribou population change?

Background Literature and Ethnography

The chapter draws on research conducted among the Inuvialuit, Gwich'in, and Sahtú peoples who inhabit the western portion of the Northwest Territories (see map 7.2). The Inuvialuit, an Inuit people, are the most northerly of the three. The Inuvialuit Settlement Region was created in 1984, as part of the settlement of the first in a series of comprehensive land claims in the Canadian Arctic (Canada, Indian and Northern Affairs Canada, 1984). From the border of the Yukon with Alaska, the region extends east along the coast of the Beaufort Sea and the Amundsen Gulf and, to the north, includes Banks Island and the western section of Victoria Island, encompassing a total area of roughly 435,000 square kilometres. The Gwich'in are a Dene (or Athabaskan) people who live along the southern slopes of the Brooks Range in northern Alaska, in the northern Yukon, and in the Mackenzie Delta region of the Northwest Territories. According to oral tradition, the Gwich'in have occupied this area since time immemorial or, by more conventional estimates, for as much as twenty thousand years.[1] Today, the Gwich'in living in Canada occupy an area defined in the 1992 Gwich'in Comprehensive Land Claim Agreement (Canada, Indian and Northern Affairs Canada, 1992). The Gwich'in Settlement Region comprises traditional lands in both the Northwest Territories and the Yukon covering an area of nearly 24,000 square kilometres. South of the Gwich'in Settlement Area is the Sahtú Settlement Area, which was defined the following year in another comprehensive land claim settlement (Canada, Indian and Northern Affairs Canada, 1993) and spans an area of approximately 41,440 square kilometres. Like the Gwich'in, the Sahtú (or North Slavey) are Dene peoples, who live in the vicinity of Sahtú, or Great Bear Lake. The Sahtú Dene Council represents four First Nations: the Behdzi Ahda' First Nation (based at Colville Lake), the Délįne First Nation (based at Deline), the K'asho Got'ine First Nation (based at Fort Good Hope), and the Begade Shotagotine First Nation (based at Tulit'a).

---

1 "The Gwich'in," Gwich'in Council International, 2009, http://www.gwichin.org/gwichin.html.

Map 7.2 Comprehensive land claims in the Northwest Territories.
Source: Canada, Office of the Auditor General of Canada 2010, 7.

Although their regions are ecologically diverse, stretching from the Arctic tundra to the boreal forest, the Inuvialuit, Gwich'in, and Sahtú communities have all traditionally depended for their livelihood upon barren ground caribou, known as *tuktu* in Inuvialuktun, *ekwe* in Sahtú, and *vadzaih* in Teetł'it Gwich'in. Throughout these regions, rich oral histories establish relationships between human beings and caribou and imbue the surrounding biophysical landscapes with meaning.

Ethnographic studies and documented oral histories about women in Inuvialuit, Gwich'in and Sahtú societies are relatively limited, although what little there is suggests a general position of powerlessness. For example, Diamond Jenness ([1932] 1972, 403) said of Gwich'in women that they "received no gentle treatment; they performed nearly all the hard work in camp, transported all the family possessions, ate only after the men had eaten, and had no voice in family or tribal affairs." Such views, while commonplace at the time, have not been borne out by academic research, nor do Aboriginal women themselves hold such views. In Dene oral traditions and histories recorded elsewhere, women are identified as leaders and guides, with natural as well as supernatural powers of endurance and healing. For example, respect is given to women who have endured physical hardship, such as those who have managed to care for others despite having been left on their own. The late Judith Catholique, of the Łutsël K'é Dene First Nation, talked about "working like a man—we had to learn to hunt for ourselves" (quoted in Parlee et al. 2001). The Łutsël K'é Dene live along the eastern arm of Great Slave Lake, not far from Parry Falls. According to Denésǫłiné oral tradition, the "old lady of the falls" is said to help care for people by providing them with guidance about the location of the caribou during fall and winter months (Parlee, Manseau, and Łutsël K'é Dene First Nation 2005, 34). Denésǫłiné women have been celebrated as powerful leaders of their peoples, as is evident in the oral histories surrounding Thanadelthur, the seventeenth-century Chipewyan woman who helped to make peace between her people and the Cree.

Although the roles of women in Inuvialuit, Gwich'in, and Sahtú cultures have been little explored, stories about the comings and goings of caribou are common in many northern Inuit and Dene narratives. In the Inuvialuit, Gwich'in, and Sahtú regions, oral history has contributed to a cautious acceptance that caribou are presently scarce and to a parallel faith in their eventual return. Elders and hunters point to a variety of ecological factors in explanation of the present decline—fire, predation, and extreme weather events, as well as disturbances brought about by resource development (Wray 2011). In numerous traditional narratives, however, women are featured as those principally responsible for the arrival or departure of caribou.

According to these explanatory frameworks, lack of respect for caribou is the central cause of their disappearance, and the restoration of that respect is key to their return. Within this dynamic, women exercise a power that can be positive or negative. If they are careful not to touch or walk over hunting tools and demonstrate respect through the careful preparation of meat and hides, so that nothing is wasted, the caribou are likely to return. Conversely, women who are not careful to use all of the caribou that has given itself to human beings will potentially be blamed by family and community if the caribou subsequently fail to return.

Contemporary ethnographic evidence speaks further to this dimension of women's power. Rituals associated with puberty are particularly important, as puberty is a critical point of transition in the development of women's power: only mature women have access to the knowledge of healing and the right to share that knowledge with other women. Although to some extent men hold a similar medicine power, women are said to possess special powers of their own, which they have to control if hunting activities are to be successful. According to an ethnographic study of Gwichya Gwich'in (Heine et al. 2001, 98), "women accepted the responsibility to exercise this control and to behave in the appropriate manner; this was one of their indirect contributions to the hunters' work."

Women and the Survival of Traditional Knowledge

It may be in recognition of this power that many Inuvialuit, Gwich'in, and Sahtú women insist on the importance of passing on their knowledge and skills to future generations. Concern appears to be growing about a generation whose capacity to connect with the land has diminished, at the same time that a push exists in the North for youth to become "strong like two people" by forging combined identities and drawing on two systems of knowledge (Martin 1991). Given that youth have relatively scant experience with living on the land, one must ask how far concepts and practices grounded in traditional knowledge hold meaning for them. Moreover, while what a community recognizes and respects as traditional knowledge varies across communities, the general tendency has been to privilege the voices of elders (mainly men) and thus to discount the knowledge and capacities of other members of the community, namely, women and youth. Young women have arguably suffered most from this bias toward elders, with policy makers as well as researchers decrying their limited understanding of traditional ways of life and their lack of connection to the land.

If it is currently difficult to say what traditional knowledge means for young women in the western Arctic, for older women, such knowledge has much to do with responsibility and care for the family. The preparation of meat and hides is generally regarded as one of a woman's most important responsibilities, one that serves a dual purpose. Such labour provides for the needs of the family, who require not only food but clothing. At the same time, by making use of the hide—that is, by not wasting any part of the cari-bou—women offer respect to the caribou, thereby ensuring their continued presence or, as the case may be, their return. Tanning a caribou hide is a labour-intensive process that must be carried out carefully. The steps in the process are described in the inset box below.

Table 7.1 The process of tanning a caribou hide

Tanning a caribou hide	
A good time to work	Spring and summer
Soaking the skin	Moose and caribou hides were soaked in the river or lake water for about one week.
Scorching the hair side	Before the water was wrung out, the hair side had to be scorched to remove most of the hair from the hide. A special pan was heated and then placed upside down on the ground, and the hide was moved across it. When the step was completed, the hide was black where it had been scorched.
Thinning out the hair side	Next, the hair side around the neck area was thinned out because that was the thickest part of the hide.
Draining out the blood	To drain out all of the blood that remained in the skin, the hide was wrung out and rinsed in clear water for the first time. For every rinse, fresh water was required.
Twisting the wet hide	To prepare the hide for twisting, small loops were cut out along the outer edge. A solid stick was placed into the ground, and about three of the loops were slipped over it at the same time. Three loops on the opposite side of the hide were slipped over a sturdy piece of driftwood about 3 feet long. The pole was then used to twist the hide. After it was twisted, the hide was rinsed and then twisted again. This continued until only clean water came out when the hide was twisted.
Soaking the hide in warm brain water	The hide was then soaked in brain water, to soften it further. After soaking, it was twisted again, then soaked again, then twisted again.
Scraping the hide on the hair side	The hide was wrapped over a pole mounted between two tripods, about 5 feet off the ground. The hide was thoroughly scraped on the hair side to eliminate the hair.

Tanning a caribou hide (cont'd)	
Scraping the hide on the inside	The inside of the hide was scraped with a stone scraper until it was more or less dry, and the dried flesh was then removed using a metal scraper. To make the scraping easier, the horizontal pole was lowered so that it was only about 3 feet above the ground.
Preparing the hide for smoking	The cleaned hide would be then smoked to soften it so that it could be used to make moccasins, pants, and coats. Before smoking, the holes would be sewn up and the edges trimmed off. The hide was hung on a stick 3 to 4 feet off the ground, with a canvas sometimes attached to the bottom to act as a funnel for the smoke.
Smoking hides	The fire used for smoking was made of rotten wood and had to be well tended so that it would not either go out or become too hot and scorch the hide. The smoking fire would be kept for almost a whole day [eight hours]. Once the inside of the hide was smoked, it was taken off and scraped to soften it.

Source: Adapted from Heine et al. 2001, 142.

A strong tradition still exists in many Arctic communities of preparing hides and sewing slippers, mitts, and mukluks. Given the current decline in caribou numbers, however, opportunities to pass on the knowledge of how to tan hides have become increasingly scarce. The predominant concern is that the youth of today will no longer have the skills to work with caribou hides, with the result that caribou will be wasted. Although themes of frustration and loss often dominate discussions of the preservation of traditional knowledge, many communities are working hard to build relationships between elders and youth and to awaken an interest among young people in their cultural heritage, with women actively participating in these efforts.

ADAPTING TO A DECLINE IN CARIBOU: THE VALUE OF WOMEN'S PERSPECTIVES

In Arctic communities, as elsewhere in the world, women play a pivotal role in household food production. They are responsible for the nutritional health of immediate and extended family, as well as for providing food at community functions and feasts. By virtue of this role, they bring a front-line perspective to bear on questions surrounding how best to adapt to changes in the availability of caribou meat. As Yvonne Hanson (2011, 1) notes, "Women's traditional relationships to food production, purchasing and preparation, and their socialized role in 'caring' for family members, aptly position them to comment on the competence of policy in creating and maintaining healthy communities and households." The perspectives of women arguably stem from three different roles that they assume within the household economy. The first of these is the role of hunter.

Figure 7.1 Dene woman hunting, ca. 1950s. NWT Archives, Henry Busse fonds, N-1979-052, item no. 4888.

Caribou hunting is a mainstay of Arctic household economies in Canada. In the decade from 1988 to 1997, for example, caribou meat harvest in Inuvialuit communities amounted to 110,730 kilograms, or 33.3 percent of the total harvest of traditional foods (Usher 2002, table 2 and 23). In the Gwich'in region, the harvest was 553,910 kilograms over five years, accounting for more than 75 percent of the total traditional food harvest (Gwich'in Renewable Resources Board 2009). A study of adaptive responses to food shortages among the K'asho Got'ine (McMillan 2011) suggests that, in the Sahtú region, caribou account for a similar percentage of the total harvest. Although a coarse measure of value, the annual replacement value of caribou meat is estimated at tens of millions of dollars in the Northwest Territories as a whole and hundreds of thousands of dollars in most of the Inuvialuit, Gwich'in, and Sahtú communities (Northwest Territories, Environment and Natural Resources 2011).

As hunters, men are primary drivers within this traditional economy. Many women in the Inuvialuit, Gwich'in, and Sahtú regions also hunt, however, and have done so for many generations (see figure 7.1). The crucial participation of women in hunting is attested by the comment of a successful Iñupiat hunter: "I'm not the great hunter, my wife is." He was referring to his wife's ability to attract animals, as well as to butcher, share meat, and sew clothing, all of which are described by the Iñupiat as hunting skills (Bodenhorn 1990). As hunters, women have a perspective similar to that of men on changes in the availability of caribou.

Women's active role in the wage economy affords them a second perspective on shifts in caribou populations. The average employment rate for women in the three regions under consideration is 48.9 percent, as opposed to 46.3 percent for men (see table 7.2). If we exclude the towns of Inuvik and Norman Wells, which have relatively large non-Aboriginal populations, the employment differential becomes even greater, with women having an employment rate of 44.1 percent versus 38.7 percent for men. As wage earners, women participate in the market economy, and they are probably more likely than men to be responsible for the purchase of store-bought foods. As a result, they have a clearer sense of the cost of alternatives to traditional foods.

A third perspective comes from the role of women as the primary caregivers within families. As such, women are responsible not only for procuring food but for storing and preparing it, and they also take part in the sharing of food (such as the caribou with which this chapter opened) with other members of their communities. With the declining availability of caribou, what kind of food choices are women making among traditional foods and store-bought alternatives? A comprehensive answer to this question would require detailed longitudinal research, but it is clear that such choices are influenced by a number of factors, in addition to matters of preference. These factors include both individual and community perceptions of the degree to which the availability of caribou is shifting, as well as various possible interpretations of the change. They also include relative ease of access to other sources of traditional foods, on the one hand, and to food purchased at grocery stores, on the other, as well as considerations of cost (see table 7.3).

Table 7.2 Employment rate for Inuvialuit, Gwich'in, and Sahtú women, 2009

Community	Employment rate female (male)	Community	Employment rate female (male)
Fort Good Hope	47.0 (40.0)	Fort McPherson	34.6 (35.0)
Colville Lake	54.1 (34.8)	Inuvik	67.3 (74.8)
Deline	47.5 (37.7)	Aklavik	41.9 (31.2)
Tulita	43.4 (40.0)	Tuktoyaktuk	44.2 (44.5)
Norman Wells	72.8 (85.9)	Paulatuk	43.8 (49.3)
Tsiigehtchic	41.2 (35.9)		

Source: Adapted from Heine et al. 2001, 142.

Investigation of the influence of such factors on harvest behaviour has so far been limited, given that harvest studies have typically focused on counts, that is, on the number of animals "struck and retrieved." As Peter Usher and George Wenzel (1987, 157) point out, although the specific objectives of such studies have varied, "wildlife management and socioeconomic analysis objectives are not easily reconciled (although it is by no means impossible to do so)." Perhaps for this reason, the socioeconomic factors driving harvest behaviour, including those that pertain especially to women, largely await exploration (see Parlee et al. forthcoming).

Table 7.3 Factors influencing food choices in response to decreased availability of caribou

Factor	Discussion	Principal consideration
Perceptions of change in availability of caribou	Depending on the location of their community and hunting area relative to the herd, individuals will read the "comings and goings" of caribou differently. Population surveys by government scientists suggest that groups dependent on the Cape Bathurst herd are experiencing more drastic changes than those in the region of the Bluenose East herd. In addition, communities located on the periphery of the fall and winter range are more likely to observe and experience a loss or decline in the availability of caribou than those who live closer to the calving areas or to areas of overwintering and migration, where caribou activity is greater. Information originating with government or the media can also influence perceptions of caribou availability. Information from such outside sources may compete with or be filtered through local knowledge and will be accepted or not accepted depending on how much trust individuals place in those providing the information and in the methods used to produce it.	Do people perceive a change in the availability of caribou?
Interpretation of change as a decline in population or a change in location	Interpretations of changes in the availability of caribou will often hinge upon past experiences, including oral histories about the "comings and goings" of caribou. Whereas some tend to assume that a decline in caribou activity must mean that because population numbers have declined, in many communities the prevailing theory is that the caribou move around and disappear for spiritual reasons, as well as in response to physical stresses such as extreme weather events and disturbances produced by development activity.	Why have the caribou moved away?

Factor	Discussion	Principal consideration
Preferences and access to other traditional foods	Although caribou are a mainstay in the diets of many Inuvialuit, Gwich'in, and Sahtú families, many other traditional foods are also valued and may, in the context of the declining availability of caribou, increase in dietary significance depending on preference and access. Considerations of access include the physical *availability* of the various foods, the traditional *knowledge and skills* required to harvest a particular food, and the relative *cost* and *convenience* of procuring the food. Access and preference are interrelated: as caribou become less available, other traditional foods may increasingly be preferred.	What other traditional foods are available?
Preferences and access to food from grocery stores	Traditional food is critical to the diets of Arctic peoples; however, food from the store may be preferred over certain traditional foods that, while offering an alternative to caribou, are not commonly consumed in these communities. In this context, considerations of access include the relative physical *availability* of each kind of food, the traditional *knowledge and skills* required for procuring traditional foods, and the *cost* and *convenience* of harvesting versus purchasing food from the store.	What are the alternatives to traditional foods?

WOMEN IN CO-MANAGEMENT

Caribou are managed through regional co-management boards made up of representatives appointed by Aboriginal communities and by the territorial and federal governments. The Porcupine Caribou Management Board, the Inuvialuit Game Council, the Wildlife Management Advisory Council (Northwest Territories and Yukon North Slope), the Gwich'in Renewable Resources Board, and the Council of Yukon First Nations have an overlapping interest in the management of the Porcupine caribou herd. The Porcupine Caribou Management Board is itself a co-management arrangement that brings together groups who dwell within the range of this herd.

The Bluenose East, Bluenose West, and Cape Bathurst herds are jointly managed by the Sahtú Renewable Resources Board, the Gwich'in Renewable Resources Board, the Inuvialuit Game Council, and the Wek'eezhii Renewable Resources Board. Each of these organizations includes representatives from Aboriginal communities; however, very few of these representatives are women. Out of forty-four positions, currently only one is occupied by a woman—a mere 2.27 percent (see table 7.4).

Table 7.4 Representation of Aboriginal women on co-management boards

Co-management board	Aboriginal women members / Total members	
Wildlife Management Advisory Council (WMAC), North Slope	0/4	No Aboriginal women are currently members of the council (one Aboriginal woman is named as an alternate).
Porcupine Caribou Management Board	0/8	No Aboriginal women are currently members of the board.
Inuvialuit Game Council	0/8	No Inuvialuit women are currently members of the council.
Gwich'in Renewable Resources Board	0/8	No Gwich'in women are currently members of the board (one Aboriginal woman is named as an alternate).
Sahtú Renewable Resources Board	1/8	One Sahtúgotine woman is a member of the board.
Wek'eezhii Renewable Resources Board	0/8	No Aboriginal women are representatives on the board.
Total	1/44 (2.27%)	

The main task of co-management boards in recent years has been harvest management planning in response to reported population declines. Starting in 2007, harvest management plans were created for the Porcupine, Cape Bathurst, and Bluenose herds through a process led by the Porcupine Caribou Management Board and the Bluenose Caribou Management Plan Working Group. In the case of the Porcupine Caribou herd, a voluntary "bulls only" harvest was promoted in 2007 through an education campaign: "Leave the Cows Alone." In addition, in 2009, the Yukon Government enacted the Porcupine Caribou Subsistence Harvest Regulation (Yukon O.I.C. 2009/159), which specified legal limits as well as requirements for reporting (see Yukon, Environment Yukon 2009). In the case of the Bluenose West herd, a quota system was put in place in the Northwest Territories in 2009 that allowed a maximum annual harvest of 700, to be divided equally between the Inuvialuit and Sahtú communities. This is thought to represent an 80 percent decrease from the harvest levels calculated through the Inuvialuit and Sahtú harvest studies. In 2010, the Bluenose East harvest limit was set at just over 1,900 animals for the Tłįchǫ and Sahtú communities, which the Government of the Northwest Territories estimated to be 30 to 40 percent of peak harvest levels. Arriving at consensus on the Harvest Management Plan was a challenge that occupied the better part of the time of staff and board members for some two to three years, and compliance by harvesters on a day-to-day basis is still a significant unknown. Caribou harvesting rights are entrenched in both the Constitution of Canada and in the regional land claim agreements of the Inuvialuit, Gwich'in, and Sahtú regions. Thus, government tracking of local harvests is politically charged and legally complex.

Concerns about overharvesting may, however, be moot. Research suggests current harvest levels are a fraction of historic levels and are declining; in that context, little evidence has been found that harvesting has a significant ecological impact (Usher 2004). The more pressing issue is arguably the sustainability of families and communities. To date, the social and health implications of declining caribou populations have largely been off the conventional caribou management table. Rather, these issues have been left to the kitchen table, around which women gather and converse. The tacit assumption is that decisions about how best to cope with matters affecting diet falls into the domain of personal responsibility and that the government should therefore play no formal role. An overemphasis on personal behaviour as a determinant of health, however, conveniently ignores the fact that socioeconomic and ecological factors often exercise a decisive influence on health. In situations of increased health risk, the assumption that people can and should control their own health "instructs people to be individually responsible at a time when they are becoming less capable as individuals of controlling their health environment," which in turn promotes victim-blaming (Crawford 1977, 671). In view of the risks to human health, we urgently need to reframe caribou population change as more than a wildlife management issue and the food choices made in the context of decreased availability as more than an issue of personal responsibility. Perhaps this can be accomplished only by linking the boardroom tables with the kitchen tables in communities in the Canadian North.

Conclusion

Our aim in this chapter has been to discuss the social dimensions of changing barren ground caribou populations in the western Arctic, with an emphasis on the role of women in adapting to these changes. In addition to taking care of their families, Inuvialuit, Gwich'in, and Sahtú women alike have responsibilities for "taking care" of caribou that reflect women's spiritual power and their ability to influence the appearance or disappearance of caribou. These women also wield traditional knowledge and skills, and, whether as hunters or wage earners, play a central role within the household economy. Given their responsibility for providing nourishing meals, they bring a practical perspective to bear on questions surrounding adaptive responses to a scarcity of caribou. And yet they largely lack a voice in co-management decision making, and their role in household economies has been neglected in research and rarely informs policy. The socioeconomic and health dimensions of caribou population change have been similarly overlooked, with the focus falling instead on the principally male domain of hunting.

What is missing, in short, is a conceptualization of the problem of declining caribou numbers that is more integrative of women's perspectives. Incorporating these perspectives would do more than simply enrich the information base on which policy rests. It would also enhance our awareness and understanding of vitally important issues such as economic hardship, cultural disruption, food insecurity, and risk of diabetes and other chronic illnesses. Such issues must be confronted if we expect to create sustainable communities and environments in the Canadian North.

References

Berman, Matthew, and Gary Kofinas. 2004. "Hunting for Models: Grounded and Rational Choice Approaches to Analyzing Climate Effects on Subsistence Hunting in an Arctic Community." *Ecological Economics* 49 (1): 31–46.

Bodenhorn, Barbara. 1990. "'I'm Not the Great Hunter, My Wife Is': Inupiat and Anthropological Models of Gender." *Études/Inuit/Studies* 14 (1–2): 55–74.

Campbell, Craig. 2004. "A Genealogy of the Concept of 'Wanton Slaughter' in Canadian Wildlife Biology." In *Cultivating Arctic Landscapes: Knowing and*

Managing Animals in the Circumpolar North, edited by David G. Anderson and Mark Nuttall, 154–71. New York: Berghahn Books.

Canada. Indian and Northern Affairs Canada. 1984. *The Western Arctic Claim: The Inuvialuit Final Agreement*. Ottawa: Government of Canada.

———.1992. *Comprehensive Land Claim Agreement Between Her Majesty the Queen in Right of Canada and the Gwich'in as Represented by the Gwich'in Tribal Council*. Ottawa: Government of Canada.

———. 1993. *Dahtu Dene and Metis Comprehensive Land Claim Agreement*. Ottawa: Government of Canada.

Canada. Office of the Auditor General. 2010. "Sustaining Development in the Northwest Territories." *Report of the Auditor General of Canada to the House of Commons, Spring 2010*, chap. 4. Ottawa: Office of the Auditor General of Canada. http://www.oag-bvg.gc.ca/internet/docs/parl_oag_201004_04_e.pdf.

Crawford, Robert. 1977. "You Are Dangerous to Your Health: The Ideology and Politics of Victim Blaming." *International Journal of Health Services* 7 (4): 663–80.

Ellis, Stephen. 2005. "Meaningful Consideration? A Review of Traditional Knowledge in Environmental Decision Making." *Arctic* 58 (1): 66–77.

Gwich'in Renewable Resources Board. 2009. "Gwich'in Harvest Study Final Report." Inuvik, NWT: Gwich'in Renewable Resources Board.

Hanson, Yvonne. 2011. *Recipes for Food Insecurity: Women's Stories from Saskatchewan*. Regina: Prairie Women's Health: Centre of Excellence.

Heine, Michael K., Alestine Andre, Ingrid Kritsch, Alma Cardinal, and the Elders of Tsiigehtchic. 2001. *Gwichya Gwich'in Googwandak: The History and Stories of the Gwichya Gwich'in As Told by the Elders of Tsiigehtchic*. Tsiigehtchic, NWT: Gwich'in Social and Cultural Institute.

Jenness, Diamond. (1932) 1972. *The Indians of Canada*. 6th ed, Toronto: University of Toronto Press.

Kruse, Jack A., Robert G. White, Howard E. Epstein, Billy Archie, Matthew Berman, Stephen R. Braund, F. Stuart Chapin III et al. 2004. "Sustainability of Arctic Communities: An Inter-disciplinary Collaboration of Researchers and Local Knowledge Holders." *Ecosystems* 7: 1–14.

Martin, Jim. 1991. *Strong Like Two People: The Development of a Mission Statement for the Dogrib Schools*. Rae-Edzo, NWT: Dogrib Divisional Board of Education.

McMillan, Roger. 2011. "Resilience to Ecological Change: Contemporary Harvesting and Food-Sharing Dynamics in the *K'asho Got'ine* Community of Fort Good Hope, Northwest Territories." MSc thesis, Department of Resource Economics and Environmental Sociology, University of Alberta, Edmonton.

Nadasdy, Paul. 2003. *Hunters and Bureaucrats: Power, Knowledge, and Aboriginal-State Relations in the Southwest Yukon*. Vancouver: University of British Columbia Press.

Northwest Territories. Bureau of Statistics. 2015. "Community Data." Government of the Northwest Territories, Yellowknife. http://www.statsnwt.ca/community-data/index.html.

Northwest Territories. Environment and Natural Resources. 2011. "Caribou Forever—Our Heritage and Responsibility: A Barren-Ground Caribou Management Strategy for the Northwest Territories, 2011–2015." Yellowknife: Department of Environment and Natural Resources.

Nuttall, Mark, Fikret Berkes, Bruce Forbes, Gary Kofinas, Tatiana Vlassova, and George Wenzel. 2005. "Hunting, Herding, Fishing, and Gathering: Indigenous Peoples and Renewable Resource Use in the Arctic." In ACIA Secretariat, *Arctic Climate Impact Assessment*, 649–90. Cambridge: Cambridge University Press.

Parlee, Brenda. 2013. "Offerings of Stewardship: Celebrating Life and Livelihood of Gwich'in Women in the Northwest Territories." In *Native Peoples: The Canadian Experience*, edited by R. Wilson and C. Fletcher. London: Oxford Press.

Parlee, Brenda, Natalie Zimmer, Roger McMillan, and Peter Boxall. Forthcoming. "Beyond the Harvest Study." In *When the Caribou Do Not Come: Perspectives on Barren Ground Caribou Population Change in the Western Arctic*, edited by Brenda Parlee, Ken Caine, Micheline Manseau, and Deborah Simmons. Vancouver: University of British Columbia Press.

Parlee, Brenda, Michline Manseau, and Łutsël K'é Dene First Nation. 2005. "Denésǫłiné Monitoring of Caribou Movements: Using Traditional Knowledge to Address Uncertainty." *Arctic* 53:1–8.

Parlee, Brenda, Marcel Basil, Nancy Casaway, and Lutsel K'e Dene First Nation. 2001. "Traditional Ecological Knowledge in the Kaché Tué Study Region: Final Report." Report submitted to the West Kitikmeot / Slave Study Society, Yellowknife.

Usher, Peter J. 2002. "Inuvialuit Use of the Beaufort Sea and Its Resources, 1960–2000." *Arctic* 55 (S1): 18–28.

———. 2004. "Caribou Crisis or Administrative Crisis? Wildlife and Aboriginal Policies on the Barren Grounds of Canada, 1947–60." In Anderson and Nuttall 2004, 172–99.

Usher, Peter J., and George W. Wenzel. 1987. "Native Harvest Surveys and Statistics: A Critique of Their Construction and Use." Arctic 40 (2): 145–60.

Vors, Liv Solveig, and Mark Stephen Boyce. 2009. "Global Declines of Caribou and Reindeer." *Global Change Biology* 15 (11): 2626–33.

Williamson, Karla Jessen, Gunhild Hoogensen, Ann Therese Lotherington, Lawrence H. Hamilton, Sarah Savage, Natalia Koukarenko, Marina Kalinina et al. 2004. "Gender Issues." *Arctic Human Development Report*, 187–205. Akureyri, Iceland: Stefansson Arctic Institute.

Wray, Kristine. 2011. "Ways We Respect Caribou: Hunting in Teetł'it Zheh (Fort McPherson, NWT)." MSc thesis, Department of Resource Economics and Environmental Sociology, University of Alberta, Edmonton.

Yukon. Environment Yukon. 2009. *Rationale for Implementing Conservation Measures to Protect the Porcupine Caribou Herd*. Whitehorse: Environment Yukon.

CHAPTER EIGHT

"This Is the Life"

Women's Role in Food Provisioning in Paulatuuq, Northwest Territories

Zoe Todd

Given the high cost of store-bought foods, hunting and fishing are vital to household food security in Paulatuuq[1], a small Arctic community in the Northwest Territories. Traditional harvesting activities do more, however, than address nutritional needs, sometimes generating a surplus that can be shared with extended family and friends. These activities are crucial to a sense of continuity, providing opportunities for Paulatuuqmiut to connect with memories of the past, to create and sustain relationships with other people and with the environment, and to pass knowledge along to children and grandchildren. Contrary to long-standing ethnographic assumptions to the effect that men hunt, while women gather and process, women in fact take an active part in household food provisioning. All the same, women's knowledge of the environment and their role in household economies

---

1 The standardized English spelling of Paulatuk is employed by federal, territorial, regional, and municipal government bodies to describe the hamlet. However, locally, Paulatuuqmiut prefer the use of the Siglitun spelling, Paulatuuq, in describing the community. Throughout this chapter I employ Paulatuuq when referring to the community, but where I refer to governance bodies that employ the English spelling of the hamlet's name, I employ the –uk suffix.

remain understudied, and their voices are typically muted in the scientific and bureaucratic discourses that undergird wildlife management in the Canadian Arctic.

In what follows, I examine women's participation in food harvesting generally and fishing in particular, focusing especially on the impact of shifts in patterns of employment. In so doing, I hope to document the multifaceted role that women play not merely in household food security but in the ongoing transmission of knowledge. Exploring women's place in food provisioning can provide much-needed insights into how households and, by extension, entire communities respond to the declining availability of country foods—a result of the combined forces of climate change and resource development, as well as the growth in waged employment. In turn, this more nuanced understanding may allow us to reorient research efforts in the North so as to capture more accurately the gendered aspects of traditional livelihoods and the complexity of interactions among human beings, bodies of knowledge, and the natural environment.

COMMUNITY LIVELIHOODS

Paulatuuq is an Inuvialuit community situated at the eastern base of the Parry Peninsula, on the coast of the Amundsen Gulf of the Beaufort Sea, roughly 400 kilometres northeast of Inuvik (see map 8.1). The population of Paulatuuq, which hovers around three hundred, stood at 304 in 2014, with men slightly outnumbering women and all but about 5 percent of the community identifying as Aboriginal. As in virtually all such Arctic communities, the local economy is mixed, with people variously engaging in waged and non-waged work. In 2014, roughly two-thirds (64.9 percent) of Paulatuuq's residents participated in some form of waged employment, whether full or part time, for at least a portion of the year. In 2008 (the most recent year for which statistics are available), over three-quarters—77.2 percent—of Paulatuuqmiut fished, hunted, or trapped, and 74.5 percent of Paulatuuq households consumed half or more of their food in the form of country foods. These figures, which clearly illustrate the importance of traditional subsistence activities, are similar to those for other Inuvialuit communities in the region but considerably higher than the corresponding figures of 50.8 percent and 26.3 percent, respectively, for the Northwest Territories as whole (NWT Bureau of Statistics 2014, 1, 3).

Although Paulatuuq was incorporated as a community only in 1987, the Inuvialuit have lived in the region for thousands of years. The area around Paulatuuq was originally inhabited by people known as the Igluyuaryungmiut, one of the groups of ancestors that today Inuvialuit identify as having lived in the region. Like most of these groups, the Igluyuaryungmiut were named for their main village, Iglulualuit, which was situated near the mouth of the Horton River, on Franklin Bay. Evidently, sometime around 1840, the village was abandoned, reportedly to pursue trade relationships influenced by British and Russian trade to the west (Usher 1971, 171). In 1840, the Hudson's Bay Company built a post on the Peel River, near the present-day community of Fort McPherson, and a fur trade emerged in the Mackenzie region (McDonnell 1983, 35).

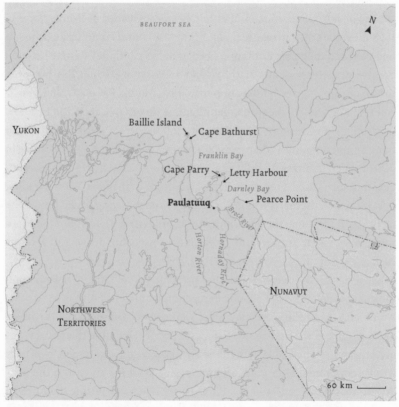

Map 8.1 A map of the fishing and harvesting sites visited during fieldwork, conducted in 2012. The Atlas of Canada - Toporama, Government of Canada.

From about 1890 to 1910, Arctic whaling brought American whalers into the Mackenzie Delta and along the coast of the Beaufort Sea, although by 1910 the value of whale oil and baleen had fallen to the point that the whaling era was essentially over. The fur trade, however, flourished in the lands around Paulatuuq. In 1916, the Hudson's Bay Company established a post at Baillie Island, off the tip of Cape Bathurst, marking the start of a local boom in furs. The Baillie Island post was followed by posts located in the more immediate vicinity of Paulatuuq, at Cape Parry, Pearce Point, and Letty Harbour. During the fox-fur trapping boom—which lasted until about 1930, when the Depression led to an abrupt decline in the demand for furs—Inuvialuit and non-Inuvialuit people alike moved outwards from the Mackenzie Delta toward the coast to capitalize on the abundant wildlife (see McDonnell 1983, 46–48; Usher 1971, 180).

In 1936, a Catholic mission that had been established at Pearce Point in 1928 moved to the current location of the Paulatuuq community, where it operated a trading post until 1954. Local families continued to move around between Cape Parry, Letty Harbour, and the coast of Darnley Bay, however, to pursue trapping and hunting opportunities (Alunik, Kolausok, and Morrison 2003, 127–28). In the 1950s, many families moved to Cape Parry to access wage opportunities at the DEW Line site, but the area was not well suited to hunting and trapping as there was far more abundant hunting and fishing in other locales in the region (McDonnell 1983, 70–71). Many community members thus advocated a return to Paulatuuq in the mid-1960s. After a trading post reopened there in 1967, more families began moving back, despite the fact that, at the time, the government was pressuring Inuvialuit families to settle in Inuvik or Tuktoyaktuk in order to consolidate delivery of services such as education (see McDonnell 1983, 56–63).

For roughly two decades after the present-day settlement at Paulatuuq took shape, fishing was a significant economic pursuit. From 1968 to 1987, Arctic char from the Hornaday River were fished commercially (Lemieux 1990, 1), and, in the mid-1980s, the feasibility of expanding this fishery was investigated (Staples 1986, 64). In the end, however, the commercial fishery was discontinued, after Paulatuuqmiut advocated for an end to the fishery, for reasons of conservation. Efforts were also made during the 1970s to support a sport-fishing industry in the community, although these proved unsuccessful (McDonnell 1983, 190). All the same, subsistence fishing remained an important activity. According to data collected by the Inuvialuit Harvest Study, in the decade from 1988 to 1997, Paulatuuqmiut harvested an annual mean catch of 2,446 Arctic char, along with 1,294 broad white-fish, 343 lake trout, 223 lake whitefish, and 100 grayling, as well as smaller quantities of other fish (Inuvialuit Joint Secretariat 2003, 118). Today, only subsistence fishing is permitted in Paulatuuq, and a strict community quota of 1,700 Arctic char per year is in place for the Hornaday River (Department of Fisheries and Oceans 1999, 2; Lemieux 1990). Traces of the sport fishery linger in the name of a fishing site along the river, Tourist Camp, at which Paulatuuqmiut continue to fish. In addition, one family in town currently runs the Bekere Lake Lodge, which offers guided tours for visiting sport hunters and sport fishers. Other guides in Paulatuuq take tourists out for occasional wildlife photography trips, as well as on hunting expeditions for polar bear and other large game.

In addition to fishing, Paulatuuqmiut hunt for a variety of animals, including caribou, polar bear, muskox, beluga whales, and seals. These large mammals are, however, subject to many hunting restrictions. For example, caribou, a staple of the local diet, is strictly regulated in Paulatuuq. All sport hunting of caribou from the regional Bluenose West herd was suspended in 2006, and an annual quota of 345 caribou is in place for Inuvialuit communities overall (Northwest Territories, Environment and Natural Resources n.d.). Such restrictions have obvious implications for local food security. By contrast, despite the quotas on Arctic char from the Hornaday and Brock rivers, community members indicated to me during research conducted in 2012 that lake trout, land-locked char, whitefish, grayling, and other varieties remain plentiful in the lakes, rivers, and coastal areas that surround the settlement, with Arctic char and lake trout regarded as especially desirable (Todd, unpublished research notes). At present, changes in natural habitats resulting both from climate change and from resource exploration and extraction in the region are taking a toll on many traditional food sources (see Keeping 1998; Mackenzie Gas Project 2004; Pearce et al. 2010). Although fish are not exempt from the effects of environmental change, access to fish is less circumscribed by conservation efforts in the form of wildlife regulations. Fish are thus an important staple in local household diets.

The cost of living in Paulatuuq constitutes a serious burden for many families. The *Inuit Health Survey, 2007–2008*, revealed that households in the Inuvialuit Settlement Region spent, on average, $1,317 per month on food—over twice the average of $609 for Canada overall—and another $1,471 on housing (Egeland 2010, 13). In the light of available household income data, these figures put many Paulatuuq households at risk of food insecurity (see Todd 2010a, 111–13; see also Todd 2010b). This risk was reaffirmed by a socio-economic survey conducted in Paulatuuq in 2012 which demonstrated a positive correlation between household income in Paulatuuq and ability to access both store-bought food and meat in the form of caribou, fish, and other game (Inuvialuit Regional Corporation 2012, 17). Data from a dietary intake study (Sharma et al. 2009), which identified nutritional deficits in the Inuvialuit Settlement Region, were used to develop Healthy Foods North, a multipronged program designed to reduce risk factors for chronic disease through dietary interventions and nutrition education. The prevalence of chronic conditions such as diabetes reflects one aspect of food insecurity— the lack of affordable access to healthy sources of nutrition.

Women's involvement in hunting and fishing, together with the knowledge that women shape, mobilize, and share through these and related activities, is an integral part of the food security equation. And yet their wisdom is seldom sought. As Joanna Kafarowski (2009) discovered in her work on women's roles in fisheries management, however, a paucity of women exists on Hunters and Trappers Organizations in Nunavut, and, in the preceding chapter (this volume), Brenda Parlee and Kristine Wray demonstrate that women are similarly underrepresented on co-management boards and wildlife agencies in the Northwest Territories. As both they and Kafarowski (2005) argue, women need to be given a greater official role in wildlife management, as the perspectives that women bring to bear shed essential light on harvesting patterns and priorities within Inuit communities. More broadly, probing the interconnections among women's harvesting activities, the knowledge generated and applied through these activities, and the need for household food security can deepen our understanding how Arctic peoples relate to one another and the environment. If we recognize that hunting and fishing serve a range of purposes beyond the purely utilitarian, we will be able to respond more appropriately to the issues—such as ecological disturbances, variations in the food supply, and the erosion of traditional customs and livelihoods—that community members identify as important to them.

Woman the Hunter (and Fisher)

As Parlee and Wray (this volume) point out, the archetype of "man the hunter" has tended to dominate ethnographic research in the circumpolar north. For many years, the assumption that men hunted either individually or with other men—in other words, the assumption that women were not involved in hunting practices—persisted not only in the literature but in the popular imagination, despite mounting evidence to the contrary. For example, in a study of hunters and trappers in the context of the modern nation-state, Harvey Feit (1982) found that the family unit was fundamental to hunting practices among the James Bay Cree. Men "did not pursue intensive hunting individually and without their families," he noted; rather, they "typically established winter hunting camps with their wives, their non-school-age children, and often some of their school-age children" (385). Along somewhat similar lines, John Kruse (1991) investigated the persistence of subsistence activities among the Alaskan Iñupiat despite the shift toward waged employment. As he discovered, in addition to participating in the wage economy, women continued to engage actively in numerous subsistence pursuits, notably fishing, gathering eggs, and assisting whaling crews (320), demonstrating a commitment by women in the study to negotiate land- and water-based subsistence activities alongside waged employment.

Although studies such as these focus overdue attention on women's roles in subsistence activities, they also tend to view these roles within a framework that arbitrarily opposes the modern world (as represented by the cash economy) to an authentic and untouchable Indigenous past (as represented by the subsistence economy). More recently, scholars have begun to emphasize the interpenetration of so-called traditional subsistence activities and contemporary realities. A study conducted by Brenda Parlee, Fikret Berkes, and the Teetl'it Gwich'in Renewable Resource Council (2005), which focused on berry harvesting among Gwich'in women in the area of Fort McPherson, explored the relationship between human and environmental well-being by identifying the values that women associate with the land, while also illustrating the role played by women's harvesting in environmental monitoring. As Robin Ridington (2001, 119) points out, subsistence technologies are "embedded in social relations that are enacted through discourse and empowered by narrative." In other words, hunting and gathering technologies presuppose certain ways in which human beings have learned to relate to each other and to the environment, and these ways are "particularly dependent on knowledge held by individuals and communicated through discourse and oral tradition" (118). These ways of understanding and relating carry forward into the present, such that the "traditional" economy includes the flexible and adaptive livelihoods that Indigenous peoples practice today.

Paulatuuqmiut well illustrate this interpenetration of past and present in the diverse livelihood strategies they have developed to meet individual and household needs. Yet little research has documented women's harvesting activities and the associated knowledge. The Inuvialuit Harvest Study compiled detailed quantitative data regarding Inuvialuit hunting, but the study mainly targeted male heads of households.[2] With regard to fishing, in particular, the situation is no better. As Usher and George Wenzel (1997, 146) point out, the recording of statistics has for the most occurred in the context of sport hunting (especially of large game animals) or commercial activities (such as the trade in furs and seal pelts). In particular, "no systemic recording of domestic fish catches" exists in the North, largely because "fisheries managers have considered it unnecessary or infeasible" to gather such data (148).[3]

Along parallel lines, Henry Stewart (2005) argues, historically, fishing has received far less detailed attention than hunting in ethnographic work conducted in the Canadian Artic. This is not to say, of course, that fishing has been entirely neglected. Reporting on the Anglo-American Polar Expedition

---

2 See Inuvialuit Joint Secretariat (2003). This report, which collects the results of annual harvest studies over a period of ten years, includes a detailed discussion of methods in section 3 of its introduction. According to section 3.3, "Harvesters (hunters) were initially defined as Inuvialuit male persons sixteen years of age and over, residing in the IRS [Inuvialuit Settlement Region]. Exceptions were made for female heads of households who hunted, or women or younger children who specifically requested to report to the survey individually" (2003, 7). This is, however, the sole mention of women in the report.

3 More broadly, Usher and Wenzel (1997, 146–47) note that statistical tracking has traditionally relied heavily on information generated by various reporting requirements and from records pertaining to the issuance of hunting and fishing permits. As they point out, however, whereas Aboriginal peoples engage in hunting and fishing primarily for purposes of subsistence, "rarely are there any systems in place to track subsistence harvests" (146). Similarly, because the right of Aboriginal peoples to hunt and fish rests on their original title to land (as recognized by treaty or through comprehensive land claims), licensing records do not capture their participation in these activities. Although the Inuvialuit Harvest Study was clearly designed to provide statistics about subsistence harvesting, its methods suggest that women's participation in these activities still largely remains under the radar.

of 1906–8, for example, Rudolph Anderson noted the pivotal role of fishing in the western Arctic:

> Fish play probably a more important part than anything else in the domestic economy of the Eskimo of the western Arctic coast. The list of food fishes is not large, but the number of individuals is so great that a family supplied with a gill-net or two can travel in summer along practically the whole Arctic coast, and be reasonably sure of catching fish for themselves and dogs at nearly every camping-place. When all the food required for a family can be obtained by merely putting out a fish-net every night and clearing it every morning, making a living is not a difficult matter. The Mackenzie delta is preëminently a fish country, fish being the staple food throughout the year—fresh in summer, and usually in a tainted or semi-putrid state in winter. (Anderson 1913, 450)

All the same, as Stewart (2005, 345–46) documents, fishing traditionally took a back seat to hunting in Arctic ethnographies—and, not surprisingly, women's role in fishing has remained largely unexplored.

One notable exception has been the work of Barbara Bodenhorn (1990) on Iñupiat whale hunting. Bodenhorn argues that the Western definition of hunting, with its emphasis on the pursuit and slaughter of an animal, is too narrow to encompass the range of activities that Iñupiat regard as hunting. An Iñupiat whaling captain's wife performs rituals that invite the whale to be hunted, she makes whaling boots and sews special mittens to be worn by her husband, and she butchers the whale in accordance with Iñupiat proto-col surrounding the proper treatment of the animal's body and soul. These activities "are needed to maintain amicable animal/human relations" (64), on which the success of the whaling expedition depends. Bodenhorn cautions against the tendency of researchers to privilege gender in analyses of Inupiat culture, suggesting that, to Iñupiat people, human-animal relationships are more important than divisions between men's work and women's work (57). Whereas Western conceptions of gender turn on a binary opposition of male to female, Iñupiat whale hunting emphasizes the interdependence of men and women, each of whom possess certain knowledge and skills that, while complementary, are inseparable from the whole.[4]

---

4 In this connection, one also thinks of Bernard Saladin d'Anglure's work on Inuit cosmologies, according to which gender is conceived not in terms of a duality but as tripartite. Saladin d'Anglure (2005) identifies a "third gender," which "straddled the boundary between two others and fulfilled a mediatory function between them"

Similarly, Kerrie Ann Shannon's (2006) research in the Inuit community of Coral Harbour, on the southern coast of Southampton Island, examines contexts in which the division of labour into men's and women's tasks begins to blur. As she notes, "Although there were aspects of daily life in Coral Harbour that readily matched the model of a gendered and complementary division of labour, there were other procurement activities that were not divided along gender lines" (13). Taking the annual fishing derby as an example of a procurement activity in which everyone participates, Shannon challenges the imposition of gender binaries:

> For a range of procurement activities, gender may influence an individual's task, but may not necessarily be a determinant of participation in the activity. For instance, in preparation for fishing, men may make the fishing handles and women may bake bannock bread to take as a snack but the activity of fishing is not considered "men's" or "women's" work. (13)

As studies such as these remind us, precisely because gender is socially constructed, it is not universally constructed in the same way. Rather than impose our own frames of references, we must respect other ways of knowing and seek, as far as possible, to understand the relational aspects of Indigenous philosophies, cosmologies, and legal orders.

In short, not only have recent studies begun to offset the historical marginalization of women in ethnographic research, but they have also provided crucial theoretical insights into our understanding of subsistence economies and our assumptions about gender. At the same time, detailed information about the role of Inuvialuit women as harvesters is lacking, and women remain underrepresented on policy-making bodies. In addition, insufficient attention has been given to women's place in the narration of culture—how they contribute to the discursive traditions through which cultural knowledge is both shaped and preserved. There is room, in this setting, to explore women's hunting and fishing in greater depth at the community level.

A MATTER OF RELATIONSHIPS: WOMEN AND HARVESTING IN PAULATUUQ

I conducted research in Paulatuuq in 2008–9 and again in 2012. The earlier research consisted of twenty semi-directed interviews with nine women and

---

(134). Although figures belonging to this third gender frequently appear in mythological narratives, the category is very much a part of living social relations.

eleven men whose employment status varied (see table 8.1). At the request of community leaders, in the summer of 2009 I organized a follow-up workshop on the subject of food security concerns. Five men and four women participated in this workshop, which focused on the ability of Paulatuuq residents to procure food from the local store. At this time, I also conducted two in-depth interviews, one with a man and one with a woman, on the subject of food security and traditional harvesting. These two interviews complemented the themes explored in the food security workshop. Both of these final interviews on food security were separate from the initial twenty interviews I conducted in 2008, which focused on harvesting, food security, and wage employment.

Table 8.1 Residents of Paulatuuq who participated in interviews, 2008

Name[a]	Gender	Amount of time spent on the land	Employment status	Age
John	M	A lot of time	Full-time harvester	61
Donald	M	A lot of time	Seasonal	45
Joseph	M	A lot of time	Seasonal (November to April)	51
Max	M	A lot of time	Self-employed (2 to 3 days a week)	55
Dave	M	A lot of time on the land outside of Paulatuuq, very little time in Paulatuuq harvesting	Full-time rotation out of town	34
Samantha	F	Some time	Retired	70
Leonard	M	Some time	Part-time, on the land	66
Rebecca	F	Some time	Part-time, in town	20
Bob	M	Some time	Part-time, in town	57
Christine	F	Some time	Seasonal (10 months of year)	49
Simon	M	Some time	Unemployed	38
Nick	M	Some time	Recently unemployed	43
Hank	M	Some time	Seasonal (10 months of year)	49
Janet	F	Some time	Full-time, in town	53

Name[a]	Gender	Amount of time spent on the land	Employment status	Age
Dorothy	F	Some time	Retired	83
Melanie	F	Very little time	Full-time, in town	26
Neve	F	Very little time	Full-time, in town	51
Karen	F	Very little time	Part-time, in town	38
Michael	M	Very little time	Full-time, in town	49
Amy	F	No time	Full-time, in town	48

[a] Names are pseudonyms.

Although interviews offer an efficient means of gathering information, they create a hierarchical relationship between questioner and questioned that can skew the results by privileging certain forms of thinking and knowing. In addition, such methods emphasize cognitive processes at the expense of embodied approaches to learning founded on direct participation in the activities through which knowledge is gained and the situations in which it is applied (see Dilley 1999; Pálsson 1994). As an Indigenous (Red River Métis) researcher, I also wanted to incorporate research methodologies that respect embodied and relational approaches to learning and articulating knowledge, drawing guidance from Inuvialuit women I worked with in Paulatuuq. Accordingly, during my fieldwork in 2012, I aimed to incorporate experiential modes of learning, seeking to understand people's relationships to the environment as these relationships are constituted through the practice of fishing itself. Learning *how* to fish, from skilled fishermen, was as critical to my understanding as learning *about* fish. Over the course of the year, three teachers—all women, from three different generations—generously shared their knowledge of fishing and the landscape with me. During these experiential learning sessions, which took place both in community settings and on the land, the hierarchy was reversed: I became the student.

Family Excursions

The fishing season in Paulatuuq extends from the early spring through to the late fall (late April through to October). Before the ice breaks up in the spring and after the fall freeze-up, people fish through holes in the ice with a homemade jigging stick, which is locally referred to as "jiggling." Local fishermen also practice net fishing, both under the ice and in open water, as well as fishing with a rod and reel. Individuals fish in the numerous small and large lakes that surround the community, along the coast (fishing, for example, for char at Lassard), and along the Hornaday and Brock rivers. Although people of all ages and genders participate in fishing, it is not entirely an inclusive activity: in order to fish, one must have time and access to equipment and supplies.

Fishing is fundamentally a social activity in Paulatuuq, usually practiced with one or more people. Both men and women fish, though in this chapter I focus on women's fishing in order to address the still under-acknowledged role of women's fishing—as a form of harvesting—in arctic ethnographic literature in Canada. Women may fish with male or female friends or family members (both men and women), often making a day trip to a nearby lake or river. Women may also fish in female-only groups when men are out hunting. For example, at Green's Island, a whaling camp to the west of the settlement at Paulatuuq, elder Anny Illasiak taught me that sometimes the women fish while the men are out on the sea in search of beluga whales. As Bob explained, fishing is a "family affair":

> The summer? It's another family affair. You, they go out. It's about ten miles from here, Argo Bay, Green's Island. They do their fishing there. Whenever caribou go passed by you get it. Basically, fishing and enjoying the July month. Also, there's beluga hunts during the month of July. August, you have your char fishing. That's another family affair. You go out, camp at the river.

As his description suggests, fishing is more than simply a utilitarian pursuit: it gives families an opportunity to spend time together on the land, especially during the warmer weather. Bob's comments also illustrate how fishing is embedded within a broader range of harvesting activities, in this case hunting caribou and beluga whales.

As became amply evident in the interviews I conducted, women take an active part in fishing. Fishing is one aspect of living on the land, which is something that women, like men, must be able to do. As Janet pointed out, she learned as a child how to live on the land:

> It's just the way that we were raised up. The first thing that we had to learn was directions, and we needed to learn each and every area in order to learn how to go out on the land. And during the spring I prac-ticed that adamantly, where right after work I would start my skidoo: the tank is full, and it's well maintained. I would go beyond Thrasher Lake immediately up to Salmon Lake and Billy Lake and even as far as

Biname Lake by myself. So long as I know where the people are—certain people—are camping to go fish, I would travel up to them, and every minute up there is not wasted. Except to eat and have some tea, but every minute is not wasted [when I'm] on "fishing time."

Although fishing, hunting, and berry picking are a big part of community life, not everyone is able to participate in these activities on a regular basis. Those who are unable to get out on the land themselves nonetheless recognize the importance of doing so and are pleased when other family members can experience what Bob called the "four corners of Paulatuuq." Melanie, a young woman who works full time in town, was grateful that her son was able to get out on the land:

This land around Paulatuuq is so beautiful, but I don't get to enjoy it as much as I used to. Like, I'll be lucky if I go out for a day trip and stuff like that, and I'm so glad that my son is going out geese hunting and caribou hunting and stuff. He's already getting ready to go out this weekend for geese hunting. They're sighting geese coming, so they're excited.

In this case, Melanie's sister, who did have time to engage in traditional harvesting, was able to take her nephew along with her and to teach him about hunting and fishing. As the individuals that I worked with in Paulatuuq reminded me throughout my research, the transmission of such traditional knowledge and skills to younger Paulatuuqmiut is crucial to enlivening Indigenous philosophies, cosmologies, and legal orders.

Again and again, those to whom I spoke emphasized the importance of family and of bringing children out onto the land. Such occasions reaffirm relationships, while also creating memories that are essential to both personal and collective identity. They also serve as a reminder of those who are no longer able to be present, thereby forging a sense of connection across time. As an activity in which both younger people and elders take part, fishing is a particularly rich site for the forging of such connections and memories. Neve, a woman in her early fifties, recalled one such occasion when relationships and kinship were reasserted by gathering together on the land to fish after the passing of family members:

One spring hunt, my parents were both gone, both died, and that spring [a] lot of, most of, my family members were out, my brothers and my sisters. The whole family, and husbands and wives, were out fishing. It was a beautiful day, just enjoying ourselves, it was. And one of my brothers said that this is the life, that's what he said. So that made it really special.

As Neve also pointed out, excursions out onto the land are inexpensive enough that the entire family can join in, unlike holidays to southern locations:

> Because we like going out on the land so much, the free time I have, instead of going down south with the family—for one thing, it costs too much to go down there, and then not all of you go out, but with on the land travel, the whole family can go out. Everything is close by. It doesn't cost that much to go out.

Neve was speaking, of course, of monetary costs. But "free" time can be very precious.

Finding Time: Women, Harvesting, and the Wage Economy

Traditional subsistence pursuits provide more than food: they afford opportunities to share knowledge with children and to revisit places of personal and family significance. In this respect, waged employment, while necessary to survival within a money economy, represents a sacrifice not merely of personal freedom but of traditions constitutive of culture. Janet, a full-time wage earner, eloquently summed up this sense of loss:

> There are times on my side that I look at the load [of] work, and when it is so big I am thinking, "Why am I not enjoying the rest of my life out on the land?" I used to envy one of my uncles, always had the freedom of going out to live on the land for a month, two months or so.

In a study of women and fishing in Arviat, a small coastal community in Nunavut, Martina Tyrell (2009) found that, although women still talk about fishing, they no longer fish on a regular basis—a shift she attributes to women's increasing involvement in full-time forms of employment. Many of the women whom I interviewed were likewise obliged to negotiate the demands of a job in order to find time to spend out on the land.

At the same time, in Arctic households, income from waged employment also serves to support traditional harvesting activities, such that a new division of labour is developing, both within and across households. As Peter Usher, Gérard Duhaime, and Edmund Searles (2003, 178) point out:

> The successful harvesting household is often also the successful wage-earning household, as this cash income is used for purchasing harvesting equipment, and especially fast means of transport. This is the key means of resolving the time allocation problem, mainly for men, between wage work and harvesting. There has also been increasing specialization

among households, so that some harvest far more than their own needs and share or exchange the surplus.

As they go on to note, access to store-bought foods relieves some of the pressure on households to procure food from the land, and such access "is probably also a key means of resolving the time allocation problem, mainly for women, between wage work and such activities as butchering, hide preparation, and making clothing" (178). Their comments suggest how important it is for researchers to interview entire households and members of extended families, as doing so will reveal how men and women employ both household- and kinship-based strategies to balance waged employment with harvesting activities.

Two of the men I interviewed, Nick and John, talked about the role their wives play in their own harvesting activities. Nick was recently unemployed when I interviewed him in 2008, so he answered the interview questions based on his most recent experiences, when he still had a full-time job. When both Nick and his wife had jobs, they would still travel on the land together, fishing throughout the year for a couple of days at a time. He would also do some caribou hunting on the weekends at the end of August and into September. His wife would join him on these trips, and she would butcher the carcasses of the animals he killed. In addition, the two would harvest berries. "In the fall time, when we're doing our caribou hunt, in late August when [my wife] comes out, then we might pick a few berries," he said. "It's mostly the aqpiks," he added, "some cranberry, [and] there's blueberries." Although Nick can hunt without his wife, he values her skills and is glad when she is able to accompany him. For her part, even though she works full-time most of the year, Nick's wife makes a point of finding opportunities to join her husband.

John's wife works ten months of the year, while he is free to hunt and fish full time. Yet, like Nick, John prefers to travel in the company of his wife, and evidently she, too, enjoys spending time on the land. "Travels with me when I travel," he declared. "I never travel alone. Everywhere I go, she goes. I leave her behind, I get an earful." Moreover, some of his hunting activities depend on his wife's ability to join him: "Yeah, caribous goes by. Make dry meat same time, and now we don't hardly do those anymore, 'cause my wife working now, so I only do it in summer now when she get off work." In much the same way, Neve pointed out that her husband prefers that she accompany him on trips onto the land, and her full-time job has complicated this arrangement. "My husband can't go out unless I go out," she said. "He has—well, he can go out hunting, but he doesn't spend all the time out there, 'cause I'm not there." As such comments suggest, a tension exists between the need for a household income and the ability to sustain customary ways of life. Yet, despite the time constraints created by waged employment, these couples continue to spend time on the land together.

In addition to participating directly in harvesting activities, whether on their own or in partnership with others, women also contribute indirectly to putting country foods on the table. A number of the women I interviewed indicated that their employment helped to support harvesting efforts in the household. Christine said that although she is able to spend only "some time" on the land herself, her income enables her sons to go hunting:

> In order for my boys to go out, they don't have a job, and I do, and I make the money. The whole family participates. Even if I don't go actually out with them, I'm very involved through my money. Through my money! [She laughs] Well, it's true—for the cost of gas, and shells.

Her situation illustrates a gendered division of labour, in which a woman's waged employment serves to support the harvesting activities of men. Besides providing financial support, however, Christine also contributed her own labour to household hunting, helping to butcher carcasses and prepare the meat.

"That's How I Grew Up": Women and Traditional Knowledge

Women, as well as men, are concerned about teaching youth what are locally called "on the land skills"—how to hunt, fish, and trap and, more broadly, how to be skilled travellers. During my fieldwork in 2012, elder Anny Illasiak described a fishing experience she shared with her grandson:

> One time my grandchild was staying with me, because I'm watching kids. (He get grown now.) He want to set net, he want to have his own net. "Okay, let's walk around and look for old net." We find one old net, we bring it home, we fix it up, we set it, he get one fish. When we set it, he get one fish. "We'll cook your fish, ah?" He said no, he's going to send it to his dad! First fish he get. He try to make his dad happy!

Anny's comments well illustrate the manner in which traditional knowledge is passed on to younger generations. The fact that, in this case, the knowledge pertained to fishing, and it was a woman who taught these skills, not only attests to women's familiarity with fishing but also demonstrates the important role that women play in teaching children how to live on the land.

Melanie's recollections of her childhood again suggest the role of women in sustaining traditional ways of life. Melanie spoke fondly of spending time on the land with her mother and brothers, absorbing knowledge of traditional ways of life. Being on the land, she said, is

> important to me because, well, when I was younger, that's how I grew up. Right up until I was about nine years old, I spent pretty much the whole year in the tree line with my mom and my brothers, at Tsoko Lake and Granite Lake. In the past, that's where they did their fox and marten and whatever other fur they can catch there in Tsoko Lake and Granite Lake. Sometimes we'd stay up pretty much a good ten months and then, after that, when we quit going to the tree line, it was just close camps like Billy's Creek, Kraut's Island, "the river," that's what they call it.

For Melanie, these memories evoked connections, both to family and to the natural worlds. She recalled "climbing trees and being there with my mom and my brothers, when we were close, you know? That was before my mom passed away, so that's a really good memory for me. A lot of scrapes and bruises from climbing trees!"

Melanie's relationship to the environment, nurtured through fishing, hunting, and playing in the woods as a child, carried through into her adult life, and she strove to ensure that her own children would also have an opportunity to live on the land. Thus, as we saw earlier, because Melanie's full-time job required her presence in town, she was glad that her son was able to go hunting with her sister. As she (and others) recognize, much of the knowledge on which culture rests is acquired through the hands-on teaching and learning of skills that can be practiced only on the land. For this reason, it is essential that young people to learn about the natural environment that surrounds Paulatuuq, and it often falls to women to create these connections among family, learning, and the land.

Conclusion: Sustaining Connections

A focus on the predominantly male activity of hunting inevitably obscures the breadth and depth of women's roles in the social, cultural, economic, and environmental relationships that characterize life in Arctic communities such as Paulatuuq. A preoccupation with hunting also has the effect of sidelining fishing—an activity in which women in fact take an active part.

As harvesters themselves, as well as by performing tasks such as butchering and preparing meat that are integral to successful hunting, women make a direct, and significant contribution to household food security. As we have seen, a woman may also serve as the family breadwinner, whose income enables others (often men) to hunt and fish. Gendered assumptions tend to leave us blind to countervailing evidence. If we wish to arrive at a more than partial understanding of household food provisioning and the environmental knowledge on which it relies, we will need to set aside our expectations and pay greater attention to women.

Despite fairly widespread recognition of the male bias that has characterized research efforts in the past, the situation has been slow to change. Detailed research into women's direct role in fishing and hunting, as well as the part that women play in transmitting the knowledge needed to acquire these skills, will serve to generate a more nuanced portrait of community harvesting and household economies, one that better captures the gendered dimension of food provisioning and responses to food insecurity. In the absence of such understanding, efforts to formulate policy, especially with regard to fish and wildlife, run the risk of creating unforeseen problems—or of compounding the problems the policies aim to address.

The residents of Paulatuuq that I worked with, like those of other Inuvialuit communities, are presently grappling with the ongoing impact of colonization. Quite apart from the introduction of a money economy, Western development—particularly in the form of plans to exploit natural resources—continues to alter ecological habitats, and climate change poses a further threat to species on which Arctic communities depend. In the face of such transformations, the pursuit of land-based activities like fishing becomes increasingly urgent. Families are already finding it difficult to sustain traditional patterns of harvesting and, by extension, cultural practices related to the use of the products of the land. As I hope this chapter has demonstrated, as holders of traditional knowledge, and often as the guardians of family relationships, women are determined to ensure that future generations do not lose their connection to the land.

The research on which this chapter is based was made possible through the financial support of the Alberta ACADRE Network, the Aurora Research Institute, the Canadian Circumpolar Institute, the Northern Scientific

Training Program, the Pierre Elliott Trudeau Foundation, the Social Economy Research Network of Northern Canada, and the Social Sciences and Humanities Research Council of Canada.

References

Alunik, Ishmael, Eddie D. Kolausok, and David A. Morrison. 2003. *Across Time and Tundra: The Inuvialuit of the Western Arctic*. Seattle: University of Washington Press.

Anderson, Rudolph Martin. 1913. "Report on the Natural History Collections of the Expedition." In *My Life with the Eskimo*, edited by Vilhjálmur Stefánsson, 436–528. New York: Macmillan.

Bodenhorn, Barbara. 1990. "'I'm Not the Great Hunter, My Wife Is': Inupiat and Anthropological Models of Gender." *Études/Inuit/Studies* 14 (1–2): 55–74.

Briggs, Jean L. 1970. *Never in Anger: Portrait of an Eskimo Family*. Cambridge, MA: Harvard University Press.

Department of Fisheries and Oceans. 1999. "Central Arctic Region DFO Science Stock Status Report D5-68 1999: Hornaday River Arctic Charr." http://fishfp. sasktelwebhosting.com/publications/Hornaday%20Arctic%20Char%20 SSR%20(1999).pdf.

Dilley, Roy. 1999. "Ways of Knowing, Forms of Power." *Cultural Dynamics* 11 (1): 33–55.

Egeland, Grace M. 2010. *Inuit Health Survey, 2007–2008: Inuvialuit Settlement Region*. Ste-Anne-de-Bellevue, QC: Centre for Indigenous Peoples' Nutrition and Environment, McGill University, Macdonald Campus. http://www.irc. inuvialuit.com/publications/pdf/ihs-report-final.pdf.

Feit, Harvey. 1982. "The Future of Hunters Within Nation-States: Anthropology and the James Bay Cree." In *Politics and History in Band Societies*, edited by Eleanor Leacock and Richard Lee, 373–411. Cambridge: Cambridge University Press.

Inuvialuit Regional Corporation. 2012. *The Economic Life of Inuvialuit Households in Paulatuk*. Inuvik, NWT: Inuvialuit Regional Corporation

Inuvialuit Joint Secretariat. 2003. "Inuvialuit Harvest Study: Data and Methods Report, 1988–1997." Inuvik, NT: Joint Secretariat.

Kafarowski, Joanna. 2005. "'Everyone Should Have a Voice, Everyone's Equal': Gender, Decision-Making and Environmental Policy in the Canadian Arctic." *Canadian Women's Studies* 24 (4): 12–17.

———. 2009. "'It's Our Land Too': Inuit Women's Involvement and Representation in Arctic Fisheries in Canada." In *Gender, Culture and*

Northern Fisheries, edited by Joanna Kafarowski, 153–70. Edmonton: Canadian Circumpolar Institute Press.

Keeping, Janet. 1998. *Thinking About Benefit Agreements: An Analytical Framework*. Northern Minerals Program. Working Paper no. 4. Yellowknife: Canadian Arctic Resources Committee.

Kruse, John A. 1991. "Alaska Inupiat Subsistence and Wage Employment Patterns: Understanding Individual Choice." *Human Organization* 50 (4): 317–26.

Lemieux, Pierre. 1990. Report on the Monitoring of the Arctic Charr Fishery at the Hornaday River 1990. Inuvik, NT: Fisheries Joint Management Committee.

Mackenzie Gas Project. 2004. "Section 6: Socio-Economic Effects Summary." In *Environmental Impact Statement for the Mackenzie Gas Project*, vol. 1, *Overview and Impact Summary*, http://www.mackenziegasproject.com/ theProject/regulatoryProcess/applicationSubmission/Documents/MGP_EIS_ Vol1_Section_6_S.pdf.

McDonnell, Sheila Margaret. 1983. "Community Resistance, Land Use and Wage Labour in Paulatuk, N.W.T." MA thesis, Department of Geography, University of British Columbia, Vancouver.

Northwest Territories. Bureau of Statistics 2014. "Paulatuk: Statistical Profile." http://www.statsnwt.ca/community-data/Profile-PDF/Paulatuk.pdf.

Northwest Territories. Environment and Natural Resources. n.d. "Barren-Ground Caribou: Northern Herds." http://www.enr.gov.nt.ca/programs/ barren-ground-caribou/northern-herds.

Pálsson, Gísli. 1994. "Enskilment at Sea." *Man* 29 (4): 901–27.

Parlee, Brenda, Fikret Berkes, and Teetl'it Gwich'in Renewable Resource Council. 2005. "Health of the Land, Health of the People: A Case Study on Gwich'in Berry Harvesting in Northern Canada." *EcoHealth* 2: 127–37

Pearce, Tristan, James Ford, Amanda Caron, Jason Prno, and Tanya Smith. 2010. *Climate Change Adaptation Action Plan: Community of Paulatuk, Northwest Territories*. Guelph, ON: Community of Paulatuk and ArcticNorth Consulting. http://jamesford.ca/wp-content/uploads/2010/05/Paulatuk-Adaptation-Action-Plan-20102.pdf.

Ridington, Robin. 2001. "Voice, Narrative and Dialogue: The Persistence of Hunter-Gatherer Discourse in North America." In *Identity and Gender in Hunting and Gathering Societies: Papers Presented at the Eighth International Conference on Hunting and Gathering Societies (CHAGS 8), National Museum of Ethnology, October 1998*, edited by Ian Keen and Takako Yamada, 117–32. Osaka: National Museum of Ethnology.

Saladin d'Anglure, Bernard. 2005. "The 'Third Gender' of the Inuit." *Diogenes* 208:134–44

Shannon, Kerrie Ann. 2006. "Everyone Goes Fishing: Understanding Procurement for Men, Women and Children in an Arctic Community." *Études/Inuit/Studies* 30 (1): 9–29.

Sharma, Sangita, Elsie De Roose, Xia Cao, Anita Pokiak, Joel Gittelsohn, and Andre Corriveau. 2009. "Dietary Intake in a Population Undergoing a Rapid Transition in Diet and Lifestyle: The Inuvialuit in the Northwest Territories of Arctic Canada." *Canadian Journal of Public Health* 100 (6): 442–48.

Staples, Lindsay. 1986. "Paulatuk Economic Development Plan and Implementation Strategy." Whitehorse: WL Staples Consulting.

Stewart, Henry. 2005. "The Fish Tale That Is Never Told: A Reconsideration of the Importance of Fishing in Inuit Societies." In *Indigenous Use and Management of Marine Resources*, edited by Nobuhiro Kishigami and James M. Savelle, 345–61. Osaka: National Museum of Ethnology.

Todd, Zoe. 2010a. "Food Security in Paulatuk, N.T.—Opportunities and Challenges of a Changing Community Economy." MSc thesis, Department of Resource Economics and Environmental Sociology, University of Alberta, Edmonton.

———. 2010b. "Food Security, Arctic Security: Why the Local Cannot Be Ignored." In *Humanizing Security in the Arctic*, edited by Michelle Daveluy, Francis Lévesque, and Jenanne Ferguson, 207–23. Edmonton: Canadian Circumpolar Institute Press.

———. 2012. Unpublished Research Notes.

Tyrrell, Martina. 2009. "'It Used to Be Women's Work': Gender and Subsistence Fishing on the Hudson Bay Coast." In *Gender, Culture and Northern Fisheries*, edited by Joanne Kafarowski, 47–65. CCI Press Occasional Publication Series no. 62. Edmonton: Canadian Circumpolar Institute Press.

Usher, Peter. 1971. "The Canadian Western Arctic: A Century of Change." In *Pilot Not Commander: Essays in Memory of Diamond Jenness*, edited by Pat Lotz and Jim Lotz, *Anthropologica* 18 (1–2): 169–84.

Usher, Peter, Gérard Duhaime, and Edmund Searles. 2003. "The Household as an Economic Unit in Arctic Aboriginal Communities, and Its Measurement by Means of a Comprehensive Survey." *Social Indicators Research* 61: 175–201.

Usher, Peter, and George Wenzel. 1997. "Native Harvest Surveys and Statistics: A Critique of Their Construction and Use." *Arctic* 40 (2): 145–60.

Contributors

Isabel Altamirano-Jiménez is Zapotec from Oaxaca, Mexico and an associate professor in the Department of Political Science and an adjunct professor in the Faculty of Native Studies at the University of Alberta, where she teaches on topics such as Indigenous peoples and globalization and Indigenous women and politics, among other topics. She is the author of *Indigenous Encounters with Neo-liberalism: Place, Women, and the Environment in Canada and Mexico*. She recently completed a three-year research project that examined the role of Indigenous women's knowledge in the stewardship of water for which she was awarded a Cluster Grant from the University of Alberta's Kule Institute for Advanced Studies.

After studying at the University of Sherbrooke and the University of California (Berkeley), **Denise Geoffroy** held various positions, including at the Canadian Parliament. She then was involved with the Naskapi Band of Schefferville, the Naskapi Construction Company, and finally was the executive director of the Naskapi Development Corporation. Since 1998, she has worked from her home office in Northern Québec.

Shalene Jobin is Cree (from her mother) and Métis (from her father) and is a member of the Red Pheasant Cree First Nation, a signatory to Treaty 6. She is an associate professor in the Faculty of Native Studies at the University of Alberta, where she also serves as the director of the Aboriginal governance programs. Her research interests lie with Indigenous perspectives on self-determination, Indigenous economies, and Indigenous ways of knowing and on the interaction of Indigenous peoples with the institutions of the state.

She holds an MA in Indigenous governance from the University of Victoria and an interdisciplinary PhD in political science and Native studies from the University of Alberta.

Kahente iontats. Askeré:wake ní:i Kanienkeháka niowehtsioton. (I am introducing myself in a traditional manner. My name is Kahente, I am bear clan, and that the earth that I come from is the place of the Mohawk) Watkanonwerahton tanon sewakwékon. (Greetings of Peace from the Kanienkehaka (Mohawk) people). I am from Kahnawà:ke, in Kanien'kehá:ka (Mohawk) territory, on the south shore of the St. Lawrence River near Montreal. My name means "she walks ahead." My work is rooted in my identity and community. I am a mother to four daughters who ground me in a rich communal family life with my mother and all of my sisters and their families. I hold a PhD from Concordia University and currently I am an assistant professor at Carleton University in the School of Canadian Studies. I teach, research and write in the areas of consensus-based decision making, Indigenous identity and belonging, and Indigenous women's issues. I work at bringing to life old traditions in the modern setting. More recently, I have begun work performing the Sky Woman narrative "We Are in Her and She Is in Us" as an act of decolonizing her story and rematriating its female elements. I work at balancing my academic activities with my creative work in beading, moccasin making, sewing, photography, and creative writing.

Nathalie Kermoal is a Breton. She is a professor in the Faculty of Native Studies at the University of Alberta. In 2011–2012, she served as Interim Dean of the Faculty of Native Studies and recently served a two-year term as special advisor to the provost on Aboriginal academic programs. From 2009 to 2015, Professor Kermoal was the Associate-Dean Academic of the Faculty of Native Studies. Her areas of interest include Métis history, Aboriginal constitutional issues, urban Aboriginal history, contemporary Aboriginal art, and Aboriginal women's issues. The author of *Les francophones de l'Alberta* (translated into English as *Alberta's Francophones*) and *Un passé métis au féminin*, in addition to numerous articles, she is currently involved in several research projects pertaining to the Métis and to urban Aboriginal issues. She holds an MA in contemporary history from Université de Nantes (France) and a PhD in Canadian history from the University of Ottawa.

Carole Lévesque is a professor at the Institut national de la recherche scientifique. She holds a PhD in social and cultural anthropology from the Sorbonne and has devoted her entire career to Aboriginal issues. She has worked closely with Québec's First Nations communities, organizations, and institutions for more than four decades and, over the years, has developed a number of applied research approaches in which Aboriginal peoples play an active role either as individuals or at a community level. She is the founder and director of DIALOG: Aboriginal Peoples Research and Knowledge Network, an interuniversity, interinstitutional, interdisciplinary, and international cluster that brings together researchers, students, and collaborators from the academic milieu and from Aboriginal organizations and communities. These diverse participants share the objectives of promoting, disseminating, and renewing research relating to Aboriginal peoples. Lévesque is also co-director, with Edith Cloutier, of the ODENA Research Alliance, dedicated to the study of Aboriginal peoples in Québec's cities. In 2015, she was awarded the Université du Québec's Prix d'excellence en recherche et création.

Leanna Parker holds a PhD in Native studies and environmental sociology from the University of Alberta. Her research interests include Indigenous resource use and management, Indigenous economies, and Indigenous economic history. Her dissertation examined the resiliency and adaptability of nineteenth-century Indigenous economies, with a focus on the participation of Indigenous peoples in the fur trade in Canada and in the whaling industry in New Zealand.

Brenda Parlee is an associate professor and Canada Research Chair in the Faculty of Native Studies and the Department of Resource Economics and Environmental Sociology at the University of Alberta. Her research into traditional ecological knowledge began in the Northwest Territories in 1995, and since that time she has carried out numerous collaborative research projects with First Nations, Inuit, and Métis communities in many parts of the North, including a four-year study of the social dimensions of changing caribou populations. Her research interests include social responses to ecological variability and change, local and traditional systems of knowledge, the health and well-being of Aboriginal communities, and the impact of resource development, including the assessment and monitoring of its cultural and socioeconomic effects. She holds a PhD in natural resources and environmental management from the University of Manitoba.

Geneviève Polèse is a trilingual (French, English, and Spanish) researcher at Institut national de la recherche scientifique at the Centre urbanisation culture société in Montréal, Canada. Her research focuses on economic development within culturally diverse societies and traditional knowledge of Indigenous populations in Québec, Canada, and abroad.

Zoe Todd is Métis and a PhD candidate in social anthropology at the University of Aberdeen. She completed a BSc in biology and an MSc in rural sociology, both at the University of Alberta. She is currently conducting research into the discourse and practice of fishing in Paulatuuq, Northwest Territories. In addition to her academic work in the North, she also writes about the issues facing the urban Aboriginal populations in Canadian Prairie cities. She is a 2011 Trudeau Scholar.

Kristine Wray holds an MSc in rural sociology from the Department of Resource Economics and Environmental Sociology at the University of Alberta and was the first graduate of the university's combined BSc/BA program in environmental and conservation sciences and Native studies. In addition to her academic interests, which include the role of Aboriginal traditional knowledge in natural resource management and institutional ethnography, she is a painter and photographer and is currently focusing her energies on developing her artistic work.